# THE HISTORY OF THE GREAT
# AMERICAN FORTUNES

# HISTORY OF THE GREAT
# AMERICAN FORTUNES

BY

## GUSTAVUS MYERS

AUTHOR OF "THE HISTORY OF TAMMANY HALL," "HISTORY OF
PUBLIC FRANCHISES IN NEW YORK CITY," ETC.

---

## VOL. II.

### GREAT FORTUNES FROM RAILROADS

---

CHICAGO
CHARLES H. KERR & COMPANY
CO-OPERATIVE

# CONTENTS

PART III

THE GREAT FORTUNES FROM RAILROADS

# HISTORY OF THE GREAT AMERICAN FORTUNES

## CHAPTER I

### THE SEIZURE OF THE PUBLIC DOMAIN

Before setting out to relate in detail the narrative of the amassing of the great individual fortunes from railroads, it is advisable to present a preliminary survey of the concatenating circumstances leading up to the time when these vast fortunes were rolled together. Without this explanation, this work would be deficient in clarity, and would leave unelucidated many important points, the absence of which might puzzle or vex the reader.

Although industrial establishments, as exemplified by mills, factories and shops, much preceded the construction of railroads, yet the next great group of fortunes to develop after, and along with, those from land were the fortunes plucked from the control and manipulation of railroad systems.

#### THE LAGGING FACTORY FORTUNES.

Under the first stages of the old chaotic competitive system, in which factory warred against factory, and an intense struggle for survival and ascendency enveloped

the whole tense sphere of manufacturing, no striking industrial fortunes were made.

Fortunate was that factory owner regarded who could
claim $50,000 clear. All of those modern and complex
factors offering such unbounded opportunities for gathering in spoils mounting into the hundreds of millions
of dollars, were either unknown or in an inchoate or rudi-
mentary state. Invention, if we may put it so, was just
blossoming forth. Hand labor was largely prevalent.
Huge combinations were undreamed of; paper capitalization as embodied in the fictitious issues of immense
quantities of bonds and stocks was not yet a part of the
devices of the factory owner, although it was a fixed
plan of the bankers and insurance companies.

The factory owner was the supreme type of that sheer
individualism which had burst forth from the re-
straints of feudalism. He stood alone fighting his commercial contests with persistent personal doggedness. Beneath his occasional benevolence and his religious professions was a wild ardor in the checkmating or bankruptcy of his competitors. These were his enemies; he
fought them with every mercantile weapon, and they him;
and none gave quarter.

Apart from the destructive character of this incessant
warfare, dooming many of the combatants, other intervening factors had the tendency of holding back the factory owners' quick progress — obstacles and drawbacks
copiously described in later and more appropriate parts
of this work.

### MIGHT OF THE RAILROAD OWNERS.

In contrast to the slow, almost creeping pace of the
factory owners in the race for wealth, the railroad own-

ers sprang at once into the lists of mighty wealth-pos-
sessers, armed with the most comprehensive and puissant powers and privileges, and vested with a sweep of
properties beside which those of the petty industrial
bosses were puny. Railroad owners, we say; the distinction is necessary between the builders of the railroads and
the owners. The one might construct, but it often happened that by means of cunning, fraud and corruption,
the builders were superseded by another set of men who
vaulted into possession.

Looking back and summing up the course of events
for a series of years, it may be said that there was created over night a number of entities empowered with
extraordinary and far-reaching rights and powers of ownership.

These entities were called corporations, and were called
into being by law. Beginning as creatures of law, the
very rights, privileges and properties obtained by means
of law, soon enabled them to become the dictators and
masters of law. The title was in the corporation, not
in the individual; hence the men who controlled the corporation swayed the substance of power and ownership.
The factory was usually a personal affair, owned by one
man or in co-partnership; to get control of this property
it was necessary to get the owner in a financial corner
and force him to sell out, for, as a rule, he had no bond
or stock issues. But the railroad corporation was a stock
corporation; whoever secured control of a majority of the
stock became the legal administrator of its policies and
property. By adroit manipulation, intimidation, superior
knavery, and the corrupt domination of law, it was always easy for those who understood the science of rig-
ging the stock market, and that of strategic undermining,
to wrest the control away from weak, or (treating the

word in a commercial sense) incompetent, holders.
This has been long shown by a succession of examples.

### THE LEGALIZING OF CUNNING

Thus this situation, so singularly conflicting with the
theoretical majesty of the law, was frequently presented:
A band of men styling themselves a corporation received
a perpetual charter with the most sweeping rights and
properties. In turn, the law interposed no effective
hindrance to the seizing of their possessions by any other
group proving its power to grasp them. All of this was
done under nominal forms of law, but differed little in
reality from the methods during medieval times when any
baron could take another baron's castle and land by armed
force, and it remained his until a stronger man came
along and proved his title likewise.

Long before the railroad had been accepted commercially as a feasible undertaking, the trading and land-owning classes, as has been repeatedly pointed out, had demonstrated very successfully how the forms of government could be perverted to enrich themselves at the expense of the working population.

Taxation laws, as we have seen, were so devised that
the burden in a direct way fell lightly on the shipping,
manufacturing, trading, banking and land-owning classes,
while indirectly it was shoved almost wholly upon the
workers, whether in shop, factory or on farm. Furthermore, the constant response of Government, municipal,
State and National, to property interests, has been touched
upon; how Government loaned vast sums of public
money, free of interest, to the traders, while at the same
time refusing to assist the impoverished and destitute;
how it granted immunity from punishment to the rich

and powerful, and inflicted the most drastic penalties upon poor debtors and penniless violators of the law; how it allowed the possessing classes to evade taxation on a large scale, and effected summarily cruel laws permitting landlords to evict tenants for non-payment of rent. These and many other partial and grievously discriminative laws have been referred to, as also the refusal of Government to interfere in the slightest with the commercial frauds and impositions constantly practiced, with all their resulting great extortions, upon the defenceless masses.

Of the long-prevailing frauds on the part of the capitalists in acquiring large tracts of public land, some significant facts have been brought out in preceding chapters. Those facts, however, are only a few of a mass. When the United States Government was organized, most of the land in the North and East was already expropriated, But immense areas of public domain still remained in the South and in the Middle West. Over much of the former Colonial land the various legislatures claimed jurisdiction, until, one after another, they ceded it to the National Government. With the Louisiana purchase, in 1805, the area of public domain was enormously extended, and consecutively so later after the Mexican war.

### THE LAND LAWS AGAINST THE POOR.

From the very beginning of the Government, the land laws were arranged to discriminate against the poor settler. Instead of laws providing simple and inexpensive ways for the poor to get land, the laws were distorted into a highly effective mechanism by which companies of capitalists. and individual capitalists, secured vast tracts

for trivial sums.  These capitalists then either held the
land, or forced settlers to pay exorbitant prices for comparatively small plots.  No laws were in existence compelling the purchaser to be a *bona fide* settler.  Absentee
landlordism was the rule.  The capitalist companies were
largely composed of Northern, Eastern and Southern
traders and bankers.  The evidence shows that they employed bribery and corruption on a great scale, either in
getting favorable laws passed, or in evading such laws as
were on the statute books by means of the systematic
purchase of the connivance of Land Office officials.

By act of Congress, passed on April 21, 1792, the Ohio
Land Company, for example, received 100,000 acres, and
in the same year it bought 892,900 acres for $642,856.66.
But this sum was not paid in money.  The bankers and
traders composing the company had purchased, at a heavy
discount, certificates of public debt and army land war-
rants, and were allowed to tender these as payment.[1]
The company then leisurely disposed of its land to settlers at an enormous profit.  Nearly all of the land companies had banking adjuncts.  The poor settler, in order
to settle on land that a short time previously had been
national property, was first compelled to pay the land
company an extortionate price, and then was forced to
borrow the money from the banking adjuncts, and give
a heavy mortgage, bearing heavy interest, on the land.[2]
The land companies always took care to select the very
best lands.  The Government documents of the time are
full of remonstrances from legislatures and individuals
complaining of these seizures, under form of law, of
the most valuable areas.  The tracts thus appropriated

[1] U. S. Senate Executive Documents, Second Session, Nineteenth Congress, Doc. No. 63.
[2] U. S. Senate Documents, First Session, Twenty-fourth Congress, 1835-36, Doc. No. 216: 16.

comprised timber and mineral, as well as **agricultural,** land.

### VAST TRACTS SECURED BY BRIBERY.

One of the most scandalous land-company transactions was that involving a group of Southern and Boston capitalists. In January, 1795, the Georgia Legislature, by special act, sold millions of acres in different parts of the State of Georgia to four land companies. The people of the State were convinced that this purchase had been obtained by bribery. It was made an election issue, and a Legislature, comprising almost wholly new members, was elected. In February, 1796, this Legislature passed a rescinding act, declaring the act of the preceding year void, on the ground of its having been obtained by " improper influence." In 1803 the tracts in question were transferred by the Georgia Legislature to the United States Government.

The Georgia Mississippi Land Company was one of the four companies. In the meantime, this company had sold its tract, for ten cents an acre, to the New England Mississippi Land Company. Although committee after committee of Congress reported that the New England Mississippi Land Company had paid little or no actual part of the purchase price, yet that company, headed by some of the foremost Boston capitalists, lobbied in Congress for eleven years for an act giving it a large indemnity. Finally, in 1814, Congress passed an indemnification act, under which the eminent Bostonians, after ten years more lobbying, succeeded in getting an award from the United States Treasury of $1,077,561.73. The total amount appropriated by Congress on the pretense of settling the claims of the various capitalists in the " Yazoo

Claims " was $1,500,000.[3]   The ground upon which this appropriation was made by Congress was that the Supreme Court of the United States had decided that, irrespective of the methods used to obtain the grant from the Georgia Legislature, the grant, once made, was in the nature of a contract which could not be revoked or impaired by subsequent legislation.   This was the first of a long line of court decisions validating grants and franchises of all kinds secured by bribery and fraud.

It was probably the scandal arising from the bribery of the Georgia Legislature that caused popular ferment, and crystallized a demand for altered laws.   In 1796 Congress declared its intention to abandon the prevailing system of selling millions of acres to companies or individuals.   The new system, it announced, was to be one adapted to the interests of both capitalist and poor man.   Land was thereafter to be sold in small quantities on credit.   Could the mechanic or farmer demand a better law?   Did it not hold out the opportunity to the poorest to get land for which payment could be gradually made?

But this law worked even better to the advantage of the capitalist class than the old.   By bribing the land officials the capitalists were able to cause the choicest lands to be fraudulently withheld, and entered by dummies.   In this way, vast tracts were acquired.   Apparently the land entries were made by a large number of intending settlers, but these were merely the intermediaries by which capi-

[3] Senate Documents, Eighteenth Congress, Second Session, 1824-25, Vol. ii, Doc. No. 14, and Senate Documents, Twenty-fourth Congress, 1836-37, Vol. ii, No. 212.   After the grants were secured, the companies attempted to swindle the State of Georgia by making payments in depreciated currency.   Georgia refused to accept it.   When the grant was rescinded, both houses of the Georgia Legislature marched in solemn state to the Capitol front and burned the deed.

talists secured great tracts in the form of many small allotments. Having obtained the best lands, the capitalists then often held them until they were in demand, and forced actual settlers to pay heavily for them. During all of this time the capitalists themselves held the land "on credit." Some of them eventually paid for the lands out of the profits made from the settlers, but a great number of the purchasers cheated the Government almost entirely out of what they owed.[4]

The capitalists of the period contrived to use the land laws wholly to their own advantage and profit. In 1824, the Illinois Legislature memorialized Congress to change the existing laws. Under them, it recited, the best selections of land had been made by non-resident speculators, and it called upon Congress to pass a law providing for selling the remaining lands at fifty cents an acre.[5] Other legislatures petitioned similarly. Yet, notwithstanding the fact that United States officials and committees of Congress were continually unearthing great frauds, no real change for the benefit of the poor settler was made.

### GREAT EXTENT OF THE LAND FRAUDS.

The land frauds were great and incessant. In a long report, the United States Senate Committee on Public Lands, reporting on June 20, 1834, declared that the evidence it had taken established the fact that in Ohio and elsewhere, combinations of capitalist speculators, at the

[4] On Sept. 30, 1822, "credit purchasers" owed the Government: In Ohio, $1,260,870.87; in Indiana, $1,212,815.28; in Illinois, $841,302.80; in Missouri, $734,108.87; in Alabama, $5,760,-728.01; in Mississippi, $684,093.50; and in Michigan, $50,584.82 — a total of nearly $10,550,000. (Executive Reports, First Session, Eighteenth Congress, 1824, Report No. 61.) Most of these creditors were capitalist land speculators.

[5] U. S. Senate Documents, Second Session, Eighteenth Congress, 1824-25, Vol. ii, Doc. No. 25.

public sales of lands, had united for the purpose of driving other purchasers out of the market and in deterring
poor men from bidding.  The committee detailed how
these companies and individuals had fraudulently bought
large tracts of land at $1.25 an acre, and sold the land
later at exorbitant prices.  It showed how, in order to
accomplish these frauds, they had bought up United
States Land Office Registers and Receivers.[6]

Another exhaustive report was handed in by the
United States Senate Committee on Lands, on March 3,
1835.  Many of the speculators, it said, filled high offices in States where public lands bought by them were
located; others were people of " wealth and intelligence."
All of them " naturally united to render this investigation odious among the people."  The committee told how
an attempt had been made to assassinate one of its members.  " The first step," it set forth, " necessary to the
success of every scheme of speculation in the public lands,
is to corrupt the land officers, by a secret understanding
between the parties that they are to receive a certain portion of the profits."[7]  The committee continued:

The States of Alabama, Mississippi and Louisiana have been
the principal theatre of speculations and frauds in buying up the
public lands, and dividing the most enormous profits between
the members of the different companies and speculators.  The
committee refers to the depositions of numerous respectable witnesses to attest the various ramifications of these speculations
and frauds, and the means by which they have been carried into
effect. . . .[8]

Describing the great frauds in Louisiana, Benjamin

[6] U. S. Senate Documents, First Session, Twenty-third Congress, 1833-34, Vol. vi, Doc. No. 461 : 1-91.
[7] U. S. Senate Documents, Second Session, Twenty-third Congress, Vol. iv, Doc. No. 151 : 2.
[8] Ibid., 3.

F. Linton, U. S. District Attorney for the Western District of Louisiana, wrote, on August 25, 1835, to President Jackson: " Governments, like corporations, are considered without souls, and according to the code of some people's morality, should be swindled and cheated on every occasion." Linton gave this picture of " a notorious speculator who has an immense extent of claims ":

He could be seen followed to and from the land office by crowds of free negroes, Indians and Spaniards, and the very lowest dregs of society, in the counties of Opelousas and Rapides, with their affidavits already prepared by himself, and sworn to before some justice of the peace in some remote county. These claims, to an immense extent, are presented and allowed. And upon what evidence? Simply upon the evidence of the parties themselves who desire to make the entry! [9]

The " credit " system was gradually abandoned by the Government, but the auction system was retained for decades. In 1847, the Government was still selling large tracts at $1.25 an acre, nominally to settlers, actually to capitalist speculators or investors. More than two million acres had been sold every year for a long period. The House Committee on Public Lands, reporting in 1847, disclosed how most of the lands were bought up by capitalists. It cited the case of the Milwaukee district where, although 6,441 land entries had been made, there were only forty actual settlers up to 1847. " This clearly shows," the committee stated, " that those who claimed the land as settlers, are either the tools of speculators, to sequester the best lands for them . . . or the claim is made on speculation to sell out." [10]

The policy of granting enormous tracts of land to

[9] U. S. Senate Documents, Second Session, Twenty-fourth Congress, 1836-37, Vol. ii, Doc. No. 168: 5.
[10] Reports of Committees, First Session, Thirtieth Congress, 1847-48, Vol. iii, Report No. 732: 6.

corporations was revived for the benefit of canal and railroad companies. The first railroad company to get a land grant from Congress was the Illinois Central, in 1850. It received as a gift 2,595,053 acres of land in Illinois. Actual settlers had to pay the company from $5 to $15 an acre.

Large areas of land bought from the Indian tribes by the Government, almost at once became the property of canal or railroad corporations by the process of Government grants. A Congressional document in 1840 (Senate Document No. 616) made public the fact that from the establishment of the Federal Government to 1839, the Indian tribes had ceded to the Government a total of 442,866,370 acres. The Indian tribes were paid either by grants of land elsewhere, or in money and merchandise. For those 442,866,370 acres they received exchange land valued at $53,757,400, and money and merchandise amounting to $31,331,403.

### THE SWAYING OF GOVERNMENT.

The trading, banking and landed class had learned well the old, all-important policy of having a Government fully susceptible to their interests, whether the governing officials were put in office by them, and were saturated with their interests, views and ideals, or whether corruption had to be resorted to in order to attain their objects. At all events, the propertied classes, in the main, secured what they wanted. And, as fast as their interests changed, so did the acts and dicta of Government change.

While the political economists were busy promulgating the doctrine that it was not the province of Government to embark in any enterprise other than that of

purely governing — a doctrine precisely suiting the traders and borrowed from their demands — the commercial
classes, early in the nineteenth century, suddenly discovered that there was an exception.  They wanted canals
built; and as they had not sufficient funds for the purpose, and did not see any immediate profit for themselves,
they clamored for the building of them by the States.  In
fine, they found that it was to their interest to have the
States put through canal projects on the ground that these
would " stimulate trade."  The canals were built, but the
commercial classes in some instances made the blunder
of allowing the ownership to rest in the people.

Never again was this mistake repeated.  If it proved
so easy to get legislatures and Congress to appropriate
millions of the public funds for undertakings profitable
to commerce, why would it not be equally simple to secure the appropriation plus the perpetual title?  Why be
satisfied with one portion, when the whole was within
reach?

True, the popular vote was to be reckoned with; it was
a time when the people scanned the tax levy with far
greater scrutiny than now; and they were not disposed
to put up the public funds only that private individuals
might reap the exclusive benefit.  But there was a way
of tricking and circumventing the electorate.  The trading and land-owning classes knew its effectiveness.  It
was they who had utilized it; who from the year 1795
on had bribed legislatures and Congress to give them
bank and other charters.  Bribery had proved a signal
success.  The performance was extended on a much
wider scale, with far greater results, and with an adroit-
ness revealing that the capitalist class had learned much
by experience, not only in reaching out for powers that
the previous generation would not have dared to grant,

but in being able to make plastic to its own purposes the electorate that believed itself to be the mainspring of political power.

## GRANTS TO CANAL CORPORATIONS.

The first great canal, built in response to the demands of the commercial class, was the Erie Canal, completed in 1825. This waterway was constructed at public expense, and was owned by New York State. The commercial men could succeed in having it managed for their purposes and profit, and the politicians could often extract plunder from the successive contracts, but there was no opportunity or possibility for the exercise of the usual capitalist methods of fraudulent diversion of land, or of over-capitalization and exorbitant rates with which to pay dividends on fictitious stock.

Very significantly, from about the very time when the Erie Canal was finished, the era of the private canal company, financed by the Government, began. One after another, canal companies came forward to solicit public funds and land grants. These companies neither had any capital of their own, nor was capital necessary. The machinery of Government, both National and State, was used to supply them with capital.

The Chesapeake and Ohio Canal Company received, up to 1839, the sum of $2,500,000 in funds appropriated by the United States Government, and $7,197,000 from the State of Maryland.

In 1824 the United States Government began giving land grants for canal projects. The customary method was the granting by Congress of certain areas of land to various States, to be expressly given to designated canal companies. The States in donating them, sometimes sold them to the canal companies at the nominal rate of $1.25 an acre. The commuting of these payments was often obtained later by corrupt legislation.

From 1824 to 1834, the Wabash and Erie Canal Company obtained land grants from the Government amounting to 826,300 acres. The Miami and Dayton Canal Company secured from the Government, in 1828 and 1833, a total grant of 333,826 acres. The St. Mary's Falls Ship Canal Company received 750,000 acres in 1852; the Portage Lake and Lake Superior Ship Canal Company, 400,000 acres in 1865–66; and the Lac La Belle Ship Canal Company, 100,000 acres in 1866. Including a grant by Congress in 1828 of 500,000 acres of public land for general canal purposes, the land grants given by the National Government to aid canal companies, totalled 4,224,073.06 acres, mostly in Indiana, Ohio, Illinois, Wisconsin and Michigan.

Whatever political corruption accompanied the building of such State-owned canals as the Erie Canal, the primary and fundamental object was to construct. In the case of the private canal companies, the primary and fundamental object was to plunder. The capitalists controlling these companies were bent upon getting rich quickly; it was to their interest to delay the work as long as possible, for by this process they could periodically go to Legislatures with this argument: That the projects were more expensive and involved more difficulties than had been anticipated; that the original appropriations were exhausted, and that if the projects were to be completed, fresh appropriations were imperative. A large part of these successive appropriations, whether in money, or land which could be sold for money, were stolen in sundry indirect ways by the various sets of capitalist directors. The many documents of the

Maryland Legislature, and the messages of the successive Governors of Maryland, do not tell the full story of how the Chesapeake and Ohio Canal project was looted, but they give abundantly enough information.

### THE GRANTS FRAUDULENTLY MANIPULATED.

Many of the canal companies, so richly endowed by the Government with great land grants, made little attempt to build canals. What some of them did was to turn about and defraud the Government out of incalculably valuable mineral deposits which were never included in the original grants.

In his annual report for 1885, Commissioner Sparks, of the United States General Land Office told (House Executive Documents, 1885–86, Vol. 11) how, by 1885, the Portage Lake " canal " was only a worthless ditch and a complete fraud. What had the company done with its large land grant? Instead of accepting the grant as intended by Congress, it had, by means of fraudulent surveys, and doubtless by official corruption, caused at least one hundred thousand acres of its grant to be surveyed in the very richest copper lands of Wisconsin.

The grants originally made by Congress were meant to cover swamp lands — that is, lands not particularly valuable for agricultural uses, but which had a certain value for other purposes. Mineral lands were strictly excluded. Such was the law: the practice was very different. The facility with which capitalists caused the most valuable mineral, grazing, agricultural and timber lands to be fraudulently surveyed as " swamp " lands, is described at length a little later on in this work. Commissioner Sparks wrote that the one hundred thousand acres appropriated in violation of explicit law " were

taken outside of legal limits, and that the lands selected
both without and within such limits were interdicted
lands on the copper range " (p. 189). Those stolen copper deposits were never recovered by the Government
nor was any attempt made to forfeit them. They comprise to-day part of the great copper mines of the Copper Trust, owned largely by the Standard Oil Company.

The St. Mary's Falls Canal Company likewise stole
large areas of rich copper deposits. This fact was clearly
revealed in various official reports, and particularly in
the suit, a few years ago, of Chandler vs. Calumet and
Hecla Mining Company (U. S. Reports, Vol. 149, pp.
79–95). This suit disclosed the fact that the mines of
the Calumet and Hecla Mining Company were located
on part of the identical alleged " swamp " lands, granted
by Congress in 1852. The plaintiff, Chandler, claimed
an interest in the mines. Concluding the court's decision, favoring the Calumet and Hecla Mining Company,
this significant note (so illustrative of the capitalist connections of the judiciary), appears: " Mr. Justice
Brown, being interested in the result, did not sit in this
case and took no part in its decision."

Whatever superficial or partial writers may say of the
benevolent origin of railroads, the fact is that railroad
construction was ushered in by a widespread corruption
of legislators that put to shame the previous debauchery
in getting bank charters. In nearly every work on the
subject the assertion is dwelt upon that railroad builders
were regarded as public benefactors; that people and legislatures were only too glad to present them with public resources. There is just a slight substance of truth
in this alleged historical writing, but nothing more. The
people, it is true, were eager, for their own convenience,
to have the railroads built, but unwilling to part with

their hard-wrung taxes, their splendid public domain, and
their rights only that a few men, part gamblers and part
men of energy and foresight, should divert the entire donation to their own aggrandizement.  For this attitude the
railroad promoters had an alluring category of arguments
ready.

### CASH THE GREAT PERSUADER.

Through the public press, and in speeches and pamphlets, the people were assured in the most seductive and
extravagant language that railroads were imperative in
developing the resources of the country; that they would
be a mighty boon and an immeasurable stimulant to progress.  These arguments had much weight, especially with
a population stretched over such a vast territory as that
of the United States.  But alone they would not have
accomplished the ends sought, had it not been for the
quantities of cash poured into legislative pockets.  The
cash was the real eloquent persuader.  In turn, the virtuous legislators, on being questioned by their constituents as to why they had voted such great subsidies, such
immense land grants and such sweeping and unprecedented privileges to private corporations, could fall back
upon the justification (and a legitimate one it' seemed)
that to get the railroads built, public encouragement and
aid were necessary.

Many of the projectors of railroads were small tradesmen, landlords, millowners, merchants, bankers, associated politicians and lawyers.  Not infrequently, however,
did it happen that some charters and grants were obtained by politicians and lawyers who, at best, were impecunious sharpers.  Their greatest asset was a devious
knowledge of how to get something for nothing.  With

a grandiloquent front and a superb bluff they would organize a company to build a railroad from this to that point; an undertaking costing millions, while perhaps they could not pay their board bill. An arrangement with a printer to turn out stock issues on credit was easy; with the promise of batches of this stock, they would then get a sufficient number of legislators to vote a charter, money and land.

After that, the future was rosy. Bankers, either in the United States or abroad, could always be found to buy out the franchise or finance it. In fact, the bankers, who themselves were well schooled in the art of bribery and other forms of corruption,[11] were often outwitted by this class of adventurers, and were only too glad to treat with them as associates, on the recognized commercial principle that success was the test of men's mettle, and that the qualities productive of such success must be immediately availed of.

In other instances a number of tradesmen and landowners would organize a company having, let us say, $250,000 among them. If they had proceeded to build a railroad with this sum, not many miles of rail would have

[11] "Schooled in the art of bribery."— In previous chapters many facts have been brought out showing the extent of corrupt methods used by the bankers. The great scandal caused in Pennsylvania in 1840 by the revelations of the persistent bribery carried on by the United States Bank for many years, was only one of many such scandals throughout the United States. One of the most characteristic phases of the reports of the various legislative investigating committees was the ironical astonishment that they almost invariably expressed at the "superior class" being responsible for the continuous bribery. Thus, in reporting in 1840, that $130,000 had been used in bribery in Pennsylvania by the United States Bank, an investigating committee of the Pennsylvania House of Representatives commented: "It is hard to come to the conclusion that men of refined education, and high and honorable character, would wink at such things, yet the conclusion is unavoidable." (Pa. House Journal, 1842, Vol. ii, Appendix, 172-531.

been laid before they would have found themselves hopelessly bankrupt.

Their wisdom was that of their class; they knew a far
better method.   This was to use the powers of government, and make the public provide the necessary means.
In the process of construction the $250,000 would have
been only a mite.   But it was quite enough to bribe a
legislature.   By expending this sum in purchasing a majority of an important committee, and a sufficient number
of the whole body, they could get millions in public loans,
vast areas of land given outright, and a succession of
privileges worth, in the long run, hundreds upon hundreds of millions of dollars.

### A WELTER OF CORRUPTION.

So the onslaught of corruption began and continued.
Corruption in Ohio was so notorious that it formed a
bitter part of the discussion in the Ohio Constitutional
Convention of 1850-51.   The delegates were droning
along over insertions devised to increase corporation
power.   Suddenly rose Delegate Charles Reemelin and
exclaimed: " Corporations always have their lobby members in and around the halls of legislation to watch and
secure their interests.   Not so with the people — they
cannot act with that directness and system that a corporation can.   No individual will take it upon himself to go
to the Capitol at his own expense, to watch the representatives of the people, and to lobby against the potent
influences of the corporation.   But corporations have the
money, and it is to their interest to expend it to secure the
passage of partial laws." [12]

Two years later, at one of the sessions of the Massa-

[12] Ohio Convention Debates, 1850-51, ii: 174.

chusetts Constitutional Convention, Delegate Walker, of
North Brookfield, made a similar statement as to conditions in that State. "I ask any man to say," he asked,
"if he believes that any measure of legislation could be
carried in this State, which was generally offensive to
the corporations of the Commonwealth? It is very rarely
the case that we do not have a majority in the legislature
who are either presidents, directors or stockholders in in-
corporated companies. This is a fact of very grave importance." [13] Two-thirds of the property in Massachusetts, Delegate Walker pointed out, was owned by
corporations.

In 1857 an acrimonious debate ensued in the Iowa Constitutional Convention over an attempt to give further
extraordinary power to the railroads. Already the State
of Iowa had incurred $12,000,000 in debts in aiding rail-
road corporations. "I fear," said Delegate Traer, "that
it is very often the case that these votes (on appropriations for railroads) are carried through by improper influences, which the people, if left alone, would, upon mature
reflection, never have adopted." [14]

### IMPOTENCE OF THE PEOPLE.

These are but a very few of the many instances of the
debauching of every legislature in the United States. No
matter how furiously the people protested at this giving
away of their resources and rights, the capitalists were
able to thwart their will on every occasion. In one case
a State legislature had been so prodigal that the people
of the State demanded a Constitutional provision forbidding the bonding of the State for railroad purposes. The

[13] Debates in the Massachusetts Convention, 1853, iii: 59.
[14] Constitutional Debates, Iowa, 1857, ii: 777.

Constitutional Convention adopted this provision.  But the members had scarcely gone to their homes before the people discovered how they had been duped.  The amendment barred the State from giving loans, but (and here was the trick) it did not forbid counties and municipalities from doing so.  Thereupon the railroad capitalists proceeded to have laws passed, and bribe county and municipal officials all over the State to issue bonds and to give them terminal sites and other valuable privileges for nothing.  In every such case the railroad owners in subsequent years sneaked legislation through in practically every State, or resorted to subterfuges, by which they were relieved from having to pay back those loans.

Hundreds of millions of dollars, exacted from the people in taxation, were turned over to the railroad corporations, and little of it was ever returned.  As for the land grants to railroads, they reached colossal proportions. From 1850 to 1872 Congress gave not less than 155,504,-994.59 acres of the public domain either direct to railroad corporations, or to the various States, to be transferred to those corporations.

Much of this immense area was given on the condition that unless the railroads were built, the grants were to be forfeited.  But the capitalists found no difficulty in getting a thoroughly corrupt Congress to extend the period of construction in cases where the construction had not been done.  Of the 155,000,000 acres, a considerable portion of it valuable mineral, coal, timber and agricultural land, only 607,741 acres were forfeited by act of Congress, and even much of these were restored to the railroads by judicial decisions.[15]  That Congress,

[15] The principal of these decisions was that of the Supreme Court of the United States in the case of Schluenberg vs. Harriman (Wallace's Supreme Court Reports, xxi: 44).  In many of the railroad grants it was provided that in case the railroad

not less than the legislatures, was honeycombed with corruption is all too evident from the disclosures of many investigations — disclosures to which we shall have pertinent occasion to refer later on. Not only did the railroad corporations loot in a gigantic way under forms of law, but they so craftily drafted the laws of both Nation and the States that fraud at all times was easy.

## DEFRAUDING THE NATION OF TAXES.

Not merely were these huge areas of land obtained by fraud, but after they were secured, fraud was further used to evade taxation. And by donations of land is not meant only that for intended railroad use or which could be sold by the railroads. In some cases, notably that of the Union Pacific Railroad, authority was given to the railroad by acts passed in 1862 and 1864 to take all of the material, such as stone, timber, etc., needed for construction, from the public lands. So, in addition to the money and lands, much of the essential material for building the railroads was supplied from the public resources. No sooner had they obtained their grants, than the railroad

lines were not completed within certain specified times, the lands unsold or unpatented should revert to the United States. The decision of the Supreme Court of the United States practically made these provisions nugatory, and indirectly legalized the crassest frauds.

The original grants excluded mineral lands, but by a subsequent fraudulent official construction, coal and iron were declared not to be covered by the term mineral.

Commissioner Sparks of the U. S. General Land Office estimated in 1885 that, in addition to the tens of millions of acres the railroad corporations had secured by fraud under form of law, they had overdrawn ten million acres, "which vast amount has been treated by the corporations as their absolute property, but is really public land of the United States recoverable to the public domain." (House Executive Docs., First Session, Forty-ninth Congress, 1885-86, ii: 184.) It has never been recovered.

corporations had law after law passed removing this restriction or that reservation until they became absolute masters of hundreds of millions of acres of land which a brief time before had been national property.

" These enormous tracts," wrote (in 1886) William A. Phillips, a member of the Committee on Public Lands of the Forty-third Congress, referring to the railroad grants, " are in their disposition subject to the will of the railroad companies.  They can dispose of them in enormous tracts if they please, and there is not a single safeguard to secure this portion of the national domain to cultivating yeomanry."  The whole machinery of legislation was not only used to exclude the farmer from getting the land, and to centralize its ownership in corporations, but was additionally employed in relieving these corporations from taxation on the land thus obtained by fraud.  " To avoid taxation," Phillips goes on, " the railroad land grant companies had an amendment enacted into law to the effect that they should not obtain their patents until they had paid a small fee to defray the expense of surveying.  This they took care not to pay, or only to pay as fast as they could sell tracts to some purchasers, on which occasions they paid the surveying fee and obtained deeds for the portion they sold.  In this way they have held millions of acres for speculative purposes, waiting for a rise in prices, without taxation, while the farmers in adjacent lands paid taxes." [16]

Phillips passes this fact by with a casual mention, as though it were one of no great significance.

It is a fact well worthy of elaboration.  Precisely as the aristocracies in the Old World had gotten their estates by force and fraud, and then had the laws so arranged as to exempt those estates from taxation, so has

[16] " Labor, Land and Law ": 338-339.

the money aristocracy of the United States proceeded on
the same plan.  As we shall see, however, the railroad
and other interests have not only put through laws relieving from direct taxation the land acquired by fraud,
but also other forms of property based upon fraud.

This survey, however, would be prejudicial and one-
sided were not the fact strongly pointed out that the railroad capitalists were by no means the only land-graspers.
Not a single part of the capitalist class was there which
could in any way profit from the theft of public domain
that did not wallow in corruption and fraud.

The very laws seemingly passed to secure to the poor
settler a homestead at a reasonable price were, as Henry
M. Teller, Secretary of the Interior, put it, perverted into
" agencies by which the capitalists secures large and valuable areas of the public land at little expense." [17]  The poor
were always the decoys with which the capitalists of the
day managed to bag their game.  It was to aid and encourage " the man of small resources " to populate the
West that the Desert Land Law was apparently enacted;

[17] Report of the Secretary of the Interior for 1883.
Reporting to Secretary of the Interior Lamar, in response to
a U. S. Senate resolution for information, William A. J. Sparks,
Commissioner of the General Land Office, gave statistics showing an enormous number of fraudulent land entries, and continued:
"It was the ease with which frauds could be perpetrated
under existing laws, and the immunity offered by a hasty issue
of patents, that encouraged the making of fictitious and fraudulent entries.  The certainty of a thorough investigation would
restrain such practices, but fraud and great fraud must inevitably exist so long as the opportunity for fraud is preserved
in the laws, and so long as it is hoped by the procurers and
promoters of fraud that examinations may be impeded or
suppressed."  If, Commissioner Sparks urged, the preëmption,
commuted-homestead, timber-land, and desert-land laws were repealed, then, "the illegal appropriation of the remaining public
lands would be reduced to a minimum."— U. S. Senate Documents, First Session, Forty-ninth Congress, 1885-1886, Vol. viii,
Doc. No. 134 : 4.

and many a pathetic and enthusiastic speech was made in Congress as this act was ostentatiously going through. Under this law, it was claimed, a man could establish himself upon six hundred and forty acres of land and, upon irrigating a portion of it, and paying $1.25 an acre, could secure a title. For once, it seemed, Congress was looking out for the interests of the man of few dollars.

### VAST THEFTS OF LAND.

But plaudits were too hasty. To the utter surprise of the people the law began to work in a perverse direction. Its provisions had read well enough on a casual scrutiny. Where lay the trouble? It lay in just a few words deftly thrown in, which the crowd did not notice. This law, acclaimed as one of great benefit to every man aspiring for a home and land, was arranged so that the capitalist cattle syndicates could get immense areas. The lever was the omission of any provision requiring *actual settlement*. The livestock corporations thereupon sent in their swarms of dummies to the " desert " lands (many of which, in reality, were not desert but excellent grazing lands), had their dummies get patents from the Government and then transfer the lands. In this way the cattlemen became possessed of enormous areas; and to-day these tracts thus gotten by fraud are securely held intact, forming what may be called great estates, for on many of them live the owners in expansive baronial style.

In numerous instances, law was entirely dispensed with. Vast tracts of land were boldly appropriated by sheep and cattle rangers who had not even a pretense of title. Enclosing these lands with fences, the rangers claimed them as their own, and hired armed guards to drive off intruders, and kill if necessary.[18]    Murder after murder was committed.    In this usurpation the august Supreme Court of the United States upheld them.    And the grounds of the decision were what?

The very extraordinary dictum that a settler could not claim any right of preëmption on public lands in possession of another who had enclosed, settled upon and improved them.    This was the very reverse of every known declaration of common and of statute law.    No court, supreme or inferior, had ever held that because the proceeds of theft were improved or were refurbished a bit,

[18] " Within the cattle region," reported Commissioner Sparks, " it is notorious that actual settlements are generally prevented and made practically impossible outside the proximity of towns, through the unlawful control of the country, maintained by cattle companies."— U. S. Senate Docs., 1885-86, Vol. viii, No. 134:4 and 5.

Acting Commissioner Harrison of the General Land Office, reporting on March 14, 1884, to Secretary of the Interior Teller, showed in detail the vast extent of the unlawful fencing of public lands. In the Arkansas Valley in Colorado at least 1,000,000 acres of public domain were illegally seized. The Prairie Cattle Company, composed of Scotch capitalists, had fenced in more than a million acres in Colorado, and a large number of other cattle companies in Colorado had seized areas ranging from 20,000 to 200,000 acres. " In Kansas," Harrison went on, " entire counties are reported as [illegally] fenced. In Wyoming, one hundred and twenty-five cattle companies are reported having fencing on the public lands. Among the companies and persons reported as having 'immense' or 'very large' areas inclosed . . . are the Dubuque, Cimarron and Renello Cattle [companies] in Colorado; the Marquis de Morales in Colorado; the Wyoming Cattle Company (Scotch) in Wyoming; and the Rankin Live Stock Company in Nebraska.

" There is a large number of cases where inclosures range from 1,000 to 25,000 acres and upwards.

" The reports of special agents show that the fraudulent entries of public land within the enclosures are extensively made by the procurement and in the interest of stockmen, largely for the purpose of controlling the sources of water supply."— " Unauthorized Fencing of Public Lands," U. S. Senate Docs., First Session, Forty-eighth Congress, 1883-84, Vol. vi, Doc. No. 127:2.

the sufferer was thereby estopped from recovery. This decision showed anew how, while the courts were ever ready to enforce the law literally against the underlings and penniless, they were as active in fabricating tortuous constructions coinciding not always, but nearly always, with the demands and interests of the capitalist class.

It has long been the fashion on the part of a certain prevalent school of writers and publicists to excoriate this or that man, this or that corporation, as the ringleader in the orgy of corruption and oppression. This practice, arising partly from passionate or ill-considered judgment, and in part from ignorance of the subject, has been the cause of much misunderstanding, popular and academic.

No one section of the capitalist class can be held solely responsible; nor were the morals and ethics of any one division different from those of the others. The whole capitalist class was coated with the same tar. Shipping merchants, traders in general, landholders, banking and railroad corporations, factory owners, cattle syndicates, public utility companies, mining magnates, lumber corporations — all were participants in various ways in the subverting of the functions of government to their own fraudulent ends at the expense of the whole producing class.

While the railroad corporations were looting the public treasury and the public domain, and vesting in themselves arbitrary powers of taxation and proscription, all of the other segments of the capitalist class were, at the same time, enriching themselves in the same way or similar ways. The railroads were much denounced; but wherein did their methods differ from those of the cattle syndicates, the industrial magnates or the lumber corporations? The lumber barons wanted their predacious share of the public domain; throughout certain parts of

the West and in the South were far-stretching, magnificent forests covered with the growth of centuries.  To
want and to get them were the same thing, with a Government in power representative of capitalism.

## SPOLIATION ON A GREAT SCALE.

The "poor settler" catspaw was again made use of.
At the behest of the lumber corporations, or of adventurers or politicians who saw a facile way of becoming
multimillionaires by the simple passage of an act, the
"Stone and Timber Act" was passed in 1878 by Congress.  An amendment passed in 1892 made frauds still
easier.  This measure was another of those benevolent-
looking laws which, on its face, extended opportunities
for the homesteader.  No longer, it was plausibly set
forth, could any man say that the Government denied
him the right to get public land for a reasonable sum.
Was ever a finer, a more glorious chance presented?
Here was the way open for any individual homesteader
to get one hundred and sixty acres of timber land for
the low price of $2.50 an acre.  Congress was over-
whelmed with outbursts of panegyrics for its wisdom and
public spirit.

Soon, however, a cry of rage went up from the duped
public.  And the cause?  The law, like the Desert Land
Law, it turned out, was filled with cunningly-drawn
clauses sanctioning the worst forms of spoliation.  Entire trainloads of people, acting in collusion with the land
grabbers, were transported by the lumber syndicates into
the richest timber regions of the West, supplied with the
funds to buy, and then each, after having paid $2.50 per
acre for one hundred and sixty acres, immediately transferred his or her allotment to the lumber corporations.

Thus, for $2.50 an acre, the lumber syndicates obtained vast tracts of the finest lands worth, at the least, according to Government agents, $100 an acre, at a time, thirty-five years ago, when lumber was not nearly so costly as now.

The next development was characteristic of the progress of onsweeping capitalism. Just as the traders, bankers, factory owners, mining and railroad magnates had come into their possessions largely (in varying degrees) by fraud, and then upon the strength of those possessions had caused themselves to be elected or appointed to powerful offices in the Government, State or National, so now some of the lumber barons used a part of the millions obtained by fraud to purchase their way into the United States Senate and other high offices. They, as did their associates in the other branches of the capitalist class, helped to make and unmake judges, governors, legislatures and Presidents; and at least one, Russell A. Alger, became a member of the President's Cabinet in 1897.

Under this one law,—the Stone and Timber Act — irrespective of other complaisant laws, not less than $57,-000,000 has been stolen in the last seven years alone from the Government, according to a statement made in Congress by Representative Hitchcock, of Nebraska, on May 5, 1908. He declared that 8,000,000 acres had been sold for $20,000,000, while the Department of the Interior had admitted in writing that the actual aggregate value of the land, at prevailing commercial prices, was $77,000,000. These lands, he asserted, had passed into the hands of the Lumber Trust, and their products were sold to the people of the United States at an advance of seventy per cent. This theft of $57,000,000 simply represented the years from 1901 to 1908; it is probable that the entire thefts for 10,395,689.96 acres sold during the whole series of years since the Stone and Timber Act was passed reaches a much vaster amount.

Stupendous as was the extent of the nation's resources already appropriated by 1876, more remained to be seized. The Government still owned 40,000,000 acres of land in the South, mainly in Alabama, Louisiana, Florida, Arkansas and Mississippi. Much of this area was valuable timber land, and a part of it, especially in Alabama, was filled with great coal and iron deposits,— a fact of which certain capitalists were well aware, although the general public did not know it.

During the Civil War nothing could be attempted in the war-ravaged South. That conflict over, a group of capitalists set about to get that land, or at least the valuable part of it. At about the time that they had their plans primed to juggle a bill through Congress, an unfortunate situation arose. A rancid public scandal ensued from the bribery of members of Congress in getting through the charters and subsidies of the Union Pacific railroad and other railroads. Congress, for the sake of appearance, had to be circumspect.

### THE "CASH SALES" ACT.

By 1876, however, the public agitation had died away. The time was propitious. Congress rushed through a bill carefully worded for the purpose. The lands were ordered sold in unlimited areas for cash. No pretense was made of restricting the sale to a certain acreage so that all any individual could buy was enough for his own use. Anyone, if he chose, could buy a million or ten million acres, provided he had the cash to pay $1.25 an acre. The way was easy for capitalists to get millions of acres of the coveted iron, coal and timber lands for practically nothing. At that very time the Government was selling coal lands in Colorado at $10 to $20 an acre, and it was recognized that even that price was absurdly low.

Hardly was this " cash sales " law passed, than the besieging capitalists pounced upon these Southern lands and scooped in eight millions of acres of coal, iron and timber lands intrinsically worth (speaking commercially) hundreds of millions of dollars. The fortunes of not a few railroad and industrial magnates were instantly and hugely increased by this fraudulent transaction.[19] Hundreds of millions of dollars in capitalist bonds and stock, representing in effect mortgages on which the people perpetually have to pay heavy interest, are to-day based upon the value of the lands then fraudulently seized.

Fraud was so continuous and widespread that we can here give only a few succinct and scattering instances. " The present system of laws," reported a special Congressional Committee appointed in 1883 to investigate what had become of the once vast public domain, " seem to invite fraud. You cannot turn to a single state paper or public document where the subject is mentioned before the year 1883, from the message of the President to the report of the Commissioner of the Land Office, but what statements of ' fraud ' in connection with the disposition of public lands are found." [20] A little later, Commissioner Sparks of the General Land Office pointed out that " the near approach of the period when the United States will have no land to dispose of has stimulated the exertions of capitalists and corporations to acquire outlying regions of public land in mass, by whatever means,

[19] "Fraudulent transaction," House Ex. Doc. 47, Part iv, Forty-sixth Congress, Third Session, speaks of the phrasing of the act as a mere subterfuge for despoilment; that the act was passed specifically " for the benefit of capitalists," and "that fraud was used in sneaking it through Congress."
[20] House Ex. Doc. 47 : 356.

legal or illegal." In the same report he further stated, "At the outset of my administration I was confronted with overwhelming evidence that the public domain was made the prey of unscrupulous speculation and the worst forms of land monopoly."[21]

## THE "EXCHANGE OF LAND" LAW.

Not pausing to deal with a multitude of other laws the purport and effect of all of which were the same — to give the railroad and other corporations a succession of colossal gifts and other special privileges — laws, many of which will be referred to later — we shall pass on to one of the final masterly strokes of the railroad magnates in possessing themselves of many of such of the last remaining valuable public lands as were open to spoliation.

This happened in 1900. What were styled the land-grant railroads, that is to say, the railroad corporations which received subsidies in both money and land from the Government, were allotted land in alternate sections. The Union Pacific manipulated Congress to "loan" it about $27,000,000 and give it outright 13,000,000 acres of land. The Central Pacific got nearly $26,000,000 and received 9,000,000 acres. To the Northern Pacific 47,-000,000 acres were given; to the Kansas Pacific, 12,100,-000; to the Southern Pacific about 18,000,000 acres. From 1850 the National Government had granted subsidies to more than fifty railroads, and, in addition to the great territorial possessions given to the six railroads enumerated, had made a cash appropriation to those six of not less than about $140,000,000. But the corruptly ob-

[21] Report of the Commissioner of the General Land Office for October, 1885: 48 and 79.

tained donations from the Government were far from being all of the bounty. Throughout the country, States, cities and counties contributed presents in the form of franchises, financial assistance, land and terminal sites.

The land grants, especially in the West, were so enormous that Parsons compares them as follows: Those in Minnesota would make two States the size of Massachusetts; in Kansas they were equal to two States the size of Connecticut and New Jersey; in Iowa the extent of the railroad grants was larger than Connecticut and Rhode Island, and the grants in Michigan and Wisconsin nearly as large; in Montana the grant to one railroad alone would equal the whole of Maryland, New Jersey and Massachusetts. The land grants in the State of Washington were about equivalent to the area of the same three States. Three States the size of New Hampshire could be carved out of the railroad grants in California.[22]

The alternate sections embraced in these States might be good or useless land; the value depended upon the locality. They might be the richest and finest of agricultural grazing, mineral or timber land or barren wastes and rocky mountain tops.

For a while the railroad corporations appeared satisfied with their appropriations and allotments. But as time passed, and the powers of government became more and more directed by them, this plan naturally occurred: Why not exchange the bad, for good, land? Having found it so easy to possess themselves of so vast and valuable an area of former public domain, they calculated that no difficulty would be encountered in putting through another process of plundering. All that was necessary was to go through the formality of ordering Congress

[22] " The Railways, the Trusts and the People ": 137.

to pass an act allowing them to exchange bad, for good, lands.

This, however, could not be done too openly. The people must be blinded by an appearance of conserving public interests. The opportunity came when the Forest Reservation Bill was introduced in Congress — a bill to establish national forest reservations. No better vehicle could have been found for the project traveling in disguise. This bill was everywhere looked upon as a wise and statesmanlike measure for the preservation of forests; capitalist interests, in the pursuit of immediate profit, had ruthlessly denuded and destroyed immense forest stretches, causing, in turn, floods and destruction of life, property and of agriculture. Part of the lands to be taken for the forest reservations included territory settled upon; it was argued as proper, therefore, that the evicted homesteaders should be indemnified by having the choice of lands elsewhere.

So far, the measure looked well. But when it went to the conference committee of the two houses of Congress, the railroad representatives artfully slipped in the four unobtrusive words, "or any other claimant." This quartet of words allowed the railway magnates to exchange millions of acres of desert and of denuded timber lands, arid hills and mountain tops covered with perpetual snow, for millions of the richest lands still remaining in the Government's much diminished hold.

So secretly was this transaction consummated that the public knew nothing about it; the subsidized newspapers printed not a word; it went through in absolute silence. The first protest raised was that of Senator Pettigrew, of South Dakota, in the United States Senate on May 31, 1900. In a vigorous speech he disclosed the vast thefts going on under this act. Congress, under the complete domination of the railroads, took no action to stop it. Only when the fraud was fully accomplished did the railroads allow Congress to go through the forms of deferring to public interests by repealing the law.[28]

## COAL LANDS EXPROPRIATED.

Not merely were the capitalist interests allowed to plunder the public domain from the people under these various acts, but another act was passed by Congress, the "Coal Land Act," purposely drawn to permit the railroads to appropriate great stretches of coal deposits. "Already," wrote President Roosevelt in a message to Congress urging the repeal of the Stone and Timber Act, the Desert Land Law, the Coal Land Act and similar enactments, "probably one-half of the total area of highgrade coals in the West has passed under private control. Including both lignite and the coal areas, these private holdings aggregate not less than 30,000,000 acres of coal fields." These urgings fell flat on a Congress that included many members who had got their millions by reason of these identical laws, and which, as a body, was fully under the control of the dominant class of the day — the Capitalist class. The oligarchy of wealth was triumphantly, gluttonously in power; it was ingenuous folly to expect it to yield where it could vanquish, and concede where it could despoil.[24]

[28] In a letter to the author Senator Pettigrew instances the case of the Northern Pacific Railroad. "The Northern Pacific," he writes, "having patented the top of Mount Tacoma, with its perpetual snow and the rocky crags of the mountains elsewhere, which had been embraced within the forest reservation, could now swap these worthless lands, every acre, for the best valley and grazing lands owned by the Government, and thus the Northern Pacific acquired about two million acres more of mineral, forest and farming lands."

[24] Nor did it yield. Roosevelt's denunciations in no way

The thefts of the public domain have continued, without intermission, up to this present day, and doubtless will not cease until every available acre is appropriated.

A recent report of H. H. Schwartz, chief of the field service of the Department of the Interior, to Secretary Garfield, of that Department, showed that in the two years from 1906 to 1908 alone, approximately $110,000,-000 worth of public land in States, principally west of the Mississippi River, had been fraudulently acquired by capitalist corporations and individuals. This report disclosed more than thirty-two thousand cases of land fraud. The frauds on the part of various capitalist corporations in obtaining vast mineral deposits in Alaska, and incalculably rich water power sites in Montana and elsewhere, constitute one of the great current public scandals. It will be described fully elsewhere in this work.

Overlooking the petty, confusing details of the last seventy years, and focusing attention upon the large developments, this is the striking result beheld: A century ago no railroads existed; to-day the railroads not only own stupendous natural resources, expropriated from the peo-

affected the steady expropriating process. In the current seizure (1909) of vast coal areas in Alaska, the long-continuing process can be seen at work under our very eyes. A controversy, in 1909, between Secretary of the Interior Ballinger and U. S. Chief Forester Gifford Pinchot brought a great scandal to a head. It was revealed that several powerful syndicates of capitalists had filed fraudulent claims to Alaskan coal lands, the value of which is estimated to be from $75,000,000 to $1,-000,000,000. At the present writing their claims, it is announced, are being investigated by the Government. The charge has been made that Secretary of the Interior Ballinger, after leaving the Land Commissioner's office — a post formerly held by him — became the attorney for the most powerful of these syndicates.

At a recent session of the Irrigation Congress at Spokane, Washington, Gov. Pardee of California charged that the timber, the minerals and the soil had long since become the booty of corporations whose political control of public servants was notorious.

ple, but, in conjunction with allied capitalist interests, they dictate what the lot, political, economic and social, of the American people shall be. All of this transformation has come about within a relatively short period, much of it in our own time. But a little while ago the railroad projectors begged and implored, tricked and bribed; and had the law been enforced, would have been adjudged criminals and consigned to prison. And now, in the blazing power of their wealth, these same men or their successors are uncrowned kings, swaying the full powers of government, giving imperial orders that Congress, legislatures, conventions and people must obey.

### AN ARRAY OF COMMANDING FACTS.

But this is not the only commanding fact. A much more important one lies in the astonishing ease with which the masses of the people have been discriminated against, exploited and oppressed. Theoretically the power of government resides in the people, down to the humblest voter. This power, however, has been made the instrument for enslaving the very people supposed to be the wielders of political action.

While Congress, the legislatures and the executive and administrative officials have been industriously giving away public domain, public funds and perpetual rights to railroad and other corporations, they have almost entirely ignored the interests of the general run of people.

The more capitalists they created, the harder it became for the poor to get settler's land on the public domain. Congress continued passing acts by which, in most cases, the land was turned over to corporations. Intending settlers had to buy it at exorbitant prices. This took place in nearly all of the States and Territories. Large num-

bers of people could not afford to pay the price demanded
by the railroads, and consequently were compelled to
herd in industrial centers. They were deliberately shut
off from possession of the land. This situation was already acute twenty-five years ago. "The area of arable
land open to settlement," pointed out Secretary of the
Interior Teller in a circular letter of May 22, 1883, "is
not great when compared with the increasing demand
and is rapidly decreasing." All other official reports con-
sistently relate the same conditions.[25]

At the same time, while being excluded from soil which
had been national property, the working and farming
class were subjected to either neglect or onerous laws.
As a class, the capitalists had no difficulty at any time
in securing whatever laws they needed; if persuasion by
argument was not effective, bribery was. Moreover, over
and above corrupt purchase of votes was the feeling ingrained in legislators by the concerted teachings of society that the man of property should be looked up to;
that he was superior to the common herd; that his interests were paramount and demanded nursing and protection. Whenever a commercial crisis occurred, the capitalists secured a ready hearing and their measures were
passed promptly. But millions of workers would be in
enforced idleness and destitution, and no move was made
to throw open public lands to them, or appropriate money,
or start public works. Such a proposed policy was considered "paternalism"—a catchword of the times implying that Governmental care should not be exercised
for the unfortunate, the weak and the helpless.

[25] "The tract books of my office show," reported Commissioner Sparks, "that available public lands are already largely
covered by entries, selections and claims of various kinds." The
actual settler was compelled to buy up these claims, if, indeed,
he was permitted to settle on the land.— U. S. Senate Ex. Docs.,
1885-86, Vol. viii, Doc. No. 134: 4.

And here was the anomaly of the so-called American democratic Government.  It was held legitimate and necessary that capital should be encouraged, but illegitimate to look out for the interests of the non-propertied.  The capitalists were very few; the non-propertied, holding nominally the overwhelming voting power, were many. Government was nothing more or less than a device for the nascent capitalist class to work out its inevitable purposes, yet the majority of the people, on whom the powers of class government severely fell, were constantly deluded into believing that the Government represented them.  Whether Federalist or anti-Federalist, Whig, Republican or Democratic party was in power, the capitalist class went forward victoriously and invincibly, the proof of which is seen in its present almost limitless power and possessions.

# CHAPTER II

## A NECESSARY CONTRAST

If the whole might of Government was used in the aggrandizement and perpetuation of a propertied aristocracy, what was its specific attitude toward the working class? Of the powerful few, whether political or industrial, the conventional histories hand down grossly biased and distorted chronicles. These few are isolated from the multitude, and their importance magnified, while the millions of obscure are nowhere adequately described. Such sterile historians proceed upon the perfunctory plan, derived from ancient usage in the days when kingcraft was supremely exalted, that it is only the mighty few whose acts are of any consequence, and that the doings of the masses are of no account.

### GOVERNMENT BY PROPERTY INTERESTS.

Hence it is that most histories are mere registers of names and dates, dull or highly-colored hackneyed splurges of print giving no insight into actual conditions.

In this respect most of the prevailing histories of the United States are the most egregious offenders. They fix the idea that this or that alleged statesman, this or that President or politician or set of politicians, have been the dominating factors in the decision and sway of public affairs. No greater error could be formulated. Behind the ostentatious and imposing public personages of the different periods, the arbiters of laws and policies have been the men of property. They it was who really ruled both the arena and the arcana of politics.

It was they, sometimes openly, but more usually covertly, who influenced and manipulated the entire sphere of government.

It was they who raised the issues which divided the people into contesting camps and which often beclouded and bemuddled the popular mind. It was their material ideals and interests that were engrafted upon the fabric of society and made the prevailing standards of the day.

From the start the United States Government was what may be called a regime swayed by property.

The Revolution, as we have seen, was a movement by the native property interests to work out their own destiny without interference by the trading classes of Great Britain. The Constitution of the United States, the various State Constitutions, and the laws, were, we have set forth, all reflexes of the interests, aims, castes and prejudices of the property owners, as opposed to the non-propertied. At first, the landholders and the shipping merchants were the dictators of laws. Then from these two classes and from the tradesmen sprang a third class, the bankers, who, after a continuous orgy of bribery, rose to a high pitch of power. At the same time, other classes of property owners were sharers in varying degrees in directing Government. One of these was the slaveholders of the South, desperately increasing their clutch on government administration the more their institutions were threatened. The factory owners were likewise participants. However bitterly some of these propertied interests might war upon one another for supremacy, there was never a time when the majority of the men who sat in Congress, the legislatures or the judges did not represent, or respond to, either the interests or the ideals of one or more of these divisions of the propertied classes.

Finally, out of the landowners, slaveowners, bankers, shippers, factory masters and tradesmen a new class of great power developed. This was the railroad-owning class. From about the year 1845 to 1890 it was the most puissant governing class in the United States, and only ceased being distinctly so when the industrial trusts became even mightier, and a time came when one trust alone, the Standard Oil Company, was able to possess itself of vast railroad systems.

These different components of the railroad-owning class had gathered in their money by either outright fraud or by the customary exploitative processes of the times. We have noted how many of the landholders secured their estates at one time or another by bribery or by invidiously fraudulent transactions; and how the bankers, who originally were either tradesmen, factory owners or landowners, had obtained their charters and privileges by widespread bribery. A portion of the money thus acquired was often used in bribing Congress and legislatures for railroad charters, public funds, immense areas of land including forests and mines, and special laws of the most extraordinary character.

### CONDITIONS OF THE NON-PROPERTIED.

Since Government was actually, although not avowedly or apparently, a property regime, what was the condition of the millions of non-propertied?

In order to get a correct understanding of both the philosophy and the significance of what manner of property rule was in force, it is necessary to give an accompanying sketch of the life of the millions of producers, and what kind of laws related to them. Merely to narrate the acts of the capitalists of the period is of no enduring value unless it be accompanied by a necessary contrast of how Government and capitalist acted toward the worker. It was the worker who tilled the ground and harvested the produce nourishing nations; whose labor, mental or manual, brought forth the thousand and one commodities, utensils, implements, articles and luxuries necessary to the material wants of civilization. Verily, what of the great hosts of toilers who have done their work and shuffled off to oblivion? What were their aspirations, difficulties, movements and struggles? While Government, controlled by both the men and the standards of property, was being used as a distributing instrument for centering resources and laws in the hands of a mere minority, what were its methods in dealing with the lowly and propertyless?

Furthermore, this contrast is indispensable for another reason. Posterity ever has a blunt way of asking the most inquisitive questions. The inquirer for truth will not be content with the simple statement that many of the factory owners and tradesmen bribed representative bodies to give them railroad charters and bountiful largess. He will seek to know how, as specifically as the records allow, they got together that money. Their nominal methods are of no weight; it is the portrayal of their real, basic methods which alone will satisfy the delver for actual facts.

This is not the place for a voluminous account of the industrial development of the United States. We cannot halt here to give the full account of the origin and growth of that factory system which has culminated in the gigantic trusts of to-day. Nor can we pause to deal with the manifold circumstances and methods in-

volved in that expansion. The full tale of the rise and
climax of industrial establishments; how they subverted
the functions of government to their own ends; stole inventions right and left and drove inventors to poverty
and to the grave; defrauded the community of incredible
amounts by evading taxation; oppressed their workers
to a degree that in future times will read like the acts of
a class outsavaging the savage; bribed without intermission; slaughtered legions of men, women and children
in the pursuit of profit; exploited the peoples of the
globe remorselessly — all of this and more, constituting
a weird chapter of horrors in the progress of the race,
will be fully described in a later part of this work.[1]

But in order to contribute a clear perspective of the
methods and morals of a period when Government was
but the mannikin of property — a period even more pronounced now — and to give a deeper insight into the
conditions against which millions had to contend at a
time when the railroad oligarchy was blown into life by
Government edict, a few important facts will be presented here.

The sonorous doctrines of the Declaration of Independence read well, but they were not meant to be applied to the worker. The independence so much vaunted
was the independence of the capitalist to do as he pleased.
Few, if any, restrictions were placed upon him; such
pseudo restrictions as were passed from time to time
were not enforced. On the other hand, the severest laws
were enacted against the worker. For a long time it
was a crime for him to go on a strike. In the first strike
in this country of which there is any record — that of
a number of sailors in New York City in 1803, for better
wages — the leader was arrested, indicted and sent to

---

[1] See "Great Fortunes from Industries."

prison. The formidable machinery of Government was employed by the ruling commercial and landed classes for a double purpose. On the one hand, they insisted that it should encourage capital, which phrase translated into action meant that it should confer grants of land, immense loans of public funds without interest, virtual immunity from taxation, an extra-legal taxing power, sweeping privileges, protective laws and clearly defined statute rights.

### THE SUPREMACY OF EMPLOYERS.

At the same time, while enriching themselves in every direction by transferring, through the powers of Government, public resources to themselves, the capitalists declared it to be a settled principle that Government should not be paternalistic; they asserted that it was not only not a proper governmental function to look out for the interests of the masses of workers, but they went even further.

With the precedents of the English laws as an example, they held that it devolved upon Government to keep the workers sternly within the bounds established by employers. In plain words, this meant that the capitalist was to be allowed to run his business as he desired. He could overwork his employees, pay them the lowest wages, and kill them off by forcing them to work under conditions in which the sacrifice of human life was held subordinate to the gathering of profits, or by forcing them to work or live in disease-breeding places.[2]

[2] The slum population of the United States increased rapidly. "According to the best estimates," stated the "Seventh Special Report of the U. S. Commissioner of Labor — The Slums of Great Cities, 1894," "the total slum population of Baltimore is about 25,000; of Chicago, 162,000; of New York, 360,000; of Philadelphia, 35,000" (p. 12). The figures of the average weekly

The law, which was the distinct expression of the interests of the capitalist, upheld his right to do all this. Yet if the workers protested; if they sought to improve their condition by joining in that community of action called a strike, the same code of laws adjudged them criminals. At once, the whole power of law, with its police, miltary and judges, descended upon them, and either drove them back to their tasks or consigned them to prison.

The conditions under which the capitalists made their profits, and under which the workers had to toil, were very oppressive to the workers. The hours of work at that period were from sunrise to sunset. Usually this rule, especially in the seasons of long days, required twelve, and very often fourteen and sixteen, hours a day. Yet the so-called statesmen and the pretentious cultured and refined classes of the day, saw nothing wrong in this exploitation. The reason was obvious. Their power, their elegant mansions, their silks and satins, their equipage and superior opportunities for enjoyment all were based upon the sweat and blood of these so-called free white men, women and children of the North, who toiled even harder than the chattel black slave of the South, and who did not receive a fraction of the care and thought bestowed, as a corrollary of property, upon the black

wages per individual of the slum population revealed why there was so large a slum population. In Baltimore these wages were $8.65½ per week; in Chicago, $9.88½; in New York, $8.36, and in Philadelphia, $8.68 per week (p. 64).

In his " Modern Social Conditions," Bailey, basing his statements upon the U. S. Census of 1900, asserted that 109,750 persons had died from tuberculosis in the United States in 1900. " Plenty of fresh air and sunlight," he wrote, " will kill the germs, and yet it is estimated that there are eight millions of people who will eventually die from consumption unless strenuous efforts are made to combat the disease. Working in a confined atmosphere, and living in damp, poorly ventilated rooms, the dwellers in the tenements of the great cities fall easy victims to the great white plague (p. 265).

slave. Already the capitalists of the North had a slavery system in force far more effective than the chattel system of the South — a system the economic superiority of which was destined to overthrow that of black slavery.

Most historians, taking their cue from the intellectual subserviency demanded of them by the ruling propertied classes, delight in picturing those times as "the good old times," when the capitalists were benevolent and amiable, and the workers lived in peace and plenty.

### AN INCESSANT WARFARE.

History in the main, thus far, has been an institution for the propagation of lies. The truth is that for thousands of years back, since the private property system came into existence, an incessant, uncompromising warfare has been going on between oppressors and oppressed. Apart from the class distinctions and the bit-terness manifested in settlement and colonial times in this country — reference to which has been given in earlier chapters — the whole of the nineteenth century, and thus far of this century, has been a continuous industrial struggle. It has been the real warfare of modern times.

In this struggle the propertied classes had the great advantage from the start. Centuries of rulership had taught them that the control of Government was the crux of the mastery. By possession of Government they had the power of making laws; of the enforcement or non-enforcement of those laws; of the directorship of police, army, navy, courts, jails and prisons — all terrible instruments for suppressing any attempt at protest, peaceful or otherwise. Notwithstanding this massing of power and force, the working class has at no time been

passive or acquiescent. It has allowed itself to be duped;
it has permitted its ranks to be divided by false issues;
it has often been blind at critical times, and has made no
concerted effort as yet to get intelligent possession of the
great strategic point,—governmental power. Nevertheless, despite these mistakes, it has been in a state of constant rebellion; and the fact that it has been so, that its
aspirations could not be squelched by jails, prisons and
cannon nor by destitution or starvation, furnishes the
sublimest record in all the annals of mankind.

### THE WORKERS' STRUGGLE FOR BETTER CONDITIONS.

Again and again the workers attempted to throw off
some of their shackles, and every time the whole dominant force of society was arrayed against them. By 1825
an agitation developed for a ten-hour workday. The politicians denounced the movement; the cultured classes
frowned upon it; the newspapers alternately ridiculed and
abused it; the officials prepared to take summary action
to put it down. As for the capitalists — the shipping
merchants, the boot and shoe manufacturers, the iron
masters and others — they not only denied the right of
the workers to organize, while insisting that they themselves were entitled to combine, but they inveighed against
the ten-hour demand as " unreasonable conditions which
the folly and caprice of a few journeymen mechanics
may dictate." " A very large sum of money," says
McNeill, " was subscribed by the merchants to defeat the
ten-hour movement." [3]    And as an evidence of the intense opposition to the workers' demands for a change
from a fourteen to a ten-hour day, McNeill quotes from
a Boston newspaper of 1832:

[3] " The Labor Movement ": 339.

Had this unlawful combination had for its object the en-
hancement of daily wages, it would have been left to its own
care; but it now strikes the very nerve of industry and good
morals by dictating the hours of labor, abrogating the good old
rule of our fathers and pointing out the most direct course to
poverty; for to be idle several of the most useful hours of the
morning and evening will surely lead to intemperance and ruin.

These, generally speaking, were the stock capitalist arguments of the day, together with the further reiterated
assertion that it was impossible to conduct business on
a ten-hour day system.  The effect of the fourteen-hour
day upon the workers was pernicious.  Having no time
for reading, self-education, social intercourse or acquaint-
ing themselves with refinement, they often developed brutal propensities.  In proportion to the length of time
and the rigor with which they were exploited, they degenerated morally and intellectually.  This was a well-
known fact, and was frequently commented upon by contemporaneous observers.  Their employers could not fail
to know it, yet, with few exceptions, they insisted that
any movement to shorten the day's labor was destructive
of good morals.

This pronouncement, however, need not arouse comment.  Ever has the propertied class set itself up as the
lofty guardian of morals although actuated by sordid
self-interest and nothing more.  Many workers were
driven to drink, crime and suicide by the exasperating
and deteriorating conditions under which they had to
labor.  The moment that they overstepped the slightest
bounds of law, in rushed the authorities with summary
punishment.  The prisons of the period were full of mechanics whom serfdom or poverty had stung on to commit
some crime or other.  However trifling the offence, or
whatever the justifiable provocation, the law made no

allowance; the letter of the statutes was strictly construed, and always administered with a heavy hand.

### THE CAPITALIST'S TACTICS.

The whole of uppermost society was aligned against the hard-driven working class. The employers deplored the audacity of the workers in forming unions and attempting to get shorter hours of labor. The capitalist changed his tactics like an acrobat. If the workers struck for a less burdensome workday he would asure them that he could not recognize such an untenable position; he might sympathize with their efforts for higher wages, but he must combat any effort for shorter hours.

But when the workers struck specifically for more wages, then the capitalist summoned the judiciary to help him out, as happened in New York City, in 1836, when twenty-one journeymen tailors were fined by Judge Edwards sums ranging from $100 to $150. As many of them could not pay it, they were despatched to jail. The clergy virulently assailed the trade-union movement. "We regret to say," read a statement of a general meeting of the mechanics of Boston and vicinity, issued on January 8, 1834, "that no one of our respected clergy are present. Application having been made to twenty-two different societies for the use of a meeting house on this day for trades unions, the doors of all were shut against us." . . .

Year after year the struggle continued for a ten-hour day throughout the North and East. Time after time the workers were driven back to their jobs by utter impoverishment. Repeatedly defeated, they renewed the attempt as often. Wherever they applied for aid or sympathy they met with hostility. In 1836 a Baltimore trades-union memorialized Congress to limit the hours of labor of those employed on the public works to ten hours a day. The pathos of this petition! So unceasingly had the workers been lied to by politicians, newspapers, clergy and employers, that they did not realize that in applying to Congress or to any legislature, that they were begging from men who represented the antagonistic interests of their own employers. After a short debate Congress laid the petition on the table. Congress at this very time was spinning out laws in behalf of capitalist interests; granting public lands, public funds, protective tariffs and manifold other measures demanded or lobbied for by existing or projected corporations.

A memorial of a " Portion of the Laboring Classes of the City of New York in Relation to The Money Market " complained to Congress in 1833 that the powers of the Government were used against the working class.

" You are not ignorant," they petitioned,

That our State Legislatures have, by a usurpation of power which is expressly withheld by our Federal Constitution, chartered many companies to engage in the manufacture of paper money; and that the necessities of the laboring classes have compelled them to give it currency.

The strongest argument against this measure is, that by licensing any man or set of men to manufacture money, instead of earning it, we virtually license them to take so much of the property of the community as they may happen to fancy, without contributing to it at all — an injustice so enormous that it is incapable of any defense and therefore needs no comment.

. . . That the profits of capital are abstracted from the earnings of labor, and that these deductions, like any other tax on industry, tend to diminish the value of money by increasing the price of all the fruits of labor, are facts beyond dispute; it is equally undeniable that there is a point which capitalists cannot exceed without injuring themselves, for when by their exertions they so far depreciate the value of money at home that it is sent abroad, many are thrown out of employ, and are not only disabled from paying their tribute, *but are forced to betake to dishonest courses or starve.*

This memorial was full of iron and stern truths, although much of its political economy was that of its own era; a very different petition, it will be noticed, from the appealing, cringing petitions sent timidly to Congress by the conservative, truckling labor leaders of later times. The memorial continued;

> The remaining laborers are then loaded with additional burdens to provide laws and prisons and standing armies to keep order; expensive wars are created merely to lull for a time the clamors for employment; each new burden aggravates the disease, and national death finally ends it.

The power of capital, was, the memorial read on, " in the nature of things, regulated by the proportion that the numbers of, and competition among, capitalists bears to the number and destitution of laborers." The only sure way of benefiting labor, " and the way best calculated to benefit all classes," was to diminish the destitution among the working classes. And the remedy proposed in the memorial? A settled principle of national policy should be laid down by Congress that the whole of the remaining of the public lands should forever continue to be the public property of the nation " and accordingly, cause them to be laid out from time to time, as the wants of the population might require, in small farms with a suitable proportion of building lots for mechanics, for the free use of any native citizen and his descendants who might be at the expense of clearing them." This policy " would establish a perpetual counterpoise to the absorbing power of capital." The memorial concluded:

> These lands have been bought with public money every cent of which is in the end derived from the earnings of the laboring classes.

And while the public money has been liberally employed to protect and foster trade, Government has never, to our knowledge, adopted but one measure (the protective tariff system) with a distinct view to promote the interests of labor; and all of the advantages of this *one* have been absorbed by the preponderating power of capital.[4]

## EMPLOYMENT OF MILITIA AGAINST THE WORKERS.

But it was not only the National Government which used the entire governing power against the workers. State and municipal authorities did likewise. In 1836 the 'longshoremen in New York City struck for an increase of wages. Their employers hurriedly substituted non-union men in their places. When the union men went from dock to dock, trying to induce the newcomers to side with them, the shipping merchants pretended that a riot was under way and made frantic calls upon the authorities for a subduing force. The mayor ordered out the militia with loaded guns. In Philadelphia similar scenes took place. Naturally, as the strikers were prevented by the soldiers from persuading their fellow workers, they lost the strikes.

Although labor-saving machinery was constantly being devised and improved to displace hand labor, and although the skilled worker was consequently producing far more goods than in former years, the masters — as the capitalists were then often termed — insisted that employees must work for the same wages and hours as had long prevailed.

By 1840, however, the labor unions had arrived at a point where they were very powerful in some of the crafts, and employers grudgingly had to recognize that

[4] Executive Documents, First Session, Twenty-third Congress, 1834, Doc. No. 104.

the time had passed by when the laborer was to be treated like a serf. A few enlightened employers voluntarily conceded the ten-hour day, not on any humane grounds, but because they reasoned that it would promote greater efficiency on the part of their workers. Many capitalists, perforce, had to yield to the demand. Other capitalists determined to break up the unions on the ground that they were a conspiracy. At the instigation of several boot and shoe manufacturers, the officials of Boston brought a suit against the Boston Journeymen Bootmakers' Society. The court ruled against the bootmakers and the jury brought in a verdict of guilty. On appeal to the Supreme Court, Robert Rantoul, the attorney for the society, so ably demolished the prosecution's points, that the court could not avoid setting aside the judgment of the inferior court.[5]

Perhaps the growing power of the labor unions had its effect upon those noble minds, the judiciary. The worker was no longer detached from his fellow workmen: he could no longer be scornfully shoved aside as a weak, helpless individual. He now had the strength of association and organization. The possibility of such strength transferred to politics affrighted the ruling classes. Where before this, the politicians had contemptuously treated the worker's petitions, certain that he could always be led blindly to vote the usual partisan tickets, it now dawned upon them that it would be wiser to make an appearance of deference and to give some concessions which, although of a slight character, could

[5] Commonwealth vs. Hunt and others; Metcalf's Supreme Court Reports, iv: 111. The prosecution had fallen back on the old English law of the time of Queen Elizabeth, making it a criminal offence for workingmen to refuse to work under certain wages. This law, Rantoul argued, had not been specifically adopted as common law in the United States after the Revolution.

be made to appear important.    The Workingmen's party of 1829 had shown a glimmer of what the worker could do when aroused to class-conscious action.

### CAJOLING THE LABOR VOTE.

Now it was that the politicians began the familiar policy of " catering to the labor vote."    Some rainbow promises of what they would do, together with a few scraps of legislation now and then — this constituted the bait held out by the politicians.    That adroit master of political chicanery, President Van Buren, hastened to issue an executive order on April 10, 1840, directing the establishment of a ten-hour day, between April and September, in the navy yards.    From the last day of October, however, until March 31, the " working hours will be from the rising to the setting of the sun "— a length of time equivalent, meal time deducted, to about ten hours.

The political trick of throwing out crumbs to the workers long proved successful.    But it was supplemented by other methods.    To draw the labor leaders away from a hostile stand to the established political parties, and to prevent the massing of workers in a party of their own, the politicians began an insidious system of bribing these leaders to turn traitors.    This was done by either appointing them to some minor political office or by giving them money.    In many instances, the labor unions in the ensuing decades were grossly betrayed.

Finally, the politicians always had large sums of election funds contributed by merchants, bankers, landowners, railroad owners — by all parts of the capitalist class. These funds were employed in corrupting the electorate and legislative bodies.    Caucuses and primaries were packed, votes bought, ballot boxes stuffed and election returns falsified. It did not matter to the corporations generally which of the old political parties was in power; some manufacturers or merchants might be swayed to one side or the other for the self-interest involved in the reënactment of the protective tariff or the establishment of free trade; but, as a rule, the corporations, as a matter of business, contributed money to both parties.

### THE BASIS OF POLITICAL PARTIES.

However these parties might differ on various issues, thy both stood for the perpetuation of the existing social and industrial system based upon capitalist ownership. The tendency of the Republican party, founded in 1856, toward the abolition of negro chattel slavery was in precise harmony with the aims and fundamental interests of the manufacturing capitalists of the North. The only peril that the capitalist class feared was the creation of a distinct, disciplined and determined workingmen's party. This they knew would, if successful, seriously endanger and tend to sweep away the injustices and oppressions upon which they, the capitalists, subsisted. To avert this, every ruse and expedient was resorted to: derision, undermining, corruption, violence, imprisonment — all of these and other methods were employed by that sordid ruling class claiming for itself so pretentious and all-embracing a degree of refinement, morality and patriotism.

Surveying historical events in a large way, however, it is by no means to be regretted that capitalism had its own unbridled way, and that its growth was not checked. Its development to the unbearable maximum had to come in order to prepare the ripe way for a newer stage in civilization. The capitalist was an outgrowth of conditions as they existed both before, and during, his time. He fitted as appropriate a part in his time as the predatory baron in feudal days.

But in this sketch we are not dealing with historical causes or sequences as much as with events and contrasts. The aim is to give a sufficient historical perspective of times when Government was manipulated by the capitalist class for its own aggrandizement, and to despoil and degrade the millions of producers.

The imminence of working-class action was an ever present and disturbing menace to the capitalists. To give one of many instances of how the workers were beginning to realize the necessity of this action, and how the capitalists met it, let us instance the resolutions of the New England Workingmen's Association, adopted in 1845. With the manifold illustrations in mind of how the powers of Government had been used and were being increasingly used to expropriate the land, the resources and the labor and produce of the many, and bond that generation and future generations under a multitude of law-created rights and privileges, this association declared in its preamble:

Whereas, we, the mechanics and workingmen of New England are convinced by the sad experience of years that under the present arrangement of society labor is and must be the slave of wealth; and, whereas, the producers of all wealth are deprived not merely of its enjoyment, but also of the social and civil rights which belong to humanity and the race; and, whereas, we are convinced that reform of those abuses must depend upon ourselves only; and, whereas, we believe that in intelligence alone is strength, we hereby declare our object to be union for power, power to bless humanity, and to further this object resolve ourselves into an association.

One of the leading spirits in this movement was Charles A. Dana, a young professional man of great promise and exceptional attainments. Subsequently he was bought off with a political office; he became not only a renegade of the most virulent type, but he leagued himself with the greatest thieves of the day — Tweed and Jay Gould, for example — received large bribes for defending them and their interests in a newspaper of which he became the owner — the New York *Sun* — and spent his last years bitterly and cynically attacking, ridiculing and misrepresenting the labor movement, and made himself the most conspicuous editorial advocate for every thieving plutocrat or capitalist measure.

The year 1884 about marked the zenith of the era of the capitalist seizing of the public domain. By that time the railroad and other corporations had possessed themselves of a large part of the area now vested in their ownership. At that very time an army of workers, estimated at 2,000,000, was out of employment. Yet it was not considered a panic year; certainly the industrial establishments of the country were not in the throes of a commercial cataclysm such as happened in 1873 and previous periods. The cities were overcrowded with the destitute and homeless; along every country road and railroad track could be seen men, singly or in pairs, tramping from place to place looking for work.

Many of those unemployed were native Americans. A large number were aliens who had been induced to migrate by the alluring statements of the steamship companies to whose profit it was to carry large batches; by the solicitations of the agents of American corporations seeking among the oppressed peoples of the Old World a generous supply of cheap, unorganized labor; or by the spontaneous prospect of bettering their condition politically or economically.

Millions of poor Europeans were thus persuaded to come over, only to find that the promises held out to them were hollow. They found that they were exploited in the United States even worse industrially than in their native country. As for political freedom their sanguine hopes were soon shattered. They had votes after a certain period of residence, it was true, but they saw — or at least the intelligent of them soon discerned — that the personnel and laws of the United States Government were determined by the great capitalists. The people were allowed to go through the form of voting; the moneyed interests, by controlling the machinery of the dominant political parties, dictated who the candidates, and what the so-called principles, of those parties should be. The same program was witnessed at every election. The electorate was stimulated with excitement and enthusiasm over false issues and dominated candidates. The more the power and wealth of the capitalist class increased, the more openly the Government became ultra-capitalistic.

## WEALTH AND THE SWAY OF DIRECT POWER

It was about this time that the Senate of the United States was undergoing a transformation clearly showing how impatient the great capitalists were of operating Government through middlemen legislators. Previously, the manufacturing, railroad and banking interests had, on the whole, deemed it wise not to exercise this power directly but indirectly. The representatives sent to Congress were largely lawyers elected by their influence and money. The people at large did not know the secret processes back of these legislators. The press, advocating, as a whole, the interests of the capitalist class, constantly portrayed the legislators as great and patriotic statesmen.

But the magnates saw that the time had arrived when some empty democratic forms of Government could be waved aside, and the power exercised openly and directly by them. Presently we find such men as Leland Stanford, of the Pacific railroad quartet, and one of the arch-bribers and thieves of the time, entering the United States Senate after debauching the California legislature; George Hearst, a mining magnate, and others of that class.

More and more this assumption of direct power increased, until now it is reckoned that there are at least eighty millionaires in Congress. Many of them have been multimillionaires controlling, or representing corporations having a controlling share in vast industries, transportation and banking systems — men such as Senator Elkins, of West Virginia; Clark, of Montana; Platt and Depew, of New York; Guggenheim, of Colorado; Knox, of Pennsylvania; Foraker, of Ohio, and a quota of others. The popular jest as to the United States Senate being a "millionaires' club" has become antiquated; much more appropriately it could be termed a "multimillionaires' club." While in both houses of Congress are legislators who represent the almost extinguished middle class, their votes are as ineffective as their declamations are flat. The Government of the United States, viewing it as an entirety, and not considering the impotent exceptions, is now more avowedly a capitalist Government than ever before. As for the various legislatures, the magnates, coveting no seats in those bodies, are content to follow the old plan of mastering them by either direct bribery or by controlling the political bosses in charge of the political machines.

Since the interests of the capitalists from the start were acutely antagonistic to those of the workers and of the people in general from whom their profits came, no cause for astonishment can be found in the refusal of Government to look out, even in trifling ways, for the workers' welfare. But it is of the greatest and most instructive interest to give a succession of contrasts. And here some complex factors intervene. Those cold, unimpassioned academicians who can perpetuate fallacies and lies in the most polished and dispassionate language, will object to the statement that the whole of governing institutions has been in the hands of thieves — great, not petty, thieves. And yet the facts, as we have seen (and will still further see), bear out this assertion. Government was run and ruled at basis by the great thieves, as it is conspicuously to-day.

### THE PASSING OF THE MIDDLE CLASS.

Yet let us not go so fast. It is necessary to remember that the last few decades have constituted a period of startling transitions.

The middle class, comprising the small business and factory men, stubbornly insisted on adhering to worn-out methods of doing business. Its only conception of industry was that of the methods of the year 1825. It refused to see that the centralization of industry was inevitable, and that it meant progress. It lamented the decay of its own power, and tried by every means at its command to thwart the purposes of the trusts. This middle class had bribed and cheated and had exploited the worker. For decades it had shaped public opinion to support the dictum that " competition was the life of trade." It had, by this shaping of opinion, enrolled on its side a large number of workers who saw only the temporary evils, and not the ultimate good, involved in the scientific organization and centralization of industry. The middle class put through anti-trust laws and other measure after measure aimed at the great combinations.

These great combinations had, therefore, a double fight on their hands. On the one hand they had to resist the trades unions, and on the other, the middle class. It was necessary to their interests that centralization of industry should continue. In fact, it was historically and economically necessary. Consequently they had to bend every effort to make nugatory any effort of Government, both National and State, to enforce the anti-trust laws. The thing had to be done no matter how. It was intolerable that industrial development could be stopped by a middle class which, for self-interest, would have kept matters at a standstill. Self-interest likewise demanded that the nascent combinations and trusts get and exercise governmental power by any means they could use.

For a while triumphant in passing certain laws which, it was fatuously expected, would wipe the trusts out of existence, the middle class was hopelessly beaten and routed. By their far greater command of resources and money, the great magnates were able to frustrate the execution of those laws, and gradually to install themselves or their tools in practically supreme power. The middle class is now becoming a mere memory. Even the frantic efforts of President Roosevelt in its behalf were of absolutely no avail; the trusts are mightier than ever before, and hold a sway the disputing of which is ineffective.

### THE TRUSTS AND THE UNEMPLOYED.

With this newer organization and centralization of industry the number of unemployed tremendously in-

creased.  In the panic of 1893 it reached about 3,000,000;
in that of 1908 perhaps 6,000,000, certainly 5,000,000.
To the appalling suffering on every hand the Government
remained indifferent.  The reasons were two-fold: Government was administered by the capitalist class whose
interest it was not to allow any measure to be passed
which might strengthen the workers, or decrease the volume of surplus labor; the second was that Government
was basically the apotheosis of the current commercial
idea that the claims of property were superior to those of
human life.

It can be said without exaggeration that high functionary after high functionary in the legislative or executive
branches of the Government, and magnate after magnate
had committed not only one violation, but constant violations, of the criminal law.  They were unmolested; having the power to prevent it they assuredly would not
suffer themselve to undergo even the farce of prosecution.  Such few prosecutions as were started with suspicious bluster by the Government against the Standard
Oil Company, the Sugar Trust, the Tobacco Trust and
other trusts proved to be absolutely harmless, and have
had no result except to strengthen the position of the
trusts.  The great magnates reaped their wealth by an
innumerable succession of frauds and thefts.  But the
moment that wealth or the basis of that wealth were
threatened in the remotest by any law or movement, the
whole body of Government, executive, legislative and
judicial, promptly stepped in to protect it intact.

The workers, however, from whom the wealth was
robbed, were regarded in law as criminals the moment
they became impoverished.  If homeless and without visible means of support, they were subject to arrest as
vagabonds.  Numbers of them were constantly sent to

prison or, in some States, to the chain-gang. If they ventured to hold mass meetings to urge the Government to start a series of public works to relieve the unemployed, their meetings were broken up and the assembled brutally clubbed, as happened in Tompkins square in New York City in the panic of 1873, in Washington in 1892, and in Chicago and in Union square, New York City, in the panic of 1908. The newspapers represented these meetings as those of irresponsible agitators, inciting the " mob " to violence. The clubbing of the unemployed and the judicial murder of their spokesman, has long been a favorite repression method of the authorities. But as for allowing them freedom of speech, considering the grievances, putting forth every effort to relieve their condition,— these do not seem to have come within the scope of that Government whose every move has been one of intense hostility — now open, again covert — to the working class.

This running sketch, which is to be supplemented by the most specific details, gives a sufficient insight into the debasement and despoiling of the working class while the capitalists were using the Government as an expropriating machine. Meanwhile, how was the great farming class faring? What were the consequences to this large body of the seizure by a few of the greater part of the public domain?

THE STATE OF THE FARMING POPULATION.

The conditions of the farming population, along with that of the working class, steadily grew worse. In the hope of improving their condition large numbers migrated from the Eastern States, ana a constant influx of agriculturists poured in from Europe.

A comparatively few of the whole were able to get land direct from the Government. Naturally the course of this extensive migration followed the path of transportation, that is to say, of the railroads. This was exactly what the railroad corporations had anticipated. As a rule the migrating farmers found the railroads or cattlemen already in possession of many of the best lands. To give a specific idea of how vast and widespread were the railroad holdings in.the various States, this tabulation covering the years up to 1883 will suffice: In the States of Florida, Louisiana, Alabama and Mississippi about 9,000,000 acres in all; in Wisconsin, 3,553,865 acres; Missouri, 2,605,251 acres; Arkansas, 2,613,631 acres; Illinois, 2,595,053 acres; Iowa, 4,181,929 acres; Michigan, 3,355,943 acres; Minnesota, 9,830,450 acres; Nebraska, 6,409,376 acres; Colorado, 3,000,000 acres; the State of Washington, 11,700,000 acres; New Mexico, 11,500,000 acres; in the Dakotas, 8,000,000 acres; Oregon, 5,800,000 acres; Montana, 17,000,000 acres; California, 16,387,000; Idaho, 1,500,000, and Utah, 1,850,-000.[6]

Prospective farmers had to pay the railroads exorbitant prices for land. Very often they had not sufficient funds; a mortgage or two would be signed; and if the farmer had a bad season or two, and could no longer pay the interest, foreclosure would result. But whether crops were good or bad, the American farmer constantly had to compete in the grain markets of the world with the cheap labor of India and Russia. And inexorably, East or West, North or South, he was caught between a double fire.

On the one hand, in order to compete with the im-

[6] "The Public Domain," House Ex. Doc. No. 47, Third Session, Forty-sixth Congress: 273.

mense capitalist farms gradually developing, he had to give up primitive implements and buy the most improved agricultural machines. For these he was charged five and six times the sum it cost the manufacturers to make and market them. Usually if he could not pay for them outright, the manufacturers took out a mortgage on his farm. Large numbers of these mortgages were fore-closed.

In addition, the time had passed when the farmer made his own clothes and many other articles. For everything that he bought he had to pay excessive prices. He, even more than the industrial working classes, had to pay an enormous manufacturer's profit, and additionally the high freight railroad rate.

On the other hand, the great capitalist agencies directly dealing with the crops — the packing houses, the gambling cotton and produce exchanges — actually owned, by a series of manipulations, a large proportion of his crops before they were out of the ground. These crops were sold to the working class at exorbitant prices. The small farmer labored incessantly, only to find himself getting poorer. It served political purpose well to describe glowingly the farmer's prosperity; but the greater crops he raised, the greater the profit to the railroad companies and to various other divisions of the capitalist class. His was the labor and worry; they gathered in the financial harvest.

## METHODS OF THE GREAT LANDOWNERS.

While thus the produce of the farmer's labor was virtually confiscated by the different capitalist combinations, the farmers of many States, particularly of the rich agricultural States of the West, were unable to stand up against the encroachments, power, and the fraudulent methods of the great capitalist landowners.

The land frauds in the State of California will serve as an example. Acting under the authority of various measures passed by Congress — measures which have been described — land grabbers succeeded in obtaining possession of an immense area in that State. Perjury, fraudulent surveys and entries, collusion with Government officials — these were a few of the many methods.

Jose Limantour, by an alleged grant from a Mexican Governor, and collusion with officials, almost succeeded in stealing more than half a million acres. Henry Miller, who came to the United States as an immigrant in 1850, is to-day owner of 14,539,000 acres of the richest land in California and Oregon. It embraces more than 22,500 square miles, a territory three times as large as New Jersey. The stupendous land frauds in all of the Western and Pacific States by which capitalists obtained " an empire of land, timber and mines " are amply described in numerous documents of the period. These land thieves, as was developed in official investigations, had their tools and associates in the Land Commissioner's office, in the Government executive departments, and in both houses of Congress. The land grabbers did their part in driving the small farmer from the soil. Bailey Millard, who extensively investigated the land frauds in California, after giving full details, says:

When you have learned these things it is not difficult to understand how one hundred men in the great Sacramento Valley have come to own over 17,000,000 acres, while in the San Joaquin Valley it is no uncommon thing for one man's name to stand for 100,000 acres. This grabbing of large tracts has discouraged immigration to California more than any other single factor. A family living on a small holding in a vast plain, with hardly a house in sight, will in time become a very lonely family indeed, and will in a few years be glad to sell out to the land king whose domain is adjacent. Thousands of small farms have in this way been acquired by the large holders at nominal prices.[7]

## SEIZURE OF IMMENSE AREAS BY FRAUD.

Official reports of the period, contemporaneous with the original seizure of these immense tracts of land, give far more specific details of the methods by which that land was obtained. Of the numerous reports of committees of the California Legislature, we will here simply quote one — that of the Swamp Land Investigating Committee of the California Assembly of 1873. Dealing with the fraudulent methods by which huge areas of the finest lands in California were obtained for practically nothing as " swamp " land, this committee reported, citing from what it termed a " mighty mass of evidence," " That through the connivance of parties, surveyors were appointed who segregated lands as ' swamp,' which were not so in fact. The corruption existing in the land department of the General Government has aided this system of fraud."

Also, the committee commented with deep irony, " the loose laws of the State, governing all classes of State lands, has enabled wealthy parties to obtain much of it under circumstances which, in some countries, where laws are more rigid and terms less refined, would be termed fraudulent, but we can only designate it as keen foresight and wise (for the land grabbers) construction of loose, unwholesome laws." [8]

[7] " The West Coast Land Grabbers." Everybody's Magazine, May, 1905.
[8] Report of the Swamp Land Investigating Committee, Appendix to California Journals of Senate and Assembly. Twentieth Session, 1874, Vol. iv, Doc. No. 5:3.

After recording its findings that it was satisfied from
the evidence that "the grossest frauds have been committed in swamp matters in this State," the committee
went on:

Formerly it was the custom to permit filings upon real or
alleged swamp lands, and to allow the applications to lie unacted
upon for an indefinite number of years, at the option of the appli-
cants. In these cases, parties on the "inside" of the Land Office
"ring" had but to wait until some one should come along who
wanted to take up these lands in good faith, and they would
"sell out" to them their "rights" to land on which they had
never paid a cent, nor intended to pay a cent.
Or, if the nature of the land was doubtful, they would post-
pone all investigation until the height of the floods during the
rainy season, when surveyors, in interest with themselves, would
be sent out to make favorable reports as to the "swampy"
character of the land. In the mountain valleys and on the
other side of the Sierras, the lands are overflowed from melting
snow exactly when the water is most wanted; but the simple
presence of the water is all that is necessary to show to the
speculators that the land is "swamp," and it therefore presents
an inviting opportunity for this grasping cupidity.[9]

In his exhaustive report for 1885, Commissioner
Sparks, of the General Land Office, described at great
length the vast frauds that had continuously been going
on in the granting of alleged "swamp" lands, and in
fraudulent surveys, in many States and Territories.[10]
"I thus found this office," he wrote, "a mere instru-
mentality in the hands of 'surveying rings.'"[11] Sixteen
townships examined in Colorado in 1885 were found to
have been surveyed on paper only, no actual surveying
having been done.[12] In twenty-two other townships ex-

[9] Report of the Swamp Land Investigating Committee, etc., 5.
[10] House Documents, First Session, Forty-ninth Congress,
1885-86, Vol. ii.
[11] Ibid., 166.
[12] Ibid., 165.

amined in Colorado, purporting to have been surveyed under a " special-deposit " contract awarded in 1881, the surveys were found wholly fraudulent in seven, while the other fifteen were full of fraud." [18]

These are a very few of the numerous instances cited by Commissioner Sparks. Although the law restricted surveys to agricultural lands and for homestead entries, yet the Land Office had long corruptly allowed what it was pleased to term certain " liberal regulations." Surveys were so construed as to include any portion of townships the " larger portion " of which was not " known " to be of a mineral character. These " regulations," which were nothing more or less than an extra-legal license to land-grabbers, also granted surveys for desert lands and timber lands under the timber-land act. By the terms of this act, it will be recalled, those who entered and took title to desert and timber lands were not required to be actual settlers. Thus, it was only necessary for the surveyors in the hire of the great land grabbers to report fine grazing, agricultural, timber or mineral land as " desert land," and vast areas could be seized by single individuals or corporations with facility.

Two specific laws directly contributed to the effectiveness of this spoliation. One act, passed by Congress on May 30, 1862, authorized surveys to be made at the expense of settlers in the townships that those settlers desired surveyed. Another act, called the Deposit Act, passed in 1871, provided that the amounts deposited by settlers should be partly applied in payment for the lands thus surveyed. Together, these two laws made the grasping of land on an extensive scale a simple process. The " settler " (which so often meant, in reality, the capitalist) could secure the collusion of the Land Office, and

[18] House Documents, etc., 1885-86, ii: 165.

have fraudulent surveys made. Under these surveys he could lay claim to immense tracts of the most valuable land and have them reported as " swamp " or " desert " lands; he could have the boundaries of original claims vastly enlarged; and the fact that part of his disbursements for surveying was considered as a payment for those lands, stood in law as virtually a confirmation of his claim.

ACTUAL SETTLERS EXCLUDED FROM PUBLIC DOMAIN.

" Wealthy speculators and powerful syndicates," reported Commissioner Sparks,

covet the public domain, and a survey is the first step in the accomplishment of this desire. The bulk of deposit surveys have been made in timber districts and grazing regions, and the surveyed lands have immediately been entered under the timber land, preëmption, commuted homestead, timber-culture and desert-land acts. So thoroughly organized has been the entire system of procuring the survey and making illegal entry of lands, that agents and attorneys engaged in this business have been advised of every official proceeding, and enabled to present entry applications for the lands at the very moment of the filing of the plots of survey in the local land offices.

Prospectors employed by lumber firms and corporations seek out and report the most valuable timber tracts in California, Oregon, Washington Territory or elsewhere; settler's applications are manufactured as a basis for survey; contracts are entered into and pushed through the General Land Office in hot haste; a skeleton survey is made . . . entry papers, made perfect in form by competent attorneys, are filed in bulk, and the manipulators enter into possession of the land. . . . This has been the course of proceeding heretofore.[14]

Commissioner Sparks described a case of where it was discovered by his special agents in California that an English firm had obtained 100,000 acres of the choicest

[14] House Documents, etc., 1885-86, ii: 167.

red-wood lands in that State. These lands were then estimated to be worth $100 an acre. The cost of procuring surveys and fraudulent entries did not probably exceed $3 an acre.[15]

"In the same manner," Commissioner Sparks continued, "extensive coal deposits in our Western territory are acquired in mass through expedited surveys, followed by fraudulent pre-emption and commuted homestead entries."[16] He went on to tell that nearly the whole of the Territory (now State) of Wyoming, and large portions of Montana, had been surveyed under the deposit system, and the lands on the streams fraudulently taken up under the desert land act, to the exclusion of actual settlers. Nearly all of Colorado, the very best cattle-raising portions of New Mexico, the rich timber lands of California, the splendid forest lands of Washington Territory and the principal part of the extensive pine lands of Minnesota had been fraudulently seized in the same way.[17] In all of the Western States and Territories these fraudulent surveys had accomplished the seizure of the best and most valuable lands. "To enable the pressing tide of Western immigration to secure homes upon the public domain," Commissioner Sparks urged, "it is necessary . . . that hundreds of millions of acres of public lands now appropriated should be wrested from illegal control."[18] But nothing was done to recover these stolen lands. At the very time Commissioner Sparks — one of the very few incorruptible Commissioners of Public Lands,— was writing this, the land-grabbing interests were making the greatest exertions to get him removed. During his tenure of office they caused him to be malevolently harassed and assailed. After he left office

[15] House Ex. Docs., etc., 1885-86, ii : 167.
[16] Ibid.      [17] Ibid., 168.      [18] Ibid.

they resumed complete domination of the Land Commissioner's Bureau.[19]

## THE GIGANTIC PRIVATE LAND CLAIM FRAUDS.

The frauds in the settlement of private land claims on alleged grants by Spain and Mexico were colossal. Vast estates in California, New Mexico, Arizona, Colorado and other States were obtained by collusion with the Government administrative officials and Congress. These were secured upon the strength of either forged documents purporting to be grants from the Spanish or Mexican authorities, or by means of fraudulent surveys.

One of the most notorious of these was the Beaubin and Miranda grant, otherwise famous thirty years ago as the Maxwell land grant. A reference to it here is indispensable. It was by reason of this transaction, as well as by other similar transactions, that one of the American multimillionaires obtained his original millions. This individual was Stephen B. Elkins, at present a powerful

[19] The methods of capitalists in causing the removal of officials who obstructed or exposed their crimes and violent seizure of property were continuous and long enduring. It was a very old practice. When Astor was debauching and swindling Indian tribes, he succeeded, it seems, by exerting his power at Washington, in causing Government agents standing in his way to be dismissed from office. The following is an extract from a communication, in 1821, of the U. S. Indian agent at Green Bay, Wisconsin, to the U. S. Superintendent of Indian Trade: "The Indians are frequently kept in a state of intoxication, giving their furs, etc., at a great sacrifice for whiskey. . . . The agents of Mr. Astor hold out the idea that they will, ere long be able to break down the factories [Government agencies]; and they menace the Indian agents and others who may interfere with them, with dismission from office through Mr. Astor. They say that a representation from Messrs. Crooks and Stewart (Mr. Astor's agents) led to the dismission of the Indian agent at Mackinac, and they also say that the Indian agent here is to be dismissed. . . ."— U. S. Senate Documents, First Session, Seventeenth Congress, 1821-22, Vol. i, Doc. No. 60: 52-53.

member of the United States Senate, and one of the ruling oligarchy of wealth. He is said to possess a fortune of at least $50,000,000, and his daughter, it is reported, is to marry the Duke of the Abruzzi, a scion of the royal family of Italy.

The New Mexico claim of Beaubin and Miranda transferred to L. B. Maxwell, was allowed by the Government in 1869, but for ninety-six thousand acres only. The owner refused to comply with the law, and in 1874 the Department of the Interior ordered the grant to be treated as public lands and thrown open to settlement. Despite this order, the Government officials in New Mexico, acting in collusion with other interested parties, illegally continued to assess it as private property. In 1877 a fraudulent tax sale was held, and the grant, fraudulently enlarged to 1,714,764.94 acres, was purchased by M. M. Mills, a member of the New Mexico Legislature. He transferred the title to T. B. Catron, the United States Attorney for New Mexico. Presently Elkins turned up as the principal owner. The details of how this claim was repeatedly shown up to be fraudulent by Land Commissioners and Congressional Committees; how the settlers in New Mexico fought it and sought to have it declared void, and the law enforced;[20] and how Elkins, for some years himself a Delegate in Congress from New Mexico, succeeded in having the grant finally validated on technical grounds, and "judicially cleared" of all taint of fraud, by an astounding decision of the Supreme Court of the United States — a decision contrary to the facts as specifically shown by successive Government

[20] "Land Titles in New Mexico and Colorado," House Reports, First Session, Fifty-second Congress, 1891-92, Vol. iv, Report No. 1253. Also, House Reports, First Session, Fifty-second Congress, 1891-92, Vol. vii, Report No. 1824. Also, House Reports, First Session, Forty-ninth Congress, 1885-86, ii: 170.

officials — all of these details are set forth fully in another part of this work.[21]

The forgeries and fraudulent surveys by which these huge estates were secured were astoundingly bold and frequent. Large numbers of private land claims, rejected by various Land Commissioners as fraudulent, were corruptly confirmed by Congress. In 1870, the heirs of one Gervacio Nolan applied for confirmation of two grants alleged to have been made to an ancestor under the colonization laws of New Mexico. They claimed more than 1,500,000 acres, but Congress conditionally confirmed their claim to the extent of forty-eight thousand acres only, asserting that the Mexican laws had limited to this area the area of public lands that could be granted to one individual. In 1880 the Land Office reopened the claim, and a new survey was made by surveyors in collusion with the claimants, and hired by them. When the report of this survey reached Washington, the Land Office officials were interested to note that the estate had grown from forty-eight thousand acres to five hundred and seventy-five thousand acres, or twelve times the legal quantity.[22] The actual settlers were then evicted. The romancer might say that the officials were amazed; they were not; such fraudulent enlargements were common.

The New Mexico estate of Francis Martinez, granted under the Mexican laws restricting a single grant to forty-eight thousand acres, was by a fraudulent survey, extended to 594,515.55 acres, and patented in 1881.[23] A New Mexico grant said to have been made to Salvador Gonzales, in 1742, comprising " a spot of land to enable

---

[21] See " The Elkins Fortune," in Vol. iii.
[22] House Reports, First Session, Forty-ninth Congress, 1885-86, ii: 171.
[23] Ibid., 172.

him to plant a cornfield for the support of his family," was fraudulently surveyed and enlarged to 103,959.31 acres — a survey amended later by reducing the area to 23,661 acres.[24] The B. M. Montaya grant in New Mexico, limited to forty-eight thousand acres, under the Mexican colonization laws, was fraudulently surveyed for 151,056.97 acres. The Estancia grant in New Mexico, also restricted under the colonization act to forty-eight thousand acres, was enlarged by a fraudulent survey to 415,036.56 acres.[25] In 1768, Ignacio Chaves and others in New Mexico petitioned for a tract of about two and one-fourth superficial leagues, or approximately a little less than ten thousand acres. A fraudulent survey magnified this claim to 243,036.43 acres.[26]

These are a very few of the large number of forged or otherwise fraudulent claims.

Some were rejected by Congress; many, despite Land Office protests, were confirmed. By these fraudulent and corrupt operations, enormous estates were obtained in New Mexico, Colorado and in other sections. The Pablo Montaya grant comprised in all, 655,468.07 acres; the Mora grant 827,621.01 acres; the Tierra Amarilla grant 594,515 acres, and the Sangre de Cristo grant 998,780.46 acres. All of these were corruptly obtained.[27] Scores of other claims were confirmed for lesser areas. During Commissioner Sparks' tenure of office, claims to 8,500,000 acres in New Mexico alone were pending before Congress. A comprehensive account of the operations of the land-grabbers, giving the explicit facts, as told in

[24] House Reports, etc., 1885-86, ii: 172.
[25] Ibid., 173.
[26] Ibid.
[27] See Resolution of House Committee on Private Land Claims, June, 1892, demanding a thorough investigation. The House took no action.— Report No. 1824, 1892.

Government and court records, of their system of fraud, is presented in the chapter on the Elkins fortune.

### FORGERY, PERJURY AND FRAUDULENT SURVEY.

Reporting, in 1881, to the Commissioner of the General Land Office, Henry M. Atkinson, U. S. Surveyor-General of New Mexico, wrote that " the investigation of this office for the past five years has demonstrated that some of the alleged grants are forgeries." He set forth that unless the court before which these claims were adjudicated could have full access to the archives, " it is much more liable to be imposed upon by fraudulent title papers." [28] In fact, the many official reports describe with what cleverness the claimants to these great areas forged their papers, and the facility with which they bought up witnesses to perjure for them.  Finding it impossible to go back of the aggregate and corroborative " evidence " thus offered, the courts were frequently forced to decide in favor of the claimants.  To use a modern colloquial phrase, the cases were " framed up."   In the case of Luis Jamarillo's claim to eighteen thousand acres in New Mexico, U. S. Surveyor-General Julian of New Mexico, in recommending the rejection of the claim and calling attention to the perjury committed, said:

When these facts are considered, in connection with the further and well-known fact that such witnesses can readily be found by grant claimants, and that in this way the most monstrous frauds have been practiced in extending the lines of such grants in New Mexico, it is not possible to accept the statement of this witness as to the west boundary of this grant, which he locates at such a distance from the east line as to include more than four times the amount of land actually granted.[29]

[28] " The Public Domain," etc.. 1124.   Also see note 29.

" The widespread belief of the people of this country," wrote Commissioner Sparks in 1885, " that the land department has been largely conducted to the advantage of speculation and monopoly, private and corporate, rather than in the public interest, I have found supported by developments in every branch of the service. . . . I am satisfied that thousands of claims without foundation in law or equity, involving millions of acres of public land, have been annually passed to patent upon the single proposition that nobody but the Government had any *adverse* interest. The vast machinery of the land department has been devoted to the chief result of conveying the title of the United States to public lands upon fraudulent entries under loose construction of law." [30] Whenever a capitalist's interest was involved, the law was always " loosely construed," but the strictest interpretation was invariably given to laws passed against the working population.

It was estimated, in 1892, that 57,000,000 acres of land in New Mexico and Colorado had, for more than thirty years, been unlawfully treated by public officers as having been ceded to the United States by Mexico. The Maxwell, Sangre de Cristo, Nolan and other grants were within this area. The House Committee on Private Land Claims reported on April 29, 1892: " A long list of alleged Mexican and Spanish grants within the limits of the Texas cession have been confirmed, or quit claimed by Congress, under the false representation that said alleged grants were located in the territory of New Mexico ceded by the treaty; an enormous area of land has long been and is now held as confirmed Mexican and Spanish

[29] Senate Executive Documents, First Session, Fiftieth Congress, 1887-88, Vol. i, Private Land Claim No. 103, Ex. Doc. No. 20: 3. Documents Nos. 3 to 11, 13 to 23, 25 to 29 and 38 in the same volume deal with similar claims.
[30] House Ex. Docs., 1885-86, ii: 156.

grants, located in the territory of Mexico ceded by the treaty when such is not the fact." [81]

In Texas the fraudulent, and often, violent methods of the seizure of land by the capitalists were fully as marked as those used elsewhere.

Upon its admittance to the Union, Texas retained the disposition of its public lands. Up to about the year 1864, almost the entire area of Texas, comprising 274,356 square miles, or 175,587,840 acres, was one vast unfenced feeding ground for cattle, horses and sheep. In about the year 1874, the agricultural movement began; large numbers of intending farmers migrated to Texas, particularly with the expectation of raising cattle, then a highly profitable business. They found huge stretches of the land already preëmpted by individual capitalists or corporations. In a number of instances, some of these individuals, according to the report of a Congressional Committee, in 1884, dealing with Texas lands, had each acquired the ownership of more than two hundred and fifty thousand acres.

" It is a notorious fact," this committee reported, " that the public land laws, although framed with the special object of encouraging the public domain, of developing its resources and protecting actual settlers, have been extensively evaded and violated. Individuals and corporations have, by purchasing the proved-up claims, or purchases of ostensible settlers, employed by them to make entry, extensively secured the ownership of large bodies of land." [82]    The committee went on to describe how, to a very considerable extent, " foreigners of large means " had obtained these great areas, and had gone into the cattle business, and how the titles to these lands were se-

[81] House Report, 1892, No. 1253:8.
[82] House Reports, Second Session, Forty-eighth Congress, 1884-85, Vol. xxix, Ex. Doc. No. 267:43.

cured not only by individuals but by foreign corporations. "Certain of these foreigners are titled noblemen. Some of them have brought over from Europe, in considerable numbers, herdsmen and other employees who sustain to them a dependent relationship characteristic of the peasantry on the large landed estates of Europe." Two British syndicates, for instance, held 7,500,000 acres in Texas.[33]

This spoliation of the public domain was one of the chief grievances of the National Greenback-Labor party in 1880. This party, to a great extent, was composed of the Western farming element. In his letter accepting the nomination of that party for President of the United States, Gen. Weaver, himself a member of long standing in Congress from Iowa, wrote:

An area of our public domain larger than the territory occupied by the great German Empire has been wantonly donated to wealthy corporations; while a bill introduced by Hon. Hendrick B. Wright, of Pennsylvania, to enable our poor people to reach and occupy the few acres remaining, has been scouted, ridiculed, and defeated in Congress. In consequence of this stupendous system of land-grabbing, millions of the young men of America, and millions more of industrious people from abroad, seeking homes in the New World, are left homeless and destitute. The public domain must be sacredly reserved to actual settlers, and where corporations have not complied strictly with the terms of their grants, the lands should be at once reclaimed.

### INCREASE OF FARM TENANTRY.

Without dwelling upon all the causative factors — involving an extended work in themselves — some significant general results will be pointed out.

The original area of public domain amounted to 1,815,-

[33] House Reports, etc., 1884-85, Doc. No. 267: 46.

504,147 acres, of which considerably more than half, embracing some of the very best agricultural, grazing, mineral and timber lands, was already alienated by the year 1880. By 1896 the alienation reached 806,532,362 acres. Of the original area, about 50,000,000 acres of forests have been withdrawn from the public domain by the Government, and converted into forest reservations. Large portions of such of the agricultural, grazing, mineral and timber lands as were not seized by various corporations and favored individuals before 1880, have been expropriated west of the Mississippi since then, and the process is still going, notably in Alaska. The nominal records of the General Land Office as to the number of homesteaders are of little value, and are very misleading. Immense numbers of alleged homesteaders were, as we have copiously seen, nothing but paid dummies by whose entries vast tracts of land were seized under color of law. It is indisputably clear that hundreds of millions of acres of the public domain have been obtained by outright fraud.

Notwithstanding the fact that only a few years before, the Government had held far more than enough land to have provided every agriculturist with a farm, yet by 1880, a large farm tenant class had already developed. Not less than 1,024,061 of the 4,008,907 farms in the United States were held by renters. One-fourth of all the farms in the United States were cultivated by men who did not own them. Furthermore, and even more impressive, there were 3,323,876 farm laborers composed of men who did not even rent land. Equally significant was the increasing tendency to the operating of large farms by capitalists with the hired labor. Of farms under cultivation, extending from one hundred to five hundred acres, there were nearly a million and a half — 1,416,618, to give the exact number — owned largely by capitalists and cultivated by laborers.[34]

Phillips, who had superior opportunities for getting at the real facts, and whose volume upon the subject issued at the time is well worthy of consideration, thus commented upon the census returns:

It will thus be seen that of the 7,670,493 persons in our country engaged in agriculture, there are 1,024,601 who pay rent to persons not cultivating the soil; 1,508,828 capitalist or speculating owners, who own the soil and employ laborers; 804,522 of well-to-do farmers who hire part of their work or employ laborers, and 670,944 who may be said to actually cultivate the soil they own: the rest are hired workers.

Phillips goes on to remark:

Another fact must be borne in mind, that a large number of the 2,984,306 farmers who own land are in debt for it to the money lenders. From the writer's observation it is probable that forty per cent. of them are so deeply in debt as to pay a rent in interest. This squeezing process is going on at the rate of eight and ten per cent., and in most cases can terminate in but one way.[35]

### A LARGELY DISPOSSESSED NATION.

These are the statistics of a Government which, it is

[34] Tenth Census, Statistics of Agriculture: 28.
[35] "Labor, Land and Law": 353.
It is difficult to get reliable statistics on the number of mortgages on farms, and on the number of farm tenants. The U. S. Industrial Commission estimated, in 1902, that fifty per cent. of the homesteads in Eastern Minnesota were mortgaged. Although admitting that such a condition had been general, it represented in its Final Report that a large number of mortgages in certain States had been paid off. According to the " Political Science Quarterly " (Vol. xi, No. 4, 1896) the United States Census of 1890 showed a marked increase, not only absolutely, but relatively in the number of farm tenants. It can hardly be doubted that farm tenantry is rapidly increasing and will under the influence of various causes increase still more,

known, seeks to make its showing as favorable as pos- ·
sible to the existing regime. They make it clear that a
rapid process of the dispossession of the industrial working, the middle and the small farming classes has been
going on unceasingly. If the process was so marked in
1900 what must it be now? All of the factors operating
to impoverish the farming population of the United
States and turn them into homeless tenants have been
a thousandfold intensified and augmented in the last
ten years, beginning with the remarkable formation of
hundreds of trusts in 1898. Even though the farmer
may get higher prices for his products, as he did in 1908
and 1909, the benefits are deceptively transient, while
the expropriating process is persistent.

There was a time when farm land in Ohio, Illinois,
Minnesota, Indiana, Wisconsin, and many other States
was considered of high value. But in the last few years
an extraordinary sight has been witnessed. Hundreds of
thousands of American farmers migrated to the virgin
fields of Northwest Canada and settled there — a portentous movement significant of the straits to which the
American farmer has been driven.

Abandoned farms in the East are numerous; in New
York State alone 22,000 are registered. Hitherto the
farmer has considered himself a sort of capitalist: if
not hostile to the industrial working classes, he has been
generally apathetic. But now he is being forced to the
point of being an absolute dependant himself, and will
inevitably align his interests with those of his brothers
in the factories and in the shops.

With this contrast of the forces at work which gave
empires of public domain to the few, while dispossessing
the tens of millions, we will now proceed to a consideration of some of the fortunes based upon railroads.

# CHAPTER III

## THE BEGINNINGS OF THE VANDERBILT FORTUNE

The first of the overshadowing fortunes to develop from the ownership and manipulation of railroads was that of Cornelius Vanderbilt. The Havemeyers and other factory owners, whose descendants are now enrolled among the conspicuous multimillionaires, were still in the embryonic stages when Vanderbilt towered aloft in a class by himself with a fortune of $105,000,000. In these times of enormous individual accumulations and centralization of wealth, the personal possession of $105,-000,000 does not excite a fraction of the astonished comment that it did at Cornelius Vanderbilt's death in 1877. Accustomed as the present generation is to the sight of billionaires or semi-billionaires, it cannot be expected to show any wonderment at fortunes of lesser proportions.

### NINETY MILLIONS IN FIFTEEN YEARS.

Yet to the people of thirty years ago, a round hundred million was something vast and unprecedented. In 1847 millionaires were so infrequent that the very word, as we have seen, was significantly italicised. But here was a man who, figuratively speaking, was a hundred millionaires rolled in one. Compared with his wealth the great fortunes of ten or fifteen years before dwindled into bagatelles. During the Civil War a fortune of $15,000,000 had been looked upon as monumental. Even the huge Astor fortune, so long far outranking all

95

competitors, lost its exceptional distinction and ceased being the sole, unrivalled standard of immense wealth. Nearly a century of fraud was behind the Astor fortune. The greater part of Cornelius Vanderbilt's wealth was massed together in his last fifteen years.

This was the amazing, unparalleled feature to his generation. Within fifteen brief years he had possessed himself of more than $90,000,000. His wealth came rushing in at the rate of $6,000,000 a year. Such an accomplishment may not impress the people of these years, familiar as they are with the ease with which John D. Rockefeller and other multimillionaires have long swept in almost fabulous annual revenues. With his yearly income of fully $80,000,000 or $85,000,000 [1] Rockefeller can look back and smile with superior disdain at the commotion raised by the contemplation of Cornelius Vanderbilt's $6,000,000.

Each period to itself, however. Cornelius Vanderbilt was the golden luminary of his time, a magnate of such combined, far-reaching wealth and power as the United States had never known. Indeed, one overruns the line of tautology in distinguishing between wealth and power. The two were then identical not less than now. Wealth was the real power. None knew or boasted of this more than old Vanderbilt when, with advancing age, he became more arrogant and choleric and less and less inclined to smooth down the storms he provoked by his contemptuous flings at the great pliable public. When threatened by competitors, or occasionally by public officials, with the invocation of the law, he habitually

[1] The " New York Commercial," an ultra-conservative financial and commercial publication, estimated in January, 1905, his annual income to be $72,000,000. Obviously it has greatly increased every year.

sneered at them and vaunted his defiance. In terse sentences, interspersed with profanity, he proclaimed the fact that money was law; that it could buy either laws or immunity from the law.

Since wealth meant power, both economic and political, it is not difficult to estimate Vanderbilt's supreme place in his day.

Far below him, in point of possessions, stretched the 50,000,000 individuals who made up the nation's population. Nearly 10,000,000 were wage laborers, and of the 10,000,000 fully 500,000 were child laborers. The very best paid of skilled workers received in the highest market not more than $1,040 a year. The usual weekly pay ran from $12 to $20 a week; the average pay of unskilled laborers was $350 a year. More than 7,500,000 persons ploughed and hoed and harvested the farms of the country; comparatively few of them could claim a decent living, and a large proportion were in debt. The incomes of the middle class, including individual employers, business and professional men, tradesmen and small middlemen, ranged from $1,000 to $10,000 a year.

How immeasurably puny they all seemed beside Vanderbilt! He beheld a multitude of many millions struggling fiercely for the dollar that meant livelihood or fortune; those bits of metal or paper which commanded the necessities, comforts and luxuries of life; the antidote of grim poverty and the guarantees of good living; which dictated the services, honorable or often dishonorable, of men, women and children; which bought brains not less than souls, and which put their sordid seal on even the most sacred qualities. Now by these tokens, he had securely 105,000,000 of these bits of metal or wealth in some form equivalent to them. Millions of people had none of these dollars; the hundreds of thousands had a few; the thousands had hundreds of thousands; the few had millions. He had more than any.

Even with all his wealth, great as it was in his day, he would scarcely be worth remembrance were it not that he was the founder of a dynasty of wealth. Therein lies the present importance of his career.

### A FORTUNE OF $700,000,000.

From $105,000,000 bequeathed at his death, the Vanderbilt fortune has grown until it now reaches fully $700,000,000. This is an approximate estimate; the actual amount may be more or less. In 1889 Shearman placed the wealth of Cornelius and William K. Vanderbilt, grandsons of the first Cornelius, at $100,000,000. each, and that of Frederick W. Vanderbilt, a brother of those two men, at $20,000,000.[2] Adding the fortunes of the various other members of the Vanderbilt family, the Vanderbilts then possessed about $300,000,000. Since that time the population and resources of the United States have vastly increased; wealth in the hold of a few has become more intensely centralized; great fortunes have gone far beyond their already extraordinary boundaries of twenty years ago; the possessions of the Vanderbilts have expanded and swollen in value everywhere, although recently the Standard Oil oligarchy has been encroaching upon their possessions. Very probable it is that the combined Vanderbilt fortune reaches fully $700,000,000, actually and potentially.

But the incidental mention of such a mass of money conveys no adequate conception of the power of this family. Nominally it is composed of private citizens

2 "Who Owns the United States?"—The Forum Magazine, November, 1889.

with theoretically the same rights and limitations of citizenship held by any other citizen and no more. But this is a fanciful picture. In reality, the Vanderbilt family is one of the dynasties of inordinately rich families ruling the United States industrially and politically. Singly it has mastery over many of the railroad and public utility systems and industrial corporations of the United States. In combination with other powerful men or families of wealth, it shares the dictatorship of many more corporations. Under the Vanderbilts' direct domination are 21,-000 miles of railroad lines, the ownership of which is embodied in $600,000,000 in stocks and $700,000,000 in bonds. One member alone, William K. Vanderbilt, is a director of seventy-three transportation and industrial combinations or corporations.

### BONDS THAT HOLD PRESENT AND POSTERITY.

Behold, in imagination at least, this mass of stocks and bonds. Heaps of paper they seem; dead, inorganic things. A second's blaze will consume any one of them, a few strokes of the fingers tear it into shapeless ribbons. Yet under the institution of law, as it exists, these pieces of paper are endowed with a terrible power of life and death that even enthroned kings do not possess. Those dainty prints with their scrolls and numerals and inscriptions are binding titles to the absolute ownership of a large part of the resources created by the labors of entire peoples.

Kingly power at best is shadowy, indefinite, depending mostly upon traditional custom and audacious assumption backed by armed force. If it fall back upon a certain alleged divine right it cannot produce documents to prove its authority. The industrial monarchs of the

United States are fortified with both power and proofs of possession. Those bonds and stocks are the tangible titles to tangible property; whoso holds them is vested with the ownership of the necessities of tens of millions of subjected people. Great stretches of railroad traverse the country; here are coal mines to whose products some ninety million people look for warmth; yonder are factories; there in the cities are street car lines and electric light and power supply and gas plants; on every hand are lands and forests and waterways — all owned, you find, by this or that dominant man or family.

The mind wanders back in amazement to the times when, if a king conquered territory, he had to erect a fortress or castle and station a garrison to hold it. They that then disputed the king's title could challenge, if they chose, at peril of death, the provisions of that title, which same provisions were swords and spears, arrows and muskets.

But nowhere throughout the large extent of the Vanderbilt's possessions or those of other ruling families are found warlike garrisons as evidence of ownership. Those uncouth barbarian methods are grossly antiquated; the part once played by armed battalions is now performed by bits of paper. A wondrously convenient change has it been; the owners of the resources of nations can disport themselves thousands of miles away from the scene of their ownership; they need never bestir themselves to provide measures for the retention of their property. Government, with its array of officials, prisons, armies and navies, undertakes all of this protection for them. So long as they hold these bits of paper in their name, Government recognizes them as the incontestable owners and safeguards their property accordingly. The very Government established on the taxation of the workers is used to enforce the means by which the workers are held in subjection.

## THEY DECREE TAXES AT WILL.

These batches of stocks and bonds betoken as much more again. A pretty fiction subsists that Government, the creator of the modern private corporation, is necessarily more powerful than its creature. This theoretical doctrine, so widely taught by university professors and at the same time so greatly at variance with the palpable facts, will survive to bring dismay in the near future to the very classes who would have the people believe it so. Instead of now being the superior of the corporation the Government has long since definitely surrendered to private corporations a tremendous taxing power amounting virtually to a decree authorizing enslavement. Upon every form of private corporation — railroad, industrial, mining, public utility — is conferred a peculiarly sweeping and insidious power of taxation the indirectness of which often obscures its frightful nature and effects.

Where, however, the industrial corporation has but one form of taxation the railroad has many forms. The trust in oil or any other commodity can tax the whole nation at its pleasure, but inherently only on the one product it controls. That single taxation is of itself confiscatory enough, as is seen in the $912,000,000 of profits gathered in by the Standard Oil Company since its inception. The trust tax is in the form of its selling price to the public. But the railroad puts its tax upon every product transported or every person who travels. Not a useful plant grows or an article is made but that, if shipped, a heavy tax must be paid on it.

This tax comes in the guise of freight or passenger rates.

The labor of hundreds of millions of people contributes incessantly to the colossal revenues enriching the railroad owners. For their producing capacity the workers are paid the meagerest wages, and the products which they make they are compelled to buy back at exorbitant prices after they pass through the hands of the various great capitalist middlemen, such as the trusts and the railroads. How enormous the revenues of the railroads are may be seen in the fact that in the ten years from 1898 to 1908 the dividends declared by thirty-five of the leading railroads in the United States reached the sum of about $1,800,000,000. This railroad taxation is a grinding, oppressive one, from which there is no appeal. If the Government taxes too heavily the people nominally can have a say; but the people have absolutely no voice in altering the taxation of corporations. Pseudo attempts have been made to regulate railroad charges, but their futility was soon evident, for the reason that owning the instruments of business the railroads and the allied trusts are in actual possession of the governmental power viewing it as a working whole.

### AND EXERCISE UNRESTRAINED POWER.

Visualizing this power one begins to get a vivid perception of the comprehensive sway of the Vanderbilts and of other railroad magnates. They levy tribute without restraint — a tribute so vast that the exactions of classic conquerors become dwarfed beside it. If this levying entailed only the seizing of money, that cold, unbreathing, lifeless substance, then human emotion might not start in horror at the consequences. But beneath it all are the tugging and tearing of human muscles and minds, the toil and sweat of an unnumbered multitude, the rending of homes, the infliction of sorrow, suffering and death.

The magnates, as we have said, hold the power of decreeing life and death; and time never was since the railroads were first built when this power was not arbitrarily exercised.

Millions have gone hungry or lived on an attenuated diet while elsewhere harvests rotted in the ground; between their needs and nature's fertility lay the railroads. Organized and maintained for profit and for profit alone, the railroads carry produce and products at their fixed rates and not a whit less; if these rates are not paid the transportation is refused. And as in these times transportation is necessary in the world's intercourse, the men who control it have the power to stand as an inflexible barrier between individuals, groups of individuals, nations and international peoples. The very agencies which should under a rational form of civilization be devoted to promoting the interests of mankind, are used as their capricious self-interest incline them by the few who have been allowed to obtain control of them. What if helpless people are swept off by starvation or by diseases superinduced by lack of proper food? What if in the great cities an increasing sacrifice of innocents goes on because their parents cannot afford the price of good milk — a price determined to a large extent by railroad tariff? All of this slaughter and more makes no impress upon the unimpressionable surfaces of these stocks and bonds, and leaves no record save in the hospitals and graveyards.

The railroad magnates have other powers. Government itself has no power to blot a town out of existence. It cannot strew desolation at will. But the railroad owners can do it and do not hesitate if sufficient profits be involved. One man sitting in a palace in New York can give an order declaring a secret discriminative tariff against the products of a place, whereupon its industries no longer able to compete with formidable competitors enjoying better rates, close down and the life of the place flickers and sometimes goes out.

These are but a very few of the immensity of extravagant powers conferred by the ownership of these railroad bonds and stocks. Bonds they assuredly are, incomparably more so than the clumsy yokes of olden days. Society has improved its outwards forms in these passing centuries. Clanking chains are no longer necessary to keep slaves in subjection. Far more effective than chains and balls and iron collars are the ownership of the means whereby men must live. Whoever controls them in large degree, is a potentate by whatever name he be called, and those who depend upon the owner of them for their sustenance are slaves by whatever flattering name they choose to go.

### HIGH AND MIGHTY POTENTATES.

The Vanderbilts are potentates. Their power is bounded by no law; they are among the handful of fellow potentates who say what law shall be and how it shall be enforced. No stern, masterful men and women are they as some future moonstruck novelist or historian bent upon creating legendary lore may portray them. Voluptuaries are most of them, sunk in a surfeit of gorgeous living and riotous pleasure. Weak, without distinction of mind or heart, they have the money to hire brains to plan, plot, scheme, advocate, supervise and work for them.  Suddenly deprived of their stocks and bonds they would find themselves adrift in the sheerest helplessness.  With these stocks and bonds they are the direct absolute masters of an army of employees. On the New York Central Railroad alone the Vanderbilt payroll embraces fifty thousand workers.  This is but one of their railroad systems.  As many more, or nearly as many, men work directly for them on their other railroad lines.

One hundred thousand men signify, let us say, as many families.  Accepting the average of five to a family, here are five hundred thousand souls whose livelihood is dependent upon largely the will of the Vanderbilt family. To that will there is no check.  To-day it may be expansively benevolent; to-morrow, after a fit of indigestion or a night of demoralizing revelry, it may flit to an extreme of parsimonious retaliation.  As the will fluctuates, so must be the fate of the hundred thousand workers.  If the will decides that the pay of the men must go down, curtailed it is, irrespective of their protests that the lopping off of their already slender wages means still keener hardship.  Apparently free and independent citizens, this army of workers belong for all essential purposes to the Vanderbilt family.  Their jobs are the hostages held by the Vanderbilts.  The interests and decisions of one family are supreme.

The germination and establishment of this immense power began with the activities of the first Cornelius Vanderbilt, the founder of this pile of wealth.  He was born in 1794.  His parents lived on Staten Island; his father conveyed passengers in a boat to and from New York — an industrious, dull man who did his plodding part and allowed his wife to manage household ex-

penses. Regularly and obediently he turned his earnings over to her. She carefully hoarded every available
cent, using an old clock as a depository.

### THE FOUNDER'S START.

Vanderbilt was a rugged, headstrong, untamable, illiterate youth. At twelve years of age he could scarcely
write his own name. But he knew the ways of the
water; when still a youth he commenced ferrying passengers and freight between Staten Island and New York
City. For books he cared nothing; the refinements of
life he scorned. His one passion was money. He was
grasping and enterprising, coarse and domineering. Of
the real details of his early life little is known except
what has been written by laudatory writers. We are
informed that as he gradually made and saved money
he built his own schooners, and went in for the coasting
trade. The invention and success of the steamboat, it
is further related, convinced him that the day of the
sailing vessel would soon be over. He, therefore, sold
his interest in his schooners, and was engaged as captain
of a steamboat plying between New York and points on
the New Jersey coast. His wife at the same time enlarged the family revenues by running a wayside tavern
at New Brunswick, N. J., whither Vanderbilt had moved.

In 1829, when his resources reached $30,000, he quit
as an employee and began building his own steamboats.
Little by little he drove many of his competitors out of
business. This he was able to do by his harsh, unscrupulous and strategic measures.[8] He was severe with

[8] Some glimpses of Vanderbilt's activities and methods in his
early career are obtainable from the court records. In 1827 he
was fined two penalties of $50 for refusing to move a steamboat
called "The Thistle," commanded by him, from a wharf on

the men who worked for him, compelling them to work long hours for little pay. He showed a singular ability in undermining competitors. They could not pay low wages but what he could pay lower; as rapidly as they set about reducing passenger and freight rates he would anticipate them. His policy at this time was to bankrupt competitors, and then having obtained a monopoly, to charge exorbitant rates. The public, which welcomed him as a benefactor in declaring cheaper rates and which flocked to patronize his line, had to pay dearly for their premature and short-sighted joy. For the first five years his profits, according to Croffut, reached $30,000 a year, doubling in successive years. By the time he was forty years old he ran steamboats to many cities on the coast, and had amassed a fortune of half a million dollars.

### DRIVING OUT COMPETITORS.

Judging from the records of the times, one of his most effective means for harassing and driving out compet-

the North River in order to give berth to "The Legislature," a competing steamboat. His defence was that Adams, the harbor master, had no authority to compel him to move. The lower courts decided against him, and the Supreme Court, on appeal, affirmed their judgment. (Adams vs. Vanderbilt. Cowen's Reports. Cases in Supreme Court of the State of New York, vii: 349-353.)

In 1841 the Eagle Iron Works sued Vanderbilt for the sum of $2,957.15 which it claimed was due under a contract made by Vanderbilt on March 8, 1838. This contract called for the payment by Vanderbilt of $10,500 in three installments for the building of an engine for the steamboat "Wave." Vanderbilt paid $7,900, but refused to pay the remainder, on the ground that braces to the connecting rods were not supplied. These braces, it was brought out in court, cost only $75 or $100. The Supreme Court handed down a judgment against Vanderbilt. An appeal was taken by Vanderbilt, and Judge Nelson, in the Supreme Court, in October, 1841, affirmed that judgment.— Vanderbilt vs. Eagle Iron Works, Wendell's Reports, Cases in the Supreme Court of the State of New York, xxv: 665-668, itors was in bribing the New York Common Council to give him, and refuse them, dock privileges. As the city owned the docks, the Common Council had the exclusive right of determining to whom they should be leased. Not a year passed but what the ship, ferry and steamboat owners, the great landlords and other capitalists bribed the aldermen to lease or give them valuable city property. Many scandals resulted, culminating in the great scandal of 1853, when the Grand Jury, on February 26, handed up a presentment showing in detail how certain aldermen had received bribes for disposal of the city's water rights, pier privileges and other property, and how enormous sums had been expended in bribes to get railroad grants in the city.[4] Vanderbilt was not openly implicated in these frauds, no more than were the Astors, the Rhinelanders, the Goelets and other very rich men who prudently kept in the background, and who managed to loot the city by operating through go-betweens.

Vanderbilt's eulogists take great pains to elaborate upon his tremendous energy, sagacity and constructive enterprise, as though these were the exclusive qualities by which he got his fortune. Such a glittering picture, common in all of the usual biographies of rich men, discredits itself and is overthrown by the actual facts. The times in which Vanderbilt lived and thrived were not calculated to inspire the masses of people with respect for the trader's methods, although none could deny that the outcropping capitalists of the period showed a fierce vigor in overcoming obstacles of man and of nature, and in extending their conquests toward the outposts of the habitable globe.

[4] Proceedings of the New York Board of Aldermen, xlviii: 423-431.

If indomitable enterprise assured permanency of wealth then many of Vanderbilt's competitors would have become and remained multimillionaires. Vanderbilt, by no means possessed a monopoly of acquisitive enterprise; on every hand, and in every line, were men fully as active and unprincipled as he. Nearly all of these men, and scores of competitors in his own sphere — dominant capitalists in their day — have become well-nigh lost in the records of time; their descendants are in the slough of poverty, genteel or otherwise. Those times were marked by the intensest commercial competition; business was a labyrinth of sharp tricks and low cunning; the man who managed to project his head far above the rest not only had to practice the methods of his competitors but to overreach and outdo them. It was in this regard that Vanderbilt showed superior ability.

In the exploitation of the workers — forcing them to work for low wages and compelling them to pay high prices for all necessities — Vanderbilt was no different from all contemporaneous capitalists. Capitalism subsisted by this process. Almost all conventional writers, it is true, set forth that it was the accepted process of the day, implying that it was a condition acquiesced in by the employer and worker. This is one of the lies disseminated for the purpose of proving that the great fortunes were made by legitimate methods. Far from being accepted by the workers it was denounced and was openly fought by them at every auspicious opportunity.

Vanderbilt became one of the largest ship and steamboat builders in the United States and one of the most formidable employers of labor. At one time he had a hundred vessels afloat. Thousands of shipwrights, me-

chanics and other workers toiled for him fourteen and
sixteen hours a day at $1.50 a day for many years. The
actual purchasing power of this wage kept declining as
the cost of rent and other necessaries of life advanced.
This was notably so after the great gold discoveries in
California, when prices of all commodities rose abnor-
mally, and the workers in every trade were forced to
strike for higher wages in order to live. Most of these
strikes were successful, but their results as far as wages
went were barren; the advance wrung from employers
was by no means equal to the increased cost of living.

### REGARDED AS A COMMERCIAL BUCCANEER.

The exploitation of labor, however, does not account
for his success as a money maker. Many other men
did the same, and yet in the vicissitudes of business went
bankrupt; the realm of business was full of wrecks.
Vanderbilt's success arose from his destructive tactics
toward his competitors. He was regarded universally
as the buccaneer of the shipping world. He leisurely
allowed other men to build up profitable lines of steamboats, and he then proceeded to carry out methods which
inevitably had one of two terminations: either his competitor had to buy him off at an exorbitant price, or he
was left in undisputed possession. His principal biographer, Croffut, whose effusion is one long chant of
praise, treats these methods as evidences of great shrewdness, and goes on: " His foible was ' opposition; ' wherever his keen eye detected a line that was making a very
large profit on its investment, he swooped down on it
and drove it to the wall by offering a better service and
lower rates." [5]  This statement is only partially true;

[5] " The Vanderbilts and the Story of Their Fortune," by W. A.
Croffut, 1886: 45-46.

its omissions are more significant than its admissions.

Far from being the " constructive genius " that he is represented in every extant biographical work and note, Vanderbilt was the foremost mercantile pirate and commercial blackmailer of his day.

Harsh as these terms may seem, they are more than justified by the facts. His eulogists, in line with those of other rich men, weave a beautiful picture for the edification of posterity, of a broad, noble-minded man whose honesty was his sterling virtue, and whose splendid ability in opening up and extending the country's resources was rewarded with a great fortune and the thanks of his generation. This is utterly false. He who has the slightest knowledge of the low practices and degraded morals of the trading class and of the qualities which insured success, might at once suspect the spuriousness of this extravagant presentation, even if the vital facts were unavailable.

But there is no such difficulty. Obviously, for every one fraudulent commercial or political transaction that comes to public notice, hundreds and thousands of such transactions are kept in concealment. Enough facts, however, remain in official records to show the particular methods Vanderbilt used in getting together his millions. Yet no one hitherto seems to have taken the trouble to disinter them; even serious writers who cannot be accused of wealth worship or deliberate misstatement have all, without exception, borrowed their narratives of Vanderbilt's career from the fiction of his literary, newspaper and oratorical incense burners. And so it is that everywhere the conviction prevails that whatever fraudulent methods Vanderbilt employed in his later career, he was essentially an honest, straightforward man who was compelled by the promptings of sheer self-preservation to fight back at unscrupulous competitors or antagonists, and who innately was opposed to underhand work or fraud in any form. Vanderbilt is in every case portrayed as an eminently high-minded man who never stooped to dissimulation, deceit or treachery, and whose first millions, at any rate, were made in the legitimate ways of trade as they were then understood.

### EXTORTION AND THEFT COMMON.

The truth is that the bulk of Vanderbilt's original millions were the proceeds of extortion, blackmail and theft.

In the established code of business the words extortion and theft had an unmistakable significance. Business men did not consider it at all dishonorable to oppress their workers; to manufacture and sell goods under false pretenses; to adulterate prepared foods and drugs; to demand the very highest prices for products upon which the very life of the people depended, and at a time when consumers needed them most; to bribe public officials and to hold up the Government in plundering schemes. These and many other practices were looked upon as commonplaces of ordinary trade.

But even as burglars will have their fine points of honor among themselves, so the business world set certain tacit limitations of action beyond which none could go without being regarded as violating the code. It was all very well as long as members of their own class plundered some other class, or fought one another, no matter how rapaciously, in accordance with understood procedure. But when any business man ventured to overstep these limitations, as Vanderbilt did, and levy a species of commercial blackmail to the extent of millions of dollars, then he was sternly denounced as an arch

COMMODORE CORNELIUS VANDERBILT,
The Founder of the Vanderbilt Fortune.

thief. If Vanderbilt had confined himself to the routine formulas of business, he might have gone down in failure. Many of the bankrupts were composed of business men who, while sharp themselves, were outgeneraled by abler sharpers. Vanderbilt was a master hand in despoiling the despoilers.

How did Vanderbilt manage to extort millions of dollars? The method was one of great simplicity; many of its features were brought out in the United States Senate in the debate of June 9, 1858, over the Mail Steamship bill. The Government had begun, more than a decade back, the policy of paying heavy subsidies to steamship companies for the transportation of mail. This subsidy, however, was not the only payment received by the steamship owners. In addition they were allowed what were called "postages"—the full returns from the amount of postage on the letters carried. Ocean postage at that time was enormous and burdensome, and was especially onerous upon a class of persons least able to bear it. About three-quarters of the letters transported by ships were written by emigrants. They were taxed the usual rate of twenty-four or twenty-nine cents for a single letter. In 1851 the amount received for trans-Atlantic postages was not less than a million dollars; three-fourths of this sum came directly from the working class.

### THE CORRUPTION OF OFFICIALS.

To get these subsidies, in conjunction with the "postages," the steamship owners by one means or another corrupted postal officials and members of Congress. "I have noticed," said Senator Toombs, in a speech in the United States Senate on June 9, 1858,

that there has never been a head of a Department strong enough
to resist steamship contracts. I have noticed them here with
your Whig party and your Democratic party for the last thirteen years, and I have never seen any head of a Department
strong enough to resist these influences. . . . . Thirteen years'
experience has taught me that wherever you allow the Postoffice
or Navy Department to do anything which is for the benefit of
contractors you may consider the thing as done. I could point
to more than a dozen of these contracts. . . . A million
dollars a year is a power that will be felt. For ten years it
amounts to ten million dollars, and I know it is felt. I know it
perverts legislation. I have seen its influence; I have seen the
public treasury plundered by it. . . .[6]

By means of this systematic corruption the steamship owners received many millions of dollars of Government funds. This was all virtually plunder; the returns from the "postages" far more than paid them
for the transportation of mails. And what became of
these millions in loot? Part went in profits to the owners, and another part was used as private capital by them
to build more and newer ships constantly. Practically
none of Vanderbilt's ships cost him a cent; the Government funds paid for their building. In fact, a careful
tracing of the history of all of the subsidized steamship
companies proves that this plunder from the Government was very considerably more than enough to build
and equip their entire lines.

One of the subsidized steamship lines was that of
E. K. Collins & Co., a line running from New York to
Liverpool. Collins debauched the postal officials and
Congress so effectively that in 1847 he obtained an appropriation of $387,000 a year, and subsequently an ad-
ditional appropriation of $475,000 for five years. To-
gether with the "postages," these amounts made a total

[6] The Congressional Globe, First Session, Thirty-fifth Congress, 1857-58, iii: 2839.

mail subsidy for that one line alone during the latter years of the contract of about a million dollars a year. The act of Congress did not, however, specify that the contract was to run for ten years.  The postal officials, by what Senator Toombs termed "a fraudulent construction," declared that it did run for ten years from 1850, and made payments accordingly.  The bill before Congress in the closing days of the session of 1858, was the usual annual authorization of the payment of this appropriation, as well as other mail-steamer appropriations.

### VANDERBILT'S HUGE LOOT.

In the course of this debate some remarkable facts came out as to how the Government was being steadily plundered, and why it was that the postal system was already burdened with a deficit of $5,000,000.  While the appropriation bill was being solemnly discussed with patriotic exclamations, lobbyists of the various steamship companies busied themselves with influencing or purchasing votes within the very halls of Congress.

Almost the entire Senate was occupied for days with advocating this or that side as if they were paid attorneys pleading for the interests of either Collins or Vanderbilt.  Apparently a bitter conflict was raging between these two millionaires.  Vanderbilt's subsidized European lines ran to Southampton, Havre and Bremen; Collins' to Liverpool.  There were indications that for years a secret understanding had been in force between Collins and Vanderbilt by which they divided the mail subsidy funds.  Ostensibly, however, in order to give no sign of collusion, they went through the public appearance of warring upon each other.  By this stratagem they were able to ward off criticism of monopoly, and each get a larger appropriation than if it were known that they were in league. But it was characteristic of business methods that while in collusion, Vanderbilt and Collins constantly sought to wreck the other.

One Senator after another arose with perfervid effusion of either Collins or Vanderbilt. The Collins supporters gave out the most suave arguments why the Collins line should be heavily subsidized, and why Collins should be permitted to change his European port to Southampton. Vanderbilt's retainers fought this move, which they declared would wipe out of existence the enterprise of a great and patriotic capitalist.

It was at this point that Senator Toombs, who represented neither side, cut in with a series of charges which dismayed the whole lobby for the time being. He denounced both Collins and Vanderbilt as plunderers, and then, in so many words, specifically accused Vanderbilt of having blackmailed millions of dollars. " I am trying," said Senator Toombs,

to protect the Government against collusion, not against conflict. I do not know but that these parties have colluded now. I have not the least doubt that all these people understand one another. I am struggling against collusion. If they have colluded, why should Vanderbilt run to Southampton for the postage when Collins can get three hundred and eighty-seven thousand dollars for running to the same place? Why may not Collins, then, sell his ships, sit down in New York, and say to Vanderbilt, 'I will give you two hundred and thirty thousand dollars and pocket one hundred and fifty-seven thousand dollars a year.' That is the plain, naked case. The Senator from Vermont says the Postmaster General will protect us. It is my duty, in the first place, to prevent collusion, and prevent the country from being plundered; to protect it by law as well as I can.'

Regarding the California mails, Senator Toombs reminded the Senate of the granting eleven years before of enormous mail subsidies to the two steamship lines running to California — the Pacific Mail Steamship Company and the United States Mail Steamship Company, otherwise called the Harris and the Sloo lines. He declared that Vanderbilt, threatening them with both competition and a public agitation such as would uncover the fraud, had forced them to pay him gigantic sums in return for his silence and inactivity. Responsible capitalists, Senator Toombs said, had offered to carry the mails to California for $550,000. "Everybody knows," he said, "that it can be done for half the money we pay now. Why, then, should we continue to waste the public money?" Senator Toombs went on:

You give nine hundred thousand dollars a year to carry the mails to California; and Vanderbilt compels the contractors to give him $56,000 a month to keep quiet. This is the effect of your subventions. Under your Sloo and Harris contracts you pay about $900,000 a year (since 1847); and Vanderbilt, by his superior skill and energy, compelled them for a long time, to disgorge $40,000 a month, and now $56,000 a month. . . . They pay lobbymen, they pay agencies, they go to law, because everybody is to have something; and I know this Sloo contract has been in chancery in New York for years.[7] The result

[7] The case in chancery referred to by Senator Toombs was doubtless that of Sloo et al. vs. Law et al. (Case No. 12,957, Federal Cases, xxii: 355-364.)
In this case argued before Judge Ingersoll in the United States Circuit Court, at New York City, on May 16, 1856, many interesting and characteristic facts came out both in the argument and in the Court decision.
From the decision (which went into the intricacies of the case at great length) it appeared that although Albert G. Sloo had formed the United States Mail Steamship Company, the incorporators were George Law, Marshall O. Roberts, Prosper M. Wetmore and Edwin Crosswell. Sloo assigned his contract to them. Law was the first president, and was succeeded by Roberts. A trust fund was formed. Law fraudulently (so the

of this system is that here comes a man — as old Vanderbilt
seems to be — I never saw him, but his operations have excited
my admiration — and he runs right at them and says disgorge
this plunder. He is the kingfish that is robbing these small
plunderers that come about the Capitol. He does not come
here for that purpose; but he says, ' Fork over $56,000 a month
of this money to me, that I may lie in port with my ships,' and
they do it.[8]

decision read) took out $700,000 of stock, and also fraudulently
appropriated large sums of money belonging to the trust fund.
This was the same Law who, in 1851 (probably with a part of
this plunder) bribed the New York Board of Aldermen, with
money, to give him franchises for the Second and Ninth Avenue
surface railway lines. Roberts appropriated $600,000 of the
United States Mail Steamship Company's stock. The huge swindles upon the Government carried on by Roberts during the Civil
War are described in later chapters in this work. Wetmore was
a notorious lobbyist. By fraud, Law and Roberts thus managed
to own the bulk of the capital stock of the United States Mail
Steamship Company. The mail contract that it had with the
Government was to yield $2,900,000 in ten years.
   Vanderbilt stepped in to plunder these plunderers. During the
time that Vanderbilt competed with that company, the price of a
single steerage passage from California to New York was $35.
After he had sold the company the steamship "North Star" for
$400,000, and had blackmailed it into paying heavily for his
silence and non-competition, the price of steerage passage was
put up to $125 (p. 364).
   The cause of the suit was a quarrel among the trustees over
the division of the plunder. One of the trustees refused to
permit another access to the books. Judge Ingersoll issued an
injunction restraining the defendant trustees from withholding
such books and papers.
   [8] The Congressional Globe, 1857-58, iii : 2843-2844.
   The acts by which the establishment of the various subsidized
ocean lines were authorized by Congress, specified that the
steamers were to be fit for ships of war in case of necessity,
and that these steamers were to be accepted by the Navy Department before they could draw subsidies. This part of the
debate in the United States Senate shows the methods used in
forcing their acceptance on the Government:
   Mr. Collamer.— The Collins line was set up by special contract?
   Mr. Toombs.— Yes, by special contract, and that was the way
with the Sloo contract and the Harris contract. They were to
build ships fit for war purposes. I know when the Collins
vessels were built; I was a member of the Committee on Ways
and Means of the other House, and I remember that the men
at the head of our bureau of yards and docks said that they

Thus, it is seen, Vanderbilt derived millions of dollars by this process of commercial blackmail. Without his having to risk a cent, or run the chance of losing a single ship, there was turned over to him a sum so large every year that many of the most opulent merchants could not claim the equal of it after a lifetime of feverish trade. It was purely as a means of blackmailing coercion that he started a steamship line to California to compete with the Harris and the Sloo interests. For his consent to quit running his ships and to give them a complete and unassailed monopoly he first extorted $480,000 a year of the postal subsidy, and then raised it to $612,000.

The matter came up in the House, June 12, 1858. Representative Davis, of Mississippi, made the same charges. He read this statement and inquired if it were true:

These companies, in order to prevent all competition to their line, and to enable them, as they do, to charge passengers double fare, have actually paid Vanderbilt $30,000 per month, and the United States Mail Steamship Company, carrying the mail between New York and Aspinwall, an additional sum of $10,000 per month, making $40,000 per month to Vanderbilt since May, 1856, which they continued to do. This $480,000 are paid to Vanderbilt per annum simply to give these two companies the entire monopoly of their lines — which sum, and much more, is charged over to passengers and freight.

were not worth a sixpence for war purposes; that a single broadside would blow them to pieces; that they could not stand the fire of their own guns; but newspapers in the cities that were subsidized commenced firing on the Secretary of the Navy, and he succumbed and took the ships. That was the way they got here.

Senator Collamer, referring to the subsidy legislation, said: "As long as the Congress of the United States makes contracts, declare who they shall be with, and how much they shall pay for them, they can never escape the generally prevailing public suspicion that there is fraud and deceit and corruption in those contracts."

Representative Davis repeatedly pressed for a definite reply as to the truth of the statement. The advocates of the bill answered with evasions and equivocations.[9]

### BLACKMAIL CHARGES TRUE.

The mail steamer appropriation bill, as finally passed by Congress, allowed large subsidies to all of the steamship interests. The pretended warfare among them had served its purpose; all got what they sought in subsidy funds. While the bill allowed the Postmaster-General to change Collins' European terminus to Southampton, that official, so it was proved subsequently, was Vanderbilt's plastic tool.

But what became of the charges against Vanderbilt? Were they true or calumniatory? For two years Congress made no effort to ascertain this. In 1860, however, charges of corruption in the postal system and other Government departments were so numerously made, that the House of Representatives on March 5, 1860, decided, as a matter of policy, to appoint an investigating committee. This committee, called the " Covode Committee," after the name of its chairman, probed into the allegations of Vanderbilt's blackmailing transactions. The charges made in 1858 by Senator Toombs and Representative Davis were fully substantiated.

Ellwood Fisher, a trustee of the United States Mail Steamship Company, testified on May 2 that during the greater part of the time he was trustee, Vanderbilt was paid $10,000 a month by the United States Mail Steamship Company, and that the Pacific Mail Steamship Company paid him $30,000 a month at the same time and for

[9] The Congressional Globe, Part iii, 1857-58: 3029. The Washington correspondent of the New York "Times" telegraphed (issue of June 2, 1858) that the mail subsidy bill was passed by the House "without twenty members knowing its details."

the same purpose. The agreement was that if competition appeared payment was to cease. In all, $480,000 a year was paid during this time. On June 5, 1860, Fisher again testified: " During the period of about four years and a half that I was one of the trustees, the earnings of the line were very large, but the greater part of the money was wrongfully appropriated to Vanderbilt for blackmail, and to others on various pretexts." [10] William H. Davidge, president of the Pacific Mail Steamship Company, admitted that the company had long paid blackmail money to Vanderbilt. " The arrangement," he said, " was based upon there being no competition, and the sum was regulated by that fact." [11] Horace F. Clark, Vanderbilt's son-in-law, one of the trustees of the United States Mail Steamship Company, likewise admitted the transaction.[12]  It is quite useless

[10] House Reports, Thirty-sixth Congress, First Session, 1859-60, v: 785-86 and 829. " Hence it was held," explained Fisher, in speaking of his fellow trustees, " that he [Vanderbilt] was interested in preventing competition, and the terror of his name and capital would be effectual upon others who might be disposed to establish steamship lines " (p. 786).
[11] Ibid., 795-796. The testimony of Fisher, Davidge and other officials of the steamship lines covers many pages of the investigating committee's report. Only a few of the most vital parts have been quoted here.
[12] Ibid., 824.
But Roberts and his associate trustees succeeded in making the Government recoup them, to a considerable extent, for the amount out of which Vanderbilt blackmailed them. They did it in this way:
A claim was trumped up by them that the Government owed a large sum, approximating about two million dollars, to the United States Mail Steamship Company for services in carrying mail in addition to those called for under the Sloo contract. In 1859 they began lobbying in Congress to have this claim recognized. The scheme was considered so brazen that Congress refused. Year after year, for eleven years, they tried to get Congress to pass an act for their benefit. Finally, on July 14, 1870, at a time when bribery was rampant in Congress, they succeeded. An act was passed directing the Court of Claims to investigate and determine the merits of the claim.

to ask whether Vanderbilt was criminally prosecuted or civilly sued by the Government. Not only was he un- molested, but two years later, as we shall see, he carried on another huge swindle upon the Government under peculiarly heinous conditions.

This continuous robbery of the public treasury ex- plains how Vanderbilt was able to get hold of millions of dollars at a time when millionaires were scarce. Van- derbilt is said to have boasted in 1853 that he had eleven million dollars invested at twenty-five per cent. A very large portion of this came directly from his bold system of commercial blackmail.[18]    The mail subsidies were the real foundation of his fortune. Many newspaper edi- torials and articles of the time mention this fact. Only a few of the important underlying facts of the character of his methods when he was in the steamboat and steam- ship business can be gleaned from the records. But these few give a clear enough insight. With a part of the proceeds of his plan of piracy, he carried on a subtle system of corruption by which he and the other steamer owners were able time after time not only to continue their control of Congress and the postal au- thorities, but to defeat postal reform measures. For fifteen years Vanderbilt and his associates succeeded in

The Court of Claims threw the case out of court. Judge Drake, in delivering the opinion of the court, said that the act was to be so construed "as to prevent the entrapping of the Government by fixing upon it liability where the intention of the legislature [Congress] was only to authorize an investigation of the question of liability" (Marshall O. Roberts et al., Trustees, vs. the United States, Court of Claims Reports, vi: 84-90). On appeal, however, the Supreme Court of the United States held that the act of Congress in referring the case to the Court of Claims was in effect *a ratification of the claim*. (Court of Claims Reports, xi: 98-126.)  Thus this bold robbery was fully validated.

[18] Undoubtedly so, but the precise proportion it is impossible to ascertain.

stifling every bill introduced in Congress for the reduction of the postage on mail.

## HE QUITS STEAMSHIPS.

The Civil War with its commerce-preying privateers was an unpropitious time for American mercantile vessels. Vanderbilt now began his career as a railroad owner.

He was at this time sixty-nine years old, a tall, robust, vigorous man with a stern face of remarkable vulgar strength. The illiteracy of his youth survived; he could not write the simplest words correctly, and his speech was a brusque medley of slang, jargon, dialect and profanity. It was said of him that he could swear more forcibly, variously and frequently than any other man of his generation. Like the Astors, he was cynical, distrustful, secretive and parsimonious. He kept his plans entirely to himself. In his business dealings he was never known to have shown the slightest mercy; he demanded the last cent due. His close-fistedness was such a passion that for many years he refused to substitute new carpets for the scandalous ones covering the floors of his house No. 10 Washington place. He never read anything except the newspapers, which he skimmed at breakfast. To his children he was unsympathetic and inflexibly harsh; Croffut admits that they feared him. The only relaxations he allowed himself were fast driving and playing whist.

This, in short, is a picture of the man who in the next few years used his stolen millions to sweep into his ownership great railroad systems. Croffut asserts that in 1861 he was worth $20,000,000; other writers say that his wealth did not exceed $10,000,000. He knew nothing of railroads, not even the first technical or supervising rudiments. Upon one thing he depended and that alone: the brute force of money with its auxiliaries, cunning, bribery and fraud.

# CHAPTER IV

## THE ONRUSH OF THE VANDERBILT FORTUNE

With the outbreak of the Civil War, and the scouring of the seas by privateers, American ship owners found themselves with an assortment of superfluous vessels on their hands. Forced to withdraw from marine commerce, they looked about for two openings. One was how to dispose of their vessels, the other the seeking of a new and safe method of making millions.

Most of their vessels were of such scandalous construction that foreign capitalists would not buy them at any price. Hastily built in the brief period of ninety days, wholly with a view to immediate profit and with but a perfunctory regard for efficiency, many of these steamers were in a dangerous condition. That they survived voyages was perhaps due more to luck than anything else; year after year, vessel after vessel similarly built and owned had gone down to the bottom of the ocean. Collins had lost many of his ships; so had other steamship companies. The chronicles of sea travel were a long, grewsome succession of tragedies; every little while accounts would come in of ships sunk or mysteriously missing. Thousands of immigrants, inhumanly crowded in the enclosures of the steerage, were swept to death without even a fighting chance for life. Cabin passengers fared better; they were given the opportunity of taking to the life-boats in cases where there was sufficient warning, time and room. At best, sea travel is a hazard; the finest of ships are liable to meet with disaster. But over much of this sacrifice of life hung grim, ugly charges of mismanagement and corruption, of insufficient crews and incompetent officers; of defective machinery and rotting timber; of lack of proper inspection and · safeguards.

### THE ANSWER FOUND.

The steamboat and steamship owners were not long lost in perplexity. Since they could no longer use their ships or make profit on ocean routes why not palm off their vessels upon the Government? A highly favorable time it was; the Government, under the imperative necessity of at once raising and transporting a huge army, needed vessels badly. As for the other question momentarily agitating the capitalists as to what new line of activity they could substitute for their own extinguished business, Vanderbilt soon showed how railroads could be made to yield a far greater fortune than commerce.

The titanic conflict opening between the North and the South found the Federal Government wholly unprepared. True, in granting the mail subsidies which established the ocean steamship companies, and which actually furnished the capital for many of them, Congress had inserted some fine provisions that these subsidized ships should be so built as to be "war steamers of the first class," available in time of war. But these provisions were mere vapor. Just as the Harris and the Sloo lines had obtained annual mail subsidy payments of $900,000 and had caused Government officials to accept their inferior vessels, so the Collins line had done the same. The report of a board of naval experts submitted to the Committee of Ways and Means of the

House of Representatives had showed that the Collins steamers had not been built according to contract; that they would crumble to pieces under the fire of their own batteries, and that a single hostile gun would blow them to splinters. Yet they had been accepted by the Navy Department.

In times of peace the commercial interests had practiced the grossest frauds in corruptly imposing upon the Government every form of shoddy supplies. These were the same interests so vociferously proclaiming their intense patriotism. The Civil War put their pretensions of patriotism to the test. If ever a war took place in which Government and people had to strain every nerve and resource to carry on a great conflict it was the Civil War. The result of that war was only to exchange chattel slavery for the more extensive system of economic slavery. But the people of that time did not see this clearly. The Northern soldiers thought they were fighting for the noblest of all causes, and the mass of the people behind them were ready to make every sacrifice to win a momentous struggle, the direct issue of which was the overthrow or retention of black slavery.

How did the capitalist class act toward the Government, or rather, let us say, toward the army and the navy so heroically pouring out their blood in battles, and hazarding life in camps, hospitals, stockades and military prisons?

### INDISCRIMINATE PLUNDERING DURING THE CIVIL WAR.

The capitalists abundantly proved their devout patriotism by making tremendous fortunes from the necessities of that great crisis. They unloaded upon the Government at ten times the cost of manufacture quantities

of munitions of war — munitions so frequently worthless
that they often had to be thrown away after their purchase.[1] They supplied shoddy uniforms and blankets
and wretched shoes; food of so deleterious a quality
that it was a fertile cause of epidemics of fevers and of
numberless deaths; they impressed, by force of corruption, worn-out, disintegrating hulks into service as army
and naval transports. Not a single possibility of profit
was there in which the most glaring frauds were not
committed. By a series of disingenuous measures the
banks plundered the Treasury and people and caused
their banknotes to be exempt from taxation. The merchants defrauded the Government out of millions of dollars by bribing Custom House officers to connive at undervaluations of imports.[2] The Custom House frauds
were so notorious that, goaded on by public opinion, the
House of Representatives was forced to appoint an investigating committee. The chairman of this committee, Representative C. H. Van Wyck, of New York, after
summarizing the testimony in a speech in the House on

[1] In a speech on February 28, 1863, on the urgency of establishing additional government armories and founderies, Representative J. W. Wallace pointed out in the House of Representatives: "The arms, ordnance and munitions of war bought by
the Government from private contractors and foreign armories
since the commencement of the rebellion have doubtless cost,
over and above the positive expense of their manufacture, ten
times as much as would establish and put into operation the
armory and founderies recommended in the resolution of the
committee. I understand that the Government, from the necessity of procuring a sufficient quantity of arms, has been paying,
on the average, about twenty-two dollars per musket, when they
could have been and could be manufactured in our national
workshops for one-half that money."—Appendix to The Congressional Globe, Thirty-seventh Congress, Third Session, 1862-
63. Part ii: 136. Fuller details are given in subsequent chapters.
[2] In his report for 1862 Salmon P. Chase, Secretary of the
Treasury, wrote: "That invoices representing fraudulent valua-
tion of merchandise are daily presented at the Custom Houses
is well known. . . ."

February 23, 1863, passionately exclaimed: "The starving, penniless man who steals a loaf of bread to save life you incarcerate in a dungeon; but the army of magnificent highwaymen who steal by tens of thousands from the people, go unwhipped of justice and are suffered to enjoy the fruits of their crimes. It has been so with former administrations: unfortunately it is so with this." [3]

The Federal armies not only had to fight an open foe in a desperately contested war, but they were at the same time the helpless targets for the profit-mongers of their own section who insidiously slew great numbers of them — not, it is true, out of deliberate lust for murder, but because the craze for profits crushed every instinct of honor and humanity, and rendered them callous to the appalling consequences. The battlefields were not more deadly than the supplies furnished by capitalist contractors. [4] These capitalists passed, and

[3] Appendix to The Congressional Globe, Thirty-seventh Congress, Third Session, 1862-63. Part ii: 118.

[4] This is one of many examples: Philip S. Justice, a gun manufacturer of Philadelphia, obtained a contract in 1861, to supply 4,000 rifles. He charged $20 apiece. The rifles were found to be so absolutely dangerous to the soldiers using them, that the Government declined to pay his demanded price for a part of them. Justice then brought suit. (See Court of Claims Reports, viii: 37-54.) In the court records, these statements are included:

William H. Harris, Second Lieutenant of Ordnance, under orders visited Camp Hamilton, Va., and inspected the arms of the Fifty-Eighth Regiment, Pennsylvania Volunteers, stationed there. He reported: "This regiment is armed with rifle muskets, marked on the barrel, 'P. S. Justice, Philadelphia,' and vary in calibre from .65 to .70. I find many of them unserviceable and irreparable, from the fact that the principal parts are defective. Many of them are made up of parts of muskets to which the stamp of condemnation has been affixed by an inspecting officer. None of the stocks have ever been approved by an officer, nor do they bear the initials of any inspector. They are made up of soft, unseasoned wood, and are defective in construction. . . . The sights are merely soldered on to the were hailed, as eminent merchants, manufacturers and bankers; they were mighty in the marts and in politics; and their praise as "enterprising" and "self-made" and "patriotic" men was lavishly diffused.

It was the period of periods when there was a kind of adoration of the capitalist taught in press, college and pulpit. Nothing is so effective, as was remarked of old, to divert attention from scoundrelism as to make a brilliant show of patriotism. In the very act of looting Government and people and devastating the army and navy, the capitalists did the most ghastly business under the mask of the purest patriotism. Incredible as it may seem, this pretension was invoked and has been successfully maintained to this very day. You

barrel, and come off with the gentlest handling. Imitative screwheads are cut on their bases. The bayonets are made up of soft iron, and, of course, when once bent remain 'set,'" etc., etc. (p. 43).

Col. (later General) Thomas D. Doubleday reported of his inspection: "The arms which were manufactured at Philadelphia, Penn., are of the most worthless kind, and have every appearance of having been manufactured from old condemned muskets. Many of them burst; hammers break off; sights fall off when discharged; the barrels are very light, not one-twentieth of an inch thick, and the stocks are made of green wood which have shrunk so as to leave the bands and trimmings loose. The bayonets are of such frail texture that they bend like lead, and many of them break off when going through the bayonet exercise. You could hardly conceive of such a worthless lot of arms, totally unfit for service, and dangerous to those using them" (p. 44).

Assistant Inspector-General of Ordnance John Buford reported: "Many had burst; many cones were blown out; many locks were defective; many barrels were rough inside from imperfect boring; and many had different diameters of bore in the same barrel. . . . *At target practice so many burst that the men became afraid to fire them*" (p. 45).

The Court of Claims, on strict technical grounds, decided in favor of Justice, but the Supreme Court of the United States reversed that decision and dismissed the case. The Supreme Court found true the Government's contention that "the arms were unserviceable and unsafe for troops to handle."

Many other such specific examples are given in subsequent chapters of this work.

can scarcely pick up a volume on the Civil War, or a biography of the statesmen or rich men of the era, without wading in fulsome accounts of the untiring patriotism of the capitalists.

## PATRIOTISM AT A SAFE DISTANCE.

But, while lustily indulging in patriotic palaver, the propertied classes took excellent care that their own bodies should not be imperilled. Inspired by enthusiasm or principle, a great array of the working class, including the farming and the professional elements, volunteered for military service. It was not long before they experienced the disappointment and demoralization of camp life. The letters written by many of these soldiers show that they did not falter at active campaigning. The prospect, however, of remaining in camp with insufficient rations, and (to use a modern expressive word) graft on every hand, completely disheartened and disgusted many of them. Many having influence with members of Congress, contrived to get discharges; others lacking this influence deserted. To fill the constantly diminishing ranks caused by deaths, resignations and desertions, it became necessary to pass a conscription act.

With few exceptions, the propertied classes of the North loved comfort and power too well to look tranquilly upon any move to force them to enlist. Once more, the Government revealed that it was but a register of the interests of the ruling classes. The Draft Act was so amended that it allowed men of property to escape being conscripted into the army by permitting them to buy substitutes. The poor man who could not raise the necessary amount had to submit to the consequences of the draft. With a few of the many dollars wrung, filched or plundered in some way or other, the capitalists could purchase immunity from military service.

As one of the foremost capitalists of the time, Cornelius Vanderbilt has been constantly exhibited as a great and shining patriot. Precisely in the same way as Croffut makes no mention of Vanderbilt's share in the mail subsidy frauds, but, on the contrary, ascribes to Vanderbilt the most splendid patriotism in his mail carrying operations, so do Croffut and other writers unctuously dilate upon the old magnate's patriotic services during the Civil War. Such is the sort of romancing that has long gone unquestioned, although the genuine facts have been within reach. These facts show that Vanderbilt was continuing during the Civil War the prodigious frauds he had long been carrying on.

When Lincoln's administration decided in 1862 to send a large military and naval force to New Orleans under General Banks, one of the first considerations was to get in haste the required number of ships to be used as transports. To whom did the Government turn in this exigency? To the very merchant class which, since the foundation of the United States, had continuously defrauded the public treasury. The owners of the ships had been eagerly awaiting a chance to sell or lease them to the Government at exorbitant prices. And to whom was the business of buying, equipping and supervising them intrusted? To none other than Cornelius Vanderbilt.

Every public man had opportunities for knowing that Vanderbilt had pocketed millions of dollars in his fraudulent hold-up arrangement with various mail subsidy lines. He was known to be mercenary and unscrupulous. Yet he was selected by Secretary of War Stanton to act as the agent for the Government. At this time Vanderbilt

was posing as a glorious patriot.  With much ostenta-
tion he had loaned to the Government for naval purposes
one of his ships — a ship that he could not put to use
himself and which, in fact, had been built with stolen
public funds.  By this gift he had cheaply attained the
reputation of being a fervent patriot.  Subsequently, it
may be added, Congress turned a trick on him by assuming that he gave this ship to the Government, and, to
his great astonishment, kept the ship and solemnly
thanked him for the present.

### VANDERBILT'S METHODS IN WAR.

The outfitting of the Banks expedition was of such a
rank character that it provoked a grave public scandal.
If the matter had been simply one of swindling the
United States Treasury out of millions of dollars, it
might have been passed over by Congress.  On all sides
gigantic frauds were being committed by the capitalists.
But in this particular case the protests of the thousands
of soldiers on board the transports were too numerous
and effective to be silenced or ignored.  These soldiers
were not regulars without influence or connections; they
were volunteers who everywhere had relatives and friends
to demand an inquiry.  Their complaints of overcrowd-
ing and of insecure, broken-down ships poured in, and
aroused the whole country.  A great stir resulted.  Congress appointed an investigating committee.

The testimony was extremely illuminative.  It showed
that in buying the vessels Vanderbilt had employed one
T. J. Southard to act as his handy man.  Vanderbilt, it
was testified by numerous ship owners, refused to charter
any vessels unless the business were transacted through
Southard, who demanded a share of the purchase money

before he would consent to do business. Any ship owner who wanted to get rid of a superannuated steamer or sailing vessel found no difficulty if he acceded to Southard's terms.

The vessels accepted by Vanderbilt, and contracted to be paid for at high prices, were in shockingly bad condition. Vanderbilt was one of the few men in the secret of the destination of Banks' expedition; he knew that the ships had to make an ocean trip. Yet he bought for $10,000 the Niagara, an old boat that had been built nearly a score of years before for trade on Lake Ontario. "In perfectly smooth weather," reported Senator Grimes, of Iowa, "with a calm sea, the planks were ripped out of her, and exhibited to the gaze of the indignant soldiers on board, showing that her timbers were rotten. The committee have in their committee room a large sample of one of the beams of this vessel to show that it has not the slightest capacity to hold a nail."[5] Senator Grimes continued:

If Senators will refer to page 18 of this report, they will see that for the steamer Eastern Queen he (Vanderbilt) paid $900 a day for the first thirty days, and $800 for the residue of the days; while she (the Eastern Queen) had been chartered by the Government, for the Burnside expedition at $500 a day, making a difference of three or four hundred dollars a day. He paid for the Quinebang $250 a day, while she had been chartered to the Government at one time for $130 a day. For the Shetucket he paid $250 a day, while she had formerly been in our employ for $150 a day. He paid for the Charles Osgood $250 a day, while we had chartered her for $150. He paid $250 a day for the James S. Green, while we had once had a charter of her for $200. He paid $450 a day for the Salvor, while she had been chartered to the Government for $300. He paid $250 a day for the Albany, while she had been chartered to the

[5] The Congressional Globe, Thirty-seventh Congress, Third Session, 1862-63, Part 1:610.

Government for $150. He paid $250 a day for the Jersey Blue, while she had been chartered to the Government for $150.[6]

These were a few of the many vessels chartered by Vanderbilt through Southard for the Government. For vessels bought outright, extravagant sums were paid. Ambrose Snow, a well-known shipping merchant, testified that " when we got to Commodore Vanderbilt we were referred to Mr. Southard; when we went to Mr. Southard, we were told that we should have to pay him a commission of five per cent." [7]

Other shipping merchants corroborated this testimony. The methods and extent of these great frauds were clear. If the ship owners agreed to pay Southard five — and very often he exacted ten per cent.[8] — Vanderbilt would agree to pay them enormous sums. In giving his testimony Vanderbilt sought to show that he was actuated by the most patriotic motives. But it was obvious that he was in collusion with Southard, and received the greater part of the plunder.

### HORRORS DONE FOR PROFIT.

On some of the vessels chartered by Vanderbilt, vessels that under the immigration act would not have been allowed to carry more than three hundred passengers, not less than nine hundred and fifty soldiers were packed. Most of the vessels were antiquated and inadequate; not a few were badly decayed. With a little superficial patching up they were imposed upon the Government. Despite his knowing that only vessels adapted for ocean

[6] The Congressional Globe, etc., 1862-63, Part i: 610.
[7] Ibid. See also Senate Report No. 84, 1863, embracing the full testimony.
[8] Senator Hale asserted that he had heard of the exacting of a brokerage equal to ten per cent. in Boston and elsewhere.

service were needed, Vanderbilt chartered craft that had hitherto been almost entirely used in navigating inland waters. Not a single precaution was taken by him or his associates to safeguard the lives of the soldiers.

It was a rule among commercial men that at least two men capable of navigating should be aboard, especially at sea. Yet, with the lives of thousands of soldiers at stake, and with old and bad vessels in use at that, Vanderbilt, in more than one instance, as the testimony showed, neglected to hire more than one navigator, and failed to provide instruments and charts. In stating these facts Senator Grimes said: " When the question was asked of Commodore Vanderbilt and of other gentlemen in connection with the expedition, why this was, and why they did not take navigators and instruments and charts on board, the answer was that the insurance companies and owners of the vessel took that risk, as though "— Senator Grimes bitingly continued —" the Government had no risk in the lives of its valiant men whom it has enlisted under its banner and set out in an expedition of this kind." [9] If the expedition had encountered a severe storm at Cape Hatteras, for instance, it is probable that most of the vessels would have been wrecked. Luckily the voyage was fair.

### FRAUDS REMAIN UNPUNISHED.

Did the Government make any move to arrest, indict and imprison Vanderbilt and his tools? None. The farcical ending of these revelations was the introduction in the United States Senate of a mere resolution censuring them as " guilty of negligence."

[9] The Congressional Globe, Thirty-seventh Congress, Third Session, 1862-63, Part i: 586.

Vanderbilt immediately got busy pulling wires; and when the resolution came up for vote, a number of Senators, led by Senator Hale, sprang up to withdraw Vanderbilt's name. Senator Grimes thereupon caustically denounced Vanderbilt. "The whole transaction," said he, "shows a chapter of fraud from beginning to end." He went on: "Men making the most open professions of loyalty and of patriotism and of perfect disinterestedness, coming before the committee and swearing that they acted from such motives solely, were compelled to admit — at least one or two were — that in some instances they received as high as six and a quarter per cent. . . . and I believe that since then the committee are satisfied in their own mind that the per cent. was greater than was in testimony before them." Senator Grimes added that he did not believe that Vanderbilt's name should be stricken from the resolution.

In vain, however, did Senator Grimes plead. Vanderbilt's name was expunged, and Southard was made the chief scapegoat. Although Vanderbilt had been tenderly dealt with in the investigation, his criminality was conclusively established. The affair deeply shocked the nation. After all, it was only another of many tragic events demonstrating both the utter inefficiency of capitalist management, and the consistent capitalist program of subordinating every consideration of human life to the mania for profits. Vanderbilt was only a type of his class; although he was found out he deserved condemnation no more than thousands of other capitalists, great and small, whose methods at bottom did not vary from his.[10]

10 One of the grossest and most prevalent forms of fraud was that of selling doctored-up horses to the Union army. Important cavalry movements were often delayed and jeoparded by this kind of fraud. In passing upon the suit of one of these horse contractors against the Government (Daniel Wormser vs. United States) for payment for horses supplied, in 1864, for

Yet such was the network of shams and falsities with which the supreme class of the time enmeshed society, that press, pulpit, university and the so-called statesmen insisted that the wealth of the rich man had its foundation in ability, and that this ability was indispensable in providing for the material wants of mankind.

Whatever obscurity may cloud many of Vanderbilt's methods in the steamship business, his methods in possessing himself of railroads are easily ascertained from official archives.

Late in 1862, at about the time when he had added to the millions that he had virtually stolen in the mail subsidy frauds, the huge profits from his manipulation of the Banks expedition, he set about buying the stock of the New York and Harlem Railroad.

### THE STORY OF A FRANCHISE.

This railroad, the first to enter New York City, had received from the New York Common Council in 1832 a franchise for the exclusive use of Fourth avenue, north of Twenty-third street — a franchise which, it was openly charged, was obtained by distributing bribes in the form of stock among the aldermen.[11]

The franchise was not construed by the city to be perpetual; certain reservations were embodied giving the

cavalry use, the Supreme Court of the United States confirmed the charge made by the Government horse inspectors that the plaintiff had been guilty of fraud, and dismissed the case. "The Government," said Justice Bradley in the court's decision, "clearly had the right to proscribe regulations for the inspection of horses, and there was great need for strictness in this regard, for frauds were constantly perpetrated. . . . It is well known that horses may be prepared and fixed up to appear bright and smart for a few hours."— Court of Claims Reports, vii: 257-262.

[11] "The History of Tammany Hall": 117.

city powers of revocation. But as we shall see, Vanderbilt not only corrupted the Legislature in 1872 to pass an act saddling one-half of the expense of depressing the tracks upon the city, but caused the act to be so adroitly worded as to make the franchise perpetual. Along with the franchise to use Fourth avenue, the railroad company secured in 1832 a franchise, free of taxation, to run street cars for the convenience of its passengers from the railroad station (then in the outskirts of New York City) south to Prince street. Subsequently this franchise was extended to Walker street, and in 1851 to Park Row. These were the initial stages of the Fourth Avenue surface line, which has been extended, and has grown into a vested value of tens of millions of dollars. In 1858 the New York and Harlem Railroad Company was forced by action of the Common Council, arising from the protests of the rich residents of Murray Hill, to discontinue steam service below Forty-second street. It, therefore, now had a street car line running from that thoroughfare to the Astor House.

This explanation of antecedent circumstances allows a clearer comprehension of what took place after Vanderbilt had begun buying the stock of the New York and Harlem Railroad. The stock was then selling at $9 a share. This railroad, as was the case with all other railroads, without exception, was run by the owners with only the most languid regard for the public interests and safety. Just as the corporation in the theory of the law was supposed to be a body to whom Government delegated powers to do certain things in the interests of the people, so was the railroad considered theoretically a public highway operated for the convenience of the people. It was upon this ostensible ground that railroad corporations secured charters, franchises, property and such privileges as the right of condemnation of necessary land. The State of New York alone had contributed $8,000,000 in public funds, and various counties, towns and municipalities in New York State nearly $31,000,000 by investment in stocks and bonds.[12] The theory was indeed attractive, but it remained nothing more than a fiction.

No sooner did the railroad owners get what they wanted, than they proceeded to exploit the very community from which their possessions were obtained, and which they were supposed to serve. The various railroads were juggled with by succeeding groups of manipulators. Management was neglected, and no attention paid to proper equipment. Often the physical layout of the railroads — the road-beds, rails and cars — were deliberately allowed to deteriorate in order that the manipulators might be able to lower the value and efficiency of the road, and thus depress the value of the stock. Thus, for instance, Vanderbilt aiming to get control of a railroad at a low price, might very well have confederates among some of. the directors or officials of that railroad who would resist or slyly thwart every attempt at improvement, and so scheme that the profits would constantly go down. As the profits decreased, so did the price of the stock in the stock market. The changing combinations of railroad capitalists were too absorbed in the process of gambling in the stock market to have any direct concern for management. It was nothing to them that this neglect caused frequent and heartrending disasters; they were not held criminally responsible for the loss of life. In fact, railroad wrecks often served their purpose in beating down the price of stocks. In-

[12] Report of the Special Committee on Railroads of the New York State Assembly, 1879, i: 7.

credible as this statement may seem, it is abundantly proved by the facts.

## VANDERBILT GETS A RAILROAD.

After Vanderbilt, by divers machinations of too intricate character to be described here, had succeeded in knocking down the price of New York and Harlem Railroad shares and had bought a controlling part, the price began bounding up. In the middle of April, 1863, it stood at $50 a share. A very decided increase it was, from $9 to $50; evidently enough, to occasion this rise, he had put through some transaction which had added immensely to the profits of the road. What was it?

Sinister rumors preceded what the evening of April 21, 1863, disclosed. He had bribed the New York City Common Council to give to the New York and Harlem Railroad a perpetual franchise for a street railway on Broadway from the Battery to Union Square. He had done what Solomon Kipp and others had done, in 1852, when they had spent $50,000 in bribing the aldermen to give them a franchise for surface lines on Sixth avenue and Eighth avenue;[13] what Elijah F. Purdy and others had done in the same year in bribing aldermen with a fund of $28,000 to give them the franchise for a surface line on Third avenue;[14] what George Law and other capitalists had done, in 1852, in bribing the aldermen to give them the franchises for street car lines on Second avenue and Ninth avenue. Only three years before — in 1860 — Vanderbilt had seen Jacob Sharp and others bribe the

[13] See presentment of Grand Jury of February 26, 1853, and accompanying testimony, Documents of the (New York) Board of Aldermen, Doc. No. XXI, Part II, No. 55.
[14] Ibid., 1333-1335.

New York Legislature (which in that same year had passed an act depriving the New York Common Council of the power of franchise granting) to give them franchises for street car lines on Seventh avenue, on Tenth avenue, on Forty-second street, on Avenue D and a franchise for the " Belt " line.  It was generally believed that the passage of these five bills cost the projectors $250,000 in money and stock distributed among the purchasable members of the Legislature.[15]

Of all the New York City street railway franchises, either appropriated or unappropriated, the Broadway line was considered the most profitable.  So valuable were its present and potential prospects estimated that in 1852 Thomas E. Davies and his associates had offered, in return for the franchise, to carry passengers for a three-cent fare and to pay the city a million-dollar bonus.  Other eager capitalists had hastened to offer the city a continuous payment of $100,000 a year.  Similar futile attempts had been made year after year to get the franchise.  The rich residents of Broadway opposed a street car line, believing it would subject them to noise and discomfort; likewise the stage owners, intent upon keeping up their monopoly, fought against it.  In 1863 the bare rights of the Broadway franchise were considered to be worth fully $10,000,000.  Vanderbilt and George Law were now frantically competing for this franchise.  While Vanderbilt was corrupting the Common Council, Law was corrupting the legislature.[16]  Such competition

---

[15] See " The History of Public Franchises in New York City.": 120-125.

[16] The business rivalry between Vanderbilt and Law was intensified by the deepest personal enmity on Law's part.  As one of the chief owners of the United States Mail Steamship Company, Law was extremely bitter on the score of Vanderbilt's having been able to blackmail him and Roberts so heavily and successfully.

on the part of capitalists in corrupting public bodies was
very frequent.

## THE ALDERMEN OUTWITTED BY VANDERBILT.

But the aldermen were by no means unschooled in the
current sharp practices of commercialism. A strong
cabal of them hatched up a scheme by which they would
take Vanderbilt's bribe money, and then ambush him for
still greater spoils. They knew that even if they gave
him the franchise, its validity would not stand the test
of the courts. The Legislature claimed the exclusive
power of granting franchises; astute lawyers assured
them that this claim would be upheld. Their plan was
to grant a franchise for the Broadway line to the New
York and Harlem Railroad. This would at once send
up the price of the stock. The Legislature, it was certain, would give a franchise for the same surface line
to Law. When the courts decided against the Common
Council that body, in a spirit of showy deference, would
promptly pass an ordinance repealing the franchise. In
the meantime, the aldermen and their political and Wall
Street confederates would contract to " sell short " large
quantities of New York and Harlem stock.

The method was simple. When that railroad stock
was selling at $100 a share upon the strength of getting
the Broadway franchise, the aldermen would find many
persons willing to contract for its delivery in a month
at a price, say, of $90 a share. By either the repealing
of the franchise ordinance or affected by adverse court
decisions, the stock inevitably would sink to a much lower
price. At this low price the aldermen and their confederates would buy the stock and then deliver it, compelling
the contracting parties to pay the agreed price of $90
a share. The difference between the stipulated price of

delivery and the value to which the stock had fallen —
$30, $40 or $50 a share —would represent the winnings.

Part of this plan worked out admirably. The Legislature passed an act giving Law the franchise. Vanderbilt countered by getting Tweed, the all-powerful political ruler of New York City and New York State, to
order his tool, Governor Seymour, to veto the measure.
As was anticipated by the aldermen, the courts pronounced that the Common Council had no power to grant
franchises. Vanderbilt's franchise was, therefore, an-
nulled. So far, there was no hitch in the plot to pluck
Vanderbilt.

But an unlooked for obstacle was encountered. Vanderbilt had somehow got wind of the affair, and with instant energy bought up secretly all of the New York and
Harlem Railroad stock he could. He had masses of
ready money to do it with; the millions from the mail
subsidy frauds and from his other lootings of the public
treasury proved an unfailing source of supply. Presently, he had enough of the stock to corner his antagonists badly. He then put his own price upon it, eventually pushing it up to $170 a share. To get the stock
that they contracted to deliver, the combination of politicians and Wall Street bankers and brokers had to buy
it from him at his own price; there was no outstanding
stock elsewhere. The old man was pitiless; he mulcted
them $179 a share. In his version, Croffut says of Van-
derbilt: " He and his partners in the bull movement took
a million dollars from the Common Council that week
and other millions from others." [17]

The New York and Harlem Railroad was now his,
as absolutely almost as the very clothes he wore. Little
it mattered that he did not hold all of the stock; he owned

[17] " The Vanderbilts," etc: 75.

a preponderance enough to rule the railroad as despotically as he pleased. Not a foot it had he surveyed or constructed; this task had been done by the mental and manual labor of thousands of wage workers not one of whom now owned the vestige of an interest in it. For their toil these wage workers had nothing to show but poverty. But Vanderbilt had swept in a railroad system by merely using in cunning and unscrupulous ways a few of the millions he had defrauded from the national treasury.

### HE ANNEXES A SECOND RAILROAD.

Having found it so easy to get one railroad, he promptly went ahead to annex other railroads. By 1864 he loomed up as the owner of a controlling mass of stock in the New York and Hudson River Railroad. This line paralleled the Hudson River, and had a terminal in the downtown section of New York City. In a way it was a competitor of the New York and Harlem Railroad.

The old magnate now conceived a brilliant idea. Why not consolidate the two roads? True, to bring about this consolidation an authorizing act of the New York Legislature was necessary. But there was little doubt of the Legislature balking. Vanderbilt well knew the means to insure its passage. In those years, when the people were taught to look upon competition as indispensable, there was deep popular opposition to the consolidating of competing interests. This, it was feared, would inflict monopoly.

The cost of buying legislators to pass an act so provocative of popular indignation would be considerable, but, at the same time, it would not be more than a trifle compared with the immense profits he would gain. The consolidation would allow him to increase, or, as the phrase went, water, the stock of the combined roads. Although substantially owner of the two railroads, he was legally two separate entities — or, rather, the corporations were.  As owner of one line he could bargain with himself as owner of the other, and could determine what the exchange purchase price should be.  So, by a juggle, he could issue enormous quantities of bonds and stocks to himself.  These many millions of bonds and stocks would not cost him personally a cent.  The sole expense — the bribe funds and the cost of engraving — he would charge against his corporations.  Immediately, these stocks and bonds would be vested with a high value, inasmuch as they would represent mortgages upon the productivity of tens of millions of people of that generation, and of still greater numbers of future generations.  By putting up traffic rates and lowering wages, dividends could be paid upon the entire outpouring of stock, thus beyond a doubt insuring its permanent · value.[18]

## CUNNING AGAINST CUNNING.

A majority of the New York Legislature was bought. It looked as if the consolidation act would go through without difficulty.  Surreptitiously, however, certain leading men in the Legislature plotted with the Wall Street opponents of Vanderbilt to repeat the trick attempted by the New York aldermen in 1863.  The bill would be

[18] Even Croffut, Vanderbilt's foremost eulogist, cynically grows merry over Vanderbilt's methods which he thus summarizes: " (1) Buy your railroad; (2) stop the stealing that went on under the other man; (3) improve the road in every practicable way within a reasonable expenditure; (4) consolidate it with any other road that can be run with it economically; (5) water its stock; (6) make it pay a large dividend."

introduced and reported favorably; every open indication would be manifested of keeping faith with Vanderbilt. Upon the certainty of its passage the market value of the stock would rise. With their prearranged plan of defeating the bill at the last moment upon some plausible pretext, the clique in the meantime would be busy selling short.

Information of this treachery came to Vanderbilt in time. He retaliated as he had upon the New York aldermen; put the price of New York and Harlem stock up to $285 a share and held it there until after he was settled with. With his chief partner, John Tobin, he was credited with pocketing many millions of dollars. To make their corner certain, the Vanderbilt pool had bought 27,000 more shares than the entire existing stock of the road. "We busted the whole Legislature," was Vanderbilt's jubilant comment," and scores of the honorable members had to go home without paying their board bills."

The numerous millions taken in by Vanderbilt in these transactions came from a host of other men who would have plundered him as quickly as he plundered them. They came from members of the Legislature who had grown rich on bribes for granting a continuous succession of special privileges, or to put it in a more comprehensible form, licenses to individuals and corporations to prey in a thousand and one forms upon the people. They came from bankers, railroad, land and factory owners, all of whom had assiduously bribed Congress, legislatures, common councils and administrative officials to give them special laws and rights by which they could all the more easily and securely grasp the produce of the many, and hold it intact without even a semblance of taxation.

The very nature of that system of gambling called stock-market or cotton or produce exchange speculation showed at once the sharply-defined disparities and discriminations in law.

Common gambling, so-called, was a crime. The gambling of the exchanges was legitimate and legalized, and the men who thus gambled with the resources of the nation were esteemed as highly respectable and responsible leaders of the community. For a penniless man to sell anything he did not own, or which was not in existence, was held a heinous crime and was severely punished by a long prison term. But the members of the all-powerful propertied class could contract to deliver stocks which they did not own or which were non-existent, or they could gamble in produce often not yet out of the ground, and the law saw no criminal act in their performances.

Far from being under the inhibition of law, their methods were duly legalized. The explanation was not hard to find. These same propertied classes had made the code of laws as it stood; and if any doubter denies that laws at all times have exactly corresponded with the interests and aims of the ruling class, all that is necessary is to compare the laws of the different periods with the profitable methods of that class, and he will find that these methods, however despicable, vile and cruel, were not only indulgently omitted from the recognized category of crimes but were elevated by prevalent teaching to be commercial virtues and ability of a high order.

With two railroads in his possession Vanderbilt cast about to drag in a third. This was the New York Central Railroad, one of the richest in the country.

Vanderbilt's eulogists, in depicting him as a masterful

constructionist, assert that it was he who first saw the waste and futility of competition, and that he organized the New York Central from the disjointed, disconnected lines of a number of previously separate little railroads. This is a gross error.

The consolidation was formed in 1853 at the time when Vanderbilt was plundering from the United States treasury the millions with which he began to buy in railroads nine years later. The New York Central arose from the union of ten little railroads, some running in the territory between Albany and Buffalo, and others merely projected, but which had nevertheless been capitalized as though they were actually in operation.

The cost of construction of these eleven roads was about $10,000,000, but they were capitalized at $23,000,000. Under the consolidating act of 1853 the capitalization was run up to about $35,000,000. This fictitious capital was partly based on roads which were never built, and existing on paper only. Then followed a series of legislative acts giving the company a further list of valuable franchises and allowing it to charge extortionate rates, inflate its stock, and virtually escape taxation. How these laws were procured may be judged from the testimony of the treasurer of the New York Central railroad before a committee of the New York State Constitutional Convention. This official stated that from about 1853 to 1867 the New York Central had spent hundreds of thousands of dollars for "legislative purposes,"— in other words, buying laws at Albany.

## ACQUISITION BY WRECKING.

Vanderbilt considered it unnecessary to buy New York Central stock to get control. He had a much better and subtler plan.  The Hudson River Railroad was at that time the only through road running from New York to Albany.  To get its passengers and freight to New York City the New York Central had to make a transfer at Albany.  Vanderbilt now deliberately began to wreck the New York Central.  He sent out an order in 1865 to all Hudson River Railroad employees to refuse to connect with the New York Central and to take no more freight. This move could not do otherwise than seriously cripple the facilities and lower the profits of the New York Central.  Consequently, the value of its stock was bound to go precipitately down.

The people of the United States were treated to an ironic sight.  Here was a man who only eight years before had been shown up in Congress as an arch plunderer; a man who had bought his railroads largely with his looted millions; a man who, if the laws had been drafted and executed justly, would have been condoning his frauds in prison;—this man was contemptuously and openly defying the very people whose interests the railroads were supposed to serve.  In this conflict between warring sets of capitalists, as in all similar conflicts, public convenience was made sport of.  Hudson River trains going north no longer crossed the Hudson River to enter Albany; they stopped half a mile east of the bridge leading into that city.  This made it impossible to transfer freight.  There in the country the trains were arbitrarily stopped for the night; locomotive fires were banked and the passengers were left to shift into Albany the best they could, whether they walked or contrived to hire vehicles.  All were turned out of the train — men, women and children — no exceptions were made for sex or infirmity.

The Legislature went through a pretense of investigat-

ing what public opinion regarded as a particularly atro-
cious outrage.    Vanderbilt covered this committee with
undisguised scorn; it provoked his wrath to be quizzed by
a committee of a body many of whose members had accepted his bribes.    When he was asked why he had so
high-handedly refused to run his trains across the river,
the old fox smiled grimly, and to their utter surprise,
showed them an old law (which had hitherto remained a
dead letter) prohibiting the New York Hudson Railroad
from running trains over the Hudson River.    This law
had been enacted in response to the demand of the New
York Central, which wanted no competitor west of Albany.    When the committee recovered its breath, its
chairman timidly inquired of Vanderbilt why he did not
run trains to the river.

"I was not there, gentlemen," said Vanderbilt.

"But what did you do when you heard of it?"

"I did not do anything."

"Why not?  Where were you?"

"I was at home, gentlemen," replied Vanderbilt with
serene impudence, "playing a rubber of whist, and I
never allow anything to interfere with me when I am
playing that game.    It requires, as you know, undivided
attention."

As Vanderbilt had foreseen, the stock of the New
York Central went down abruptly; at its lowest point he
bought in large quantities.    His opponents, Edward
Cunard, John Jacob Astor, John Steward and other
owners of the New York Central thus saw the directorship pass from their hands.    The dispossession they had
worked to the Pruyns, the Martins, the Pages and others
was now being visited upon them.    They found in this
old man of seventy-three too cunning and crafty a man
to defeat.    Rather than lose all, they preferred to choose

him as their captain; his was the sort of ability which they could not overcome and to which they must attach themselves. On November 12, 1867, they surrendered wholly and unreservedly. Vanderbilt now installed his own subservient board of directors, and proceeded to put through a fresh program of plunder beside which all his previous schemes were comparatively insignificant.

## CHAPTER V

### THE VANDERBILT FORTUNE INCREASES MANIFOLD

Vanderbilt's ambition was to become the richest man in America. With three railroads in his possession he now aggressively set out to grasp a fourth — the Erie Railroad. This was another of the railroads built largely with public money. The State of New York had contributed $3,000,000, and other valuable donations had been given.

At the very inception of the railroad corruption began.[1] The tradesmen, landowners and bankers who composed the company bribed the Legislature to relinquish the State's claim, and then looted the railroad with such consummate thoroughness that in order to avert its bankruptcy they were obliged to borrow funds from Daniel Drew. This man was an imposing financial personage in his day. Illiterate, unscrupulous, picturesque in his very iniquities, he had once been a drover, and had gone into the steamboat business with Vanderbilt. He had scraped in wealth partly from that line of traffic, and in part from a succession of buccaneering operations. His loan remaining unpaid, Drew indemnified himself by taking over, in 1857, by foreclosure, the control of the Erie Railroad.

For the next nine years Drew manipulated the stock at will, sending the price up or down as suited his gambling schemes. The railroad degenerated until travel upon

[1] Report of the New York and Erie Railroad Company, New York State Assembly Document No. 50, 1842.

it became a menace; one disaster followed another. Drew imperturbably continued his manipulation of the stock market, careless of the condition of the road. At no time was he put to the inconvenience of even being questioned by the public authorities. On the contrary, the more millions he made the greater grew his prestige and power, the higher his standing in the community. Ruling society, influenced solely by money standards, saluted him as a successful man who had his millions, and made no fastidious inquiries as to how he got them. He was a potent man; his villainies passed as great astuteness, his devious cunning as marvelous sagacity.

### GOULD OVERREACHES VANDERBILT.

Vanderbilt resolved to wrest the Erie Railroad out of Drew's hands. By secretly buying its stock he was in a position in 1866 to carry out his designs. He threw Drew and his directors out, but subsequently realizing Drew's usefulness, reinstated him upon condition that he be fully pliable to the Vanderbilt interests. Thereupon Drew brought in as fellow directors two young men, then obscure but of whom the world was to hear much — James Fisk, Jr., and Jay Gould. The narrative of how these three men formed a coalition against Vanderbilt; how they betrayed and then outgeneraled him at every turn; proved themselves of a superior cunning; sold him large quantities of spurious stock; excelled him in corruption; defrauded more than $50,000,000, and succeeded — Gould, at any rate — in keeping most of the plunder — this will be found in detail where it more properly belongs — in the chapter of the Gould fortune describing that part of Gould's career connected with the Erie Railroad.

Baffled in his frantic contest to keep hold of that railroad — a hold that he would have turned into many
millions of dollars of immediate loot by fraudulently
watering the stock, and then bribing the Legislature to
legalize it as Gould did — Vanderbilt at once set in motion a fraudulent plan of his own by which he extorted
about $44,000,000 in plunder, the greater portion of which
went to swell his fortune.

The year 1868 proved a particularly busy one for
Vanderbilt. He was engaged in a desperately devious
struggle with Gould. In vain did his agents and lobbyists
pour out stacks of money to buy legislative votes enough
to defeat the bill legalizing Gould's fraudulent issue of
stock. Members of the Legislature impassively took
money from both parties. Gould personally appeared at
Albany with a satchel containing $500,000 in greenbacks
which were rapidly distributed. One Senator, as was disclosed by an investigating committee, accepted $75,000
from Vanderbilt and then $100,000 from Gould, kept both
sums,— and voted with the dominant Gould forces. It
was only by means of the numerous civil and criminal
writs issued by Vanderbilt judges that the old man contrived to force Gould and his accomplices into paying for
the stock fraudulently unloaded upon him. The best terms
that he could get was an unsatisfactory settlement which
still left him to bear a loss of about two millions. The
veteran trickster had never before been overreached; all
his life, except on one occasion,[2] he had been the successful sharper; but he was no match for the more agile and
equally sly, corrupt and resourceful Gould. It took
some time for Vanderbilt to realize this; and it was
only after several costly experiences with Gould, that

[2] In 1837 when he had advanced funds to a contractor carrying the mails between Washington and Richmond, and had
taken security which proved to be worthless.

he could bring himself to admit that he could not hope to
outdo Gould.

## A NEW CONSOLIDATION PLANNED.

However, Vanderbilt quickly and multitudinously re-
couped himself for the losses encountered in his Erie assault. Why not, he argued, combine the New York
Central and the Hudson River companies into one corporation, and on the strength of it issue a vast amount of
additional stock?

The time was ripe for a new mortgage on the labor of
that generation and of the generations to follow. Population was wondrously increasing, and with it trade.
For years the New York Central had been paying a
dividend of eight per cent. But this was only part of
the profits. A law had been passed in 1850 authorizing
the Legislature to step in whenever the dividends rose
above ten per cent. on the railroad's actual cost, and to
declare what should be done with the surplus. This law
was nothing more or less than a blind to conciliate the
people of the State, and let them believe that they would
get some returns for the large outlay of public funds
advanced to the New York Central. No returns ever
came. Vanderbilt, and the different groups before him,
in control of the road had easily evaded it, just as in every
direction the whole capitalist class pushed aside law whenever law conflicted with its aims and interests. It was
the propertyless only for whom the execution of law was
intended. Profits from the New York Central were far
more than eight per cent.; by perjury and frauds the directors retained sums that should have gone to the State.
Every year they prepared a false account of their
revenues and expenditures which they submitted to the

State officials; they pretended that they annually spent millions of dollars in construction work on the road — work, in reality, never done.[3]   The money was pocketed by them under this device — a device that has since become a favorite of many railroad and public utility corporations.

Unenforced as it was, this law was nevertheless an obstacle in the way of Vanderbilt's plans.   Likewise was another, a statute prohibiting both the New York Central Railroad and the Hudson River Railroad from increasing their stock.   To understand why this latter law was passed it is necessary to remember that the middle class — the factory owners, jobbers, retail tradesmen and employing farmers — were everywhere seeking by the power of law to prevent the too great development of corporations.   These, they apprehended, and with reason, would ultimately engulf them and their fortunes and importance. They knew that each new output of watered stock meant either that the prevailing high freight rates would remain unchanged or would be increased; and while all the charges had to be borne finally by the working class, the middle class sought to have an unrestricted market on its own terms.

## ALARM OF THE TRADING CLASSES.

It was the opposition of the various groups of this class that Vanderbilt expected and provided against.   He was fully aware that the moment he revealed his plan of consolidation boards of trade everywhere would rise in their wrath, denounce him, call together mass meetings, insist upon railroad competition and send pretentious, fire-breathing delegates to the State Capitol.   Let them thun-

[3] See Report of New York Special Assembly Committee on Railroads, 1879, iv: 3,894.

der, said Vanderbilt placidly. While they were explod-
ing in eruptions of talk he would concentrate at Albany
a mass of silent arguments in the form of money and
get the necessary legislative votes, which was all he cared
about.

Then ensued one of the many comedies familiar to
observers of legislative proceedings. It was amusing to
the sophositicated to see delegations indignantly betake
themselves to Albany, submit voluminous briefs which
legislators never read, and with immense gravity argue
away for hours to committees which had already been
bought. The era was that of the Tweed regime, when
the public funds of New York City and State were being
looted on a huge scale by the politicians in power, and
far more so by the less vulgar but more crafty business
classes who spurred Tweed and his confederates on to
fresh schemes of spoliation.

Laws were sold at Albany to the highest bidder. " It
was impossible," Tweed testified after his downfall, " to
do anything there without paying for it; money had to be
raised for the passing of bills." [4]  Decades before this,
legislators had been so thoroughly taught by the landowners and bankers how to exchange their votes for cash
that now, not only at Albany and Washington, but everywhere in the United States, both legislative and administrative officials haggled in real astute business style for the
highest price that they could get.

One noted lobbyist stated in 1868 that for a favorable
report on a certain bill before the New York Senate,
$5,000 apiece was paid to four members of the committee
having it in charge. On the passage of the bill, a further

[4] Statement of William M. Tweed before a Special Investigating Committee of the New York Board of Aldermen. Documents of the Board of Aldermen, 1877, Part II. Document No.
8: 15-16.

$5,000 apiece with contingent expenses was added. In another instance, where but a solitary vote was needed to put a bill through, three Republicans put their figures up to $25,000 each; one of them was bought. About thirty Republicans and Democrats in the New York Legislature organized themselves into a clique (long styled the " Black Horse Cavalry "), under the leadership of an energetic lobbyist, with a mutual pledge to vote as directed.[5] " Any corporation, however extensive and comprehensive the privileges it asked "— to quote from " The History of Tammany Hall "—" and however much oppression it sought to impose upon the people in the line of unjust grants, extortionate rates or monopoly, could convince the Legislature of the righteousness of its request upon ' producing ' the proper sum."

## A LEGALIZED THEFT OF $44,000,000.

One act after another was slipped through the Legislature by Vanderbilt in 1868 and 1869. On May 20, 1869, Vanderbilt secured, by one bill alone, the right to consolidate railroads, a free grant of franchises, and other rights worth hundreds of millions of dollars, and the right to water stock and bonds to an enormous extent.

The printing presses were worked overtime in issuing more than $44,000,000 of watered stock. The capital stock of the two roads was thus doubled. Pretending that the railroads embraced in the consolidation had a great surplus on hand, Vanderbilt, instead of distributing this alleged surplus, apportioned the watered stock among the stockholders as a premium. The story of the surplus was, of course, only a pretense. Each holder of a $100 share received a certificate for $180 — that is to say, $80

[5] Documents of the Board of Aldermen, 1877, Part II, No. 8; 212-213.

in plunder for every $100 share that he held.[6]  " Thus,"
reported the " Hepburn Committee " (the popular name
for the New York State Assembly investigating committee of 1879), " as calculated by this expert, $53,507,-
060 were wrongfully added to the capital stock of these
roads."   Of this sum $44,000,000 was issued in 1869; the
remainder in previous years.   " The only answer made
by the roads was that the legislature authorized it," the
committee went on.   " It is proper to remark that the
people are quite as much indebted to the venality of the
men elected to represent them in the Legislature as to the
rapacity of the railroad managers for this state of affairs."[7]

Despite the fact that the report of the committee
recorded that the transaction was piracy, the euphemistic
wording of the committee's statement was characteristic
of the reverence shown to the rich and influential, and
the sparing of their feelings by the avoidance of harsh
language.  " Wrongfully  added "  would  have  been
quickly changed into such inconsiderate terms as theft
and robbery had the case been even a trivial one of some
ordinary citizen lacking wealth and power.   The facts
would have immediately been presented to the proper
officials for criminal prosecution.

But not a suggestion was forthcoming of haling
Vanderbilt to the criminal bar; had it been made, nothing except a farce would have resulted, for the reason
that the criminal machinery, while extraordinarily active
in hurrying petty lawbreakers to prison, was a part of
the political mechanism financed by the big criminals and
subservient to them.

" The $44,000,000," says Simon Sterne, a noted lawyer
who, as counsel for various commercial organizations, un-

[6] Report of Assembly Committee on Railroads, testimony of
Alexander Robertson, an expert accountant, 1879, i: 994-999.
  [7] Ibid., i: 21.

ravelled the whole matter before the "Hepburn Committee," in 1879, " represented no more labor than it took to print the script." It was notorious, he adds, " that the cost of the consolidated railroads was less than $44,000,000," [8] In increasing the stock to $86,000,000 Vanderbilt and his confederates therefore stole the difference between the cost and the maximum of the stock issue. So great were the profits, both open and concealed, of the consolidated railroads that notwithstanding, as Charles Francis Adams computed, " $50,000 of absolute water had been poured out for each mile of road between New York and Buffalo," the market price of the stock at once shot up in 1869 from $75 a share to $120 and then to $200.

And what was Vanderbilt's share of the $44,000,000? His inveterate panegyrist, Croffut, in smoothly defending the transaction gives this illuminating depiction of the joyous event: " One night, at midnight, he (Cornelius Vanderbilt) carried away from the office of Horace F. Clark, his son-in-law, $6,000,000 in greenbacks as a part of his share of the profits, and he had $20,000,000 more in new stock." [9]

By this coup Vanderbilt about doubled his previous wealth. Scarcely had the mercantile interests recovered from their utter bewilderment at being routed than Vanderbilt, flushed with triumph, swept more railroads into his inventory of possessions.

[8] "Life of Simon Sterne," by John Foord, 1903: 179-181.
[9] "The Vanderbilts": 103. Croffut in a footnote tells this anecdote:
"When the Commodore's portrait first appeared on the bonds of the Central, a holder of some called one day and said: ' Commodore, glad to see your face on them bonds. It's worth ten per cent. It gives everybody confidence.' The Commodore smiled grimly, the only recognition he ever made of a compliment. ' 'Cause,' explained the visitor, ' when we see that fine, noble brow, it reminds us that you'll never let anybody else steal anything.' "

His process of acquisition was now working with almost automatic ease.

First, as we have narrated, he extorted millions of dollars in blackmail. With these millions he bought, or rather manipulated into his control, one railroad after another, amid an onslaught of bribery and glaring violations of the laws. Each new million that he seized was an additional resource by which he could bribe and manipulate; progressively his power advanced; and it became ridiculously easier to get possession of more and more property. His very name became a terror to those of lesser capital, and the mere threat of pitting his enormous wealth against competitors whom he sought to destroy was generally a sufficient warrant for their surrender. After his consummation of the $44,000,000 theft in 1869 there was little withstanding of him. By the most favorable account — that of Croffut — his own allotment of the plunder amounted to $26,000,000. This sum, immense, and in fact of almost inconceivable power in that day, was enough of itself, independent of Vanderbilt's other wealth, to force through almost any plan involving a seizing of competing property.

### HE SCOOPS UP MORE RAILROADS.

Vanderbilt did not wait long. The ink on the $44,000,-000 had barely dried, before he used part of the proceeds to buy a controlling interest in the Lake Shore Railroad, a competing line. Then rapidly, by the same methods, he took hold of the Canada Southern and Michigan Central.

The commercial interests looked on dumfounded. Under their very eyes a process of centralization was going on, of which they but dimly, stupidly, grasped the purport. That competition which they had so long shouted for as the only sensible, true and moral system, and which they had sought to buttress by enacting law after law, was being irreverently ground to pieces.

Out of their own ranks were rising men, trained in their own methods, who were amplifying and intensifying those methods to shatter the class from which they had sprung. The different grades of the propertied class, from the merchant with his fortune of $250,000 to the retail tradesman, felt very comfortable in being able to look down with a conscious superiority upon the working class from whom their money was wrung. Scoffing at equality, they delighted in setting themselves up as a class infinitely above the toilers of the shop and factory; let him who disputes this consult the phrases that went the rounds — phrases, some of which are still current — as, for instance, the preaching that the moderately well-to-do class is the solid, substantial element of any country.

Now when this mercantile class saw itself being far overtopped and outclassed in the only measurement to which it attached any value — that of property — by men with vast riches and power, it began to feel its relegation. Although its ideal was money, and although it set up the acquisition of wealth as the all-stimulating incentive and goal of human effort, it viewed sullenly and enviously the development of an established magnate class which could look haughtily and dictatorially down upon it even as it constantly looked down upon the working class. The factory owner and the shopkeeper had for decades commanded the passage of summary legislation by which they were enabled to fleece the worker and render him incapable of resistance. To keep the worker in subjection and in their power they considered a justifiable proceeding. But when they saw the railroad magnates applying those same methods to themselves, by first wiping out competition, and then by enforcing edicts regardless of their interests, they burst out in furious rage.

### VANDERBILT AND HIS CRITICS.

They denounced Vanderbilt as a bandit whose methods were a menace to the community.   To the onlooker this campaign of virulent assault was extremely suggestive. If there was any one line of business in which fraud was not rampant, the many official reports and court proceedings of the time do not show it.

This widespread fraud was not occasional; it was persistent.   In one of the earlier chapters, the prevalence, more than a century ago, of the practise of fraudulent substitution of drugs and foods was adverted to.   In the middle of the nineteenth century it was far more extensive.   In submitting, on June 2, 1848, a mass of expert evidence on the adulteration of drugs, to the House of Representatives, the House Select Committee on the Importation of Drugs pointed out:

For a long series of years this base traffic has been constantly increasing, until it has become frightfully enormous.   It would be presumed, from the immense quantities, and the great variety of inferior drugs that pass our custom houses, and particularly the custom-house at New York, in the course of a single year, that this country had become the great mart and receptacle of all of the refuse merchandise of that description, not only from the European warehouses, but from the whole Eastern market.[9a]

In presenting a formidable array of expert testimony,

[9a] Reports of Committees, First Session, Thirtieth Congress, 1847-48, Vol. iii, Report No. 664:3 — The committee reported that opium was adulterated with licorice paste and bitter vegetable extract; calomel, with chalk and sulphate of barytes; quinine, with silicine, chalk and sulphate of barytes; castor, with dried blood, gum and ammonia; gum assafœtida with inferior gums, chalk and clay, etc., etc. (pp. 10 and 11).

and in giving a list of cases of persons having died from eating foods and drugs adulterated with poisonous substances, the House Committee on Epidemic Diseases, of the Forty-Sixth Congress, reported on February 4 1881:

That they have investigated, as far as they could . . . the injurious and poisonous compounds used in the preparation of food substances, and in the manufacture of wearing apparel and other articles, and find from the evidence submitted to them that the adulteration of articles used in the every day diet of vast numbers of people has grown, and is now practised, to such an extent as to seriously endanger the public health, and to call loudly for some sort of legislative correction. Drugs, liquors, articles of clothing, wall paper and many other things are subjected to the same dangerous process.[10] ‑

The House Committee on Commerce, reporting the next year, on March 4, stated that " the evidence regarding the adulterations of food indicates that they are largely of the nature of frauds upon the consumer . . . and injure both the health and morals of the people." The committee declared that the practise of fraudulent substitutions " had become universal." [11]

These few significant extracts, from a mass of official reports, show that the commercial frauds were continuous, and began long before Commodore Vanderbilt's time, and have prevailed up to the present.

Everywhere was fraud; even the little storekeepers, with their smug pretensions to homely honesty, were profiting by some of the vilest, basest forms of fraud, such as robbing the poor by the light-weight and short-weight trick,[12] or (far worse) by selling skim milk, or poisonous

[10] House Reports, Third Session, Forty-sixth Congress, 1880-81, Vol. i, Report No. 199: 1. The committee drafted a bill for the prevention of these frauds; the capitalists concerned smothered it.

[11] House Reports, First Session, Forty-seventh Congress, 1881-82, Vol. ii, Report No. 634: 1-5.

[12] These forms of cheating exist at present to a greater extent

drugs or adulterated food or shoddy material. These practises were so prevalent, that the exceptions were rarities indeed.

If any administration had dared seriously to stop these forms of theft the trading classes would have resisted and struck back in political action. Yet these were the men — these traders — who vociferously come forth with their homiletic trades against Vanderbilt's criminal transactions, demanding that the power of him and his kind be curbed.

It was not at all singular that they put their protests on moral grounds. In a form of society where each man is compelled to fight every other man in a wild, demoralizing struggle for self-preservation, self-interest naturally usurps the supreme functions, and this self-interest becomes transposed, by a comprehensible process, into moralities. That which is profitable is perverted into a moral code; the laws passed, the customs introduced and persisted in, and the weight of the dominant classes all conspire to put the stamp of morality on practices arising from the lowest and most sordid aims. Thus did the trading class make a moral profession of its methods

than ever before. It is estimated that manufacturers and shop-keepers cheat the people of the United States out of $200,000,000 a year by the light-weight and short-weight frauds. In 1907 the New York State Sealer of Weights and Measures asserted that, in that State alone, $20,000,000 was robbed from the consumers annually by these methods. Recent investigations by the Bureau of Standards of the United States Department of Commerce and Labor have shown that immense numbers of "crooked" scales are in use. It has been conclusively established by the investigations of Federal, State and municipal inspectors of weights and measures that there is hardly an article put up in bottled or canned form that is not short of the weight for which it is sold, nor is there scarcely a retail dealer who does not swindle his customers by the light-weight fraud. There are manufacturers who make a specific business of turning out fraudulent scales, and who freely advertise the cheating merits of these scales.

of exploitation; it congratulated and sanctified itself on its purity of life and its saving stability.

From this class — a class interpenetrated in every direction with commercial frauds — was largely empanelled the men who sat on those grand juries and petit juries solemnly passing verdict on the poor wretches of criminals whom environment or poverty had driven into crime. They were the arbiters of justice, but it was a justice that was never allowed to act against themselves. Examine all the penal codes of the period; note the laws proscribing long sentences in prison for thefts of property; the larceny of even a suit of clothes was severely punishable, and begging for alms was a misdemeanor. Then contrast these asperities of law with the entire absence of adequate protection for the buyer of merchandise. Following the old dictum of Roman jurisprudence, " Let the buyer beware," the factory owner could at will oppress his workers, and compel them, for the scantiest wages, to make for his profit goods unfit for consumption. These articles the retailer sold without scruple over his counter; when the buyer was cheated or overcharged, as happened with great frequency, he had practically no redress in law. If the merchant were robbed of even ever so little he could retaliate by sending the guilty one to prison. But the merchant himself could invidiously and continuously rob the customer without fear of any law. All of this was converted into a code of moralities; and any bold spirit who exposed its cant and sham was denounced as an agitator and as an enemy of law and order.[18]

[18] A few progressive jurists in the International Prison Congress are attempting to secure the recognition in law of the principle that society, as a supreme necessity, is obligated to protect its members from being made the victims of the cunning and unscrupulous. They have received no encouragement, and

Vanderbilt did better than expose it; he improved upon, and enlarged, it and made it a thing of magnitude; he and others of his quality discarded petty larceny and ascended into a sphere of superlative grand larceny. They knew with a cynical perception that society, with all its pompous pretensions to morality, had evolved a rule which worked with almost mathematical certainty. This rule was the paradoxical, but nevertheless true, one that the greater the theft the less corresponding danger there was of punishment.

### THE WISDOM OF GRAND LARCENY.

Now it was that one could see with greater clearness than ever before, how the mercenary ideal of the ruling class was working out to its inevitable conclusion. Society had made money its god and property its yardstick; even in its administration of justice, theoretically supposed to be equal, it had made " justice " an expensive luxury available, in actual practice, to the rich only. The defrauder of large sums could, if prosecuted, use a part of that plunder, easily engage a corps of shrewd, experienced lawyers, get evidence manufactured, fight out the case on technicalities, drag it along for years, call in political and social influence, and almost invariably escape in the end.

But beyond this power of money to make a mockery of justice was a still greater, though more subtle, factor, which was ever an invaluable aid to the great thief. Every section of the trading class was permeated with a profound admiration, often tangibly expressed, for the craft that got away with an impressive pile of loot. The

will receive none, from a trading class profiting from the very methods which it is sought to place under the inhibition of criminal law.

contempt felt for the pickpocket was the antithesis of the general mercantile admiring view of the man who stole in grand style, especially when he was one of their own class. In speaking of the piratical operations of this or that magnate, it was common to hear many business men interject, even while denouncing him, " Well, I wish I were as smart as he." These same men, when serving on juries, were harsh in their verdicts on poor criminals, and unctuously flattered themselves with being, and were represented as, the upholders and conservers of law and moral conduct.

Departing from the main facts as this philosophical digression may seem, it is essential for a number of reasons. One of these is the continual necessity for keeping in mind a clear, balanced perspective. Another lies in the need of presenting aright the conditions in which Vanderbilt and magnates of his type were produced. Their methods at basis were not a growth independent of those of the business world and isolated from them. They were simply a development, and not merely one of standards as applied to morals, but of the mechanism of the social and industrial organization itself. Finally it is advisable to give flashlight glimpses into the modes and views of the time, inasmuch as it was in Vanderbilt's day that the great struggle between the old principle of competition, as upheld by the small capitalists, and the superseding one of consolidation, as incarnated in him and others, took on vigorous headway.

### HE CONTINUES THE BUYING OF LAWS.

Protest as it did against Vanderbilt's merging of railroads, the midldle class found itself quite helpless. In rapid succession he put through one combination after another, and caused theft after theft to be legalized, utterly disdainful of criticism or opposition. In State after State he bought the repeal of old laws, or the passage of new laws, until he was vested with authority to connect various railroads that he had secured between Buffalo and Chicago, into one line with nearly 1,300 miles of road. The commercial classes were scared at the sight of such a great stretch of railroad — then considered an immense line — in the hands of one man, audacious, all-conquering, with power to enforce tribute at will. Again, Vanderbilt patronized the printing presses, and many more millions of stock, all fictitious capital, were added to the already flooded capital of the Lake Shore and Michigan Southern Railroad Company. Of the total of $62,000,000 of capital stock in 1871, fully one-half was based upon nothing but the certainty of making it valuable as a dividend payer by the exaction of high freight and passenger rates. A little later, the amount was run up to $73,000,000, and this was increased subsequently.

Vanderbilt now had a complete railroad system from New York to Chicago, with extensive offshoots. It is at this point that we have to deal with a singular commendation of his methods thrust forward glibly from that day to this. True, his eulogists admitted then, as they admit now, Vanderbilt was not overscrupulous in getting property that he wanted. But consider, they urge, the improvements he brought about on the railroads that came into his possession; the renovation of the roadbed, the institution of new locomotives and cars, the tearing down of the old, worn-out stations. This has been the praise showered upon him and his methods.

Inquiry, however, reveals that this appealing picture, like all others of its sort, has been ingeniously distorted.

The fact was, in the first place, that these improvements were not made out of regard to public convenience, but for two radically different reasons. The first consideration was that if the dividends were to be paid on the huge amount of fabricated stock, the road, of necessity, had to be put into a condition of fair efficiency to meet or surpass the competing facilities of other railroads running to Chicago. Second, the number of damage claims for accident or loss of life arising largely from improper appliances. and insufficient safeguards, was so great that it was held cheaper in the long run to spend millions for improvements.

### PUBLIC FUNDS FOR PRIVATE USE.

Instead of paying for these improvements with even a few millions of the proceeds of the watered stock, Vanderbilt (and all other railroad magnates in like cases did the same) forced the public treasury to defray a large part of the cost. A good illustration of his methods was his improvement of his passenger terminus in New York City. The entrance of the New York Central and the Harlem Railroads is by way of Park (formerly Fourth) avenue. This franchise, as we have seen, was obtained by bribery in 1832. But it was a qualified franchise. It reserved certain nominal restrictions in behalf of the people by inserting the right of the city to order the removal of the tracks at any time that they became an obstruction. These terms were objectionable to Vanderbilt; a perpetual franchise could be capitalized for far more than a limited or qualified one. A perpetual franchise was what he wanted.

The opportunity came in 1872. From the building of the railroad, the tracks had been on the surface of Fourth avenue. Dozens of dangerous crossings had resulted in much injury to life and many deaths. The public demand that the tracks be depressed below the level of the street had been resisted.

Instead of longer ignoring this demand, Vanderbilt now planned to make use of it; he saw how he could utilize it not only to foist a great part of the expense upon the city, but to get a perpetual franchise. Thus, upon the strength of the popular cry for reform, he would extort advantages calculated to save him millions and at the same time extend his privileges. It was but another illustration of the principle in capitalist society to which we have referred before (and which there will be copious occasion to mention again and again) that after energetically contesting even those petty reforms for which the people have contended, the ruling classes have ever deftly turned about when they could no longer withstand the popular demands, and have made those very reforms the basis for more spoliation and for a further intrenchment of their power.[14]

The first step was to get the New York City Common Council to pass, with an assumption of indignation, an ordinance requiring Vanderbilt to make the desired improvements, and committing the city to bear one-half

[14] Commodore Vanderbilt's descendants, the present Vanderbilts, have been using the public outcry for a reform of conditions on the West Side of New York City, precisely as the original Vanderbilt utilized that for the improvement of Fourth avenue. The Hudson River division of the New York Central and Hudson River Railroad has hitherto extended downtown on the surface of Tenth and Eleventh Avenues and other thoroughfares. Large numbers of people have been killed and injured. For decades there has been a public demand that these dangerous conditions be remedied or removed. The Vanderbilts have as long resisted the demand; the immense numbers of casualties had no effect upon them. When the public demand became too strong to be ignored longer, they set about to exploit it in order to get a comprehensive franchise with incalculable new privileges.

the expense and giving him a perpetual franchise. This was in Tweed's time when the Common Council was composed largely of the most corrupt ward heelers, and when Tweed's puppet, Hall, was Mayor. Public opposition to this grab was so great as to frighten the politicians; at any rate, whatever his reasons, Mayor Hall vetoed the ordinance.

Thereupon, in 1872, Vanderbilt went to the Legislature — that Legislature whose members he had so often bought like so many cattle. This particular Legislature, however, was elected in 1871, following the revelations of the Tweed "ring" frauds. It was regarded as a "model reform body." As has already been remarked in this work, the pseudo "reform" officials or bodies elected by the American people in the vain hope of overthrowing corruption, will often go to greater lengths in the disposition of the people's rights and interests than the most hardened politicians, because they are not suspected of being corrupt, and their measures have the appearance of being enacted for the public good. The Tweed clique had been broken up, but the capitalists who had assiduously bribed its members and profited so hugely from its political acts, were untouched and in greater power than ever before. The source of all this corruption had not been struck at in the slightest. Tweed, the politician, was sacrificed and went to prison and died there; the capitalists who had corrupted representative bodies everywhere in the United States, before and during his time, were safe and respected, and in a position to continue their work of corruption. Tweed made the classic, unforgivable blunder of going into politics as a business, instead of into commercialism. The very capitalists who had profited so greatly by his corruption, were the first to express horror at his acts.

From the " reform " Legislature of 1872 Vanderbilt secured all that he sought. The act was so dexterously worded that while not nominally giving a perpetual franchise, it practically revoked the qualified parts of the charter of 1832. It also compassionately relieved him of the necessity of having to pay out about $4,000,000, in replacing the dangerous roadway, by imposing that cost upon New York City. Once these improvements were made, Vanderbilt bonded them as though they had been made with private money.

## " REFORM " AS IT WORKS OUT.

But these were not his only gifts from the " reform " Legislature. The Harlem Railroad owned, as we have seen, the Fourth avenue surface line of horse cars. Although until this time it extended to Seventy-ninth street only, this line was then the second most profitable in New York City. In 1864, for instance, it carried nearly six million passengers, and its gross earnings were $735,000. It did not pay, nor was required to pay, a single cent in taxation. By 1872 the city's population had grown to 950,000. Vanderbilt concluded that the time was fruitful to gather in a few more miles of the public streets.

The Legislature was acquiescent. Chapter 325 of the Laws of 1872 allowed him to extend the line from Seventy-ninth street to as far north as Madison avenue should thereafter be opened. " But see," said the Legislature in effect, " how mindful of the public interests we have been. We have imposed a tax of five per cent. on all gross receipts above Seventy-ninth street." When, however, the time came to collect, Vanderbilt innocently pretended that he had no means of knowing whether the fares were taken in on that section of the line, free of taxation, below Seventy-ninth street, or on the taxed portion above it. Behind that fraudulent subterfuge the city officials have never been inclined to go, nor have they made any effort. As a consequence the only revenue that the city has since received from that line has been a meager few thousand dollars a year.

At the very time that he was watering stock, sliding through legislatures corrupt grants of perpetual franchises, and swindling cities and States out of huge sums in taxes,[15] Vanderbilt was forcing the drivers and conductors on the Fourth avenue surface line to work an average of fifteen hours out of twenty-four, and reducing their daily wages from $2.25 to $2.

Vanderbilt made the pretense that it was necessary to economize; and, as was the invariable rule of the capitalists, the entire burden of the economizing process was thrown upon the already overloaded workers. This subtraction of twenty-five cents a day entailed upon the drivers and conductors and their families many severe deprivations; working for such low wages every cent obviously counted in the management of household affairs. But the methods of the capitalist class in deliberately pyramiding its profits upon the sufferings of the working class were evidenced in this case (as they had been, and since have been, in countless other instances) by the announcement in the Wall Street reports that this reduction in wages was followed by an instant rise in the price of the stock of the Fourth avenue surface line. The lower the wages, the greater the dividends.

[15] Not alone he. In a tabulated report made public on February 1, 1872, the New York Council of Political Reform charged that in the single item of surface railways, New York City for a long period had been swindled annually out of at least a million dollars. This was an underestimate. All other sections of the capitalist class swindled likewise in taxes.

The further history of the Fourth avenue surface line cannot here be pursued in detail. Suffice to say that the Vanderbilts, in 1894, leased this line for 999 years to the Metropolitan Street Railway Company, controlled by those eminent financiers, William C. Whitney and others, whose monumental briberies, thefts and piracies have frequently been uncovered in official investigations. For almost a thousand years, unless a radical change of conditions comes, the Vanderbilts will draw a princely revenue from the ownership of this franchise alone.

It is not necessary to enter into a narrative of all the laws that Vanderbilt bribed Legislature after Legislature, and Common Council after Common Council, into passing — laws giving him for nothing immensely valuable grants of land, shore rights and rights to land under water, more authorizations to make further consolidations and to issue more watered stock. Nor is it necessary to deal with the numerous bills he considered adverse to his interests, that he caused to be smothered in legislative committees by bribery.

### VANDERBILT'S CHIEF OF STAFF.

His chief instrument during all those years was a general utility lawyer, Chauncey M. Depew, whose specialty was to hoodwink the public by grandiloquent exhibitions of mellifluent spread-eagle oratory, while bringing the " proper arguments " to bear upon legislators and other public officials.[16]  Every one who could in any way be used, or whose influence required subsidizing, was, in the phrase of the day, " taken care of."

---

[16] Roscoe Conkling, a noted Republican politician, said of him: " Chauncey Depew? Oh, you mean the man that Vanderbilt sends to Albany every winter to say 'haw' and 'gee' to his cattle up there."

Great sums of money were distributed outright in bribes in the legislatures by lobbyists in Vanderbilt's pay. Supplementing this, an even more insidious system of bribery was carried on. Free passes for railroad travel were lavishly distributed; no politician was ever refused; newspaper and magazine editors, writers and reporters were always supplied with free transportation for the asking, thus insuring to a great measure their good will, and putting them under obligations not to criticise or expose plundering schemes or individuals. All railroad companies used this form, as well as other forms, of bribery.

It was mainly by means of the free pass system that Depew, acting for the Vanderbilts, secured not only a general immunity from newspaper criticism, but continued to have himself and them portrayed in luridly favorable lights. Depending upon the newspapers for its sources of information, the public was constantly deceived and blinded, either by the suppression of certain news, or by its being tampered with and grossly colored. This Depew continued as the wriggling tool of the Vanderbilt family for nearly half a century. Astonishing as it may seem, he managed to pass among the uninformed as a notable man; he was continuously eulogized; at one time he was boomed for the nomination for President of the United States, and in 1905 when the Vanderbilt family decided to have a direct representative in the United States Senate, they ordered the New York State Legislature, which they practically owned, to elect him to that body. It was while he was a United States Senator that the investigations, in 1905, of a committee of the New York Legislature into the affairs of certain life insurance companies revealed that Depew had long since been an advisory party to the gigantic swindles and briberies carried on by Hyde, the founder and head of the Equitable Life Assurance Society.

The career of Depew is of no interest to posterity, excepting in so far as it shows anew how the magnates were able to use intermediaries to do their underground work for them, and to put those intermediaries into the highest official positions in the country. This fact alone was responsible for their elevation to such bodies as the United States Senate, the President's Cabinet and the courts. Their long service as lobbyists or as retainers was the surest passport to high political or judicial position; their express duty was to vote or decide as their masters' interest bid them. So it was (as it is now) that men who had bribed right and left, and who had put . their cunning or brains at the complete disposal of the magnates, filled Congress and the courts. These were, to a large extent, the officials by whose votes or decisions all measures of value to the working class were defeated; and reversely, by whose actions all or nearly all bills demanded by the money interests, were passed and sustained.

Here we are again forced to notice the truism thrusting itself forward so often and conspicuously; that law was essentially made by the great criminals of society, and that, thus far it has been a frightful instrument, based upon force, for legalizing theft on a large scale. By law the great criminals absolve themselves and at the same time declare drastic punishment for the petty criminals. The property obtained by theft is converted into a sacred vested institution; the men who commit the theft or their hirelings sit in high places, and pass laws surrounding the proceeds of that theft with impregnable fortifications of statutes; should any poor devil, goaded on by the exasperations of poverty, venture to help himself to even the tiniest part of that property, the severest penalty, enacted by those same plunderers, is mercilessly visited upon him.

After having bribed legislatures to legalize his enormous issue of watered stock, what was Vanderbilt's next move? The usual fraudulent one of securing exemption from taxation. He and other railroad owners sneaked through law after law by which many of their issues of stock were made non-taxable.

So now old shaggy Vanderbilt loomed up the richest magnate in the United States. His ambition was consummated; what mattered it to him that his fortune was begot in blackmail and extortion, bribery and theft? Now that he had his hundred millions he had the means to demand adulation and the semblance of respect, if not respect itself. The commercial world admired, even while it opposed, him; in his methods it saw at bottom the abler application and extension of its own, and while it felt aggrieved at its own declining importance and power, it rendered homage in the awed, reverential manner in which it viewed his huge fortune.

Over and over again, even to the point of wearisome repetition, must it be shown, both for the sake of true historical understanding and in justice to the founders of the great fortunes, that all mercantile society was permeated with fraud and subsisted by fraud. But the prevalence of this fraud did not argue its practitioners to be inherently evil. They were victims of a system inexorably certain to arouse despicable qualities. The memorable difference between the two classes was that the workers, as the sufferers, were keenly alive to the abominations of the system, while the capitalists not only insisted upon the right to benefit from its continuance, but harshly sought to repress every attempt of the workers to agitate for its modification or overthrow.

## REPRESSION BY STARVATION.

These repressive tactics took on a variety of forms, some of which are not ordinarily included in the definitions of repression.

The usual method was that of subsidizing press and pulpit in certain subtle ways. By these means facts were concealed or distorted, a prejudicial state of public opinion created, and plausible grounds given for hostile interference by the State. But a far more powerful engine of repression was the coercion exercised by employers in forcing their workers to remain submissive on instant peril of losing their jobs. While, at that time, manufacturers, jobbers and shopkeepers throughout the country were rising in angry protest against the accumulation of plundering power in the hands of such men as Vanderbilt, Gould and Huntington, they were themselves exploiting and bribing on a widespread scale. Their great pose was that of a thorough commercial respectability; it was in this garb that they piously went to legislatures and demanded investigations into the rascally methods of the railroad magnates. The facts, said they, should be made public, so as to base on them appropriate legislation which would curtail the power of such autocrats. Contrasted with the baseness and hypocrisy of the trading class, Vanderbilt's qualities of brutal candor and selfishness shine out as brilliant virtues.[17]

[17] No observation could be truer. As a class, the manufacturers were flourishing on stolen inventions. There might be exceptions, but they were very rare. Year after year, decade after decade, the reports of the various Commissioners of Patents pointed out the indiscriminate theft of inventions by the capi-

These same manufacturers objected in the most indignant manner, as they similarly do now, to any legislative investigations of their own methods. Eager to have the practices of Vanderbilt and Gould probed into, they were acrimoniously opposed to even criticism of their factory system. For this extreme sensitiveness there was the amplest reason. The cruelties of the factory system transcended belief. In, for instance, the State of Massachusetts, vaunting itself for its progressiveness, enlightenment and culture, the textile factories were a horror beyond description. The Convention of the Boston Eight Hour League, in 1872, did not overstate when it declared of the factory system that " it employs tens of thousands

talists. In previous chapters we have referred to the plundering of Whitney and Goodyear. But they were only two of a vast number of inventors similarly defrauded.

In speaking of the helplessness of inventors, J. Holt, Commissioner of Patents, wrote in his Annual Report for 1857: " The insolence and unscrupulousness of capital, subsidizing and leading on its minions in the work of pirating some valuable invention held by powerless hands, can scarcely by conceived by those not familiar with the records of such cases as I have referred to. Inventors, however gifted in other respects, are known to be confiding and thriftless; and being generally without wealth, and always without knowledge of the chicaneries of law, they too often prove but children in those rude conflicts which they are called on to endure with the stalwart fraud and cunning of the world." (U. S. Senate Documents, First Session, Thirty-fifth Congress, 1857-58, viii: 9-10). In his Annual Report for 1858, Commissioner Holt described how inventors were at the mercy of professional perjurers whom the capitalists hired to give evidence.

The bribing of Patent office officials was a common occurrence. " The attention of Congress," reported Commissioner of Patents Charles Mason in 1854, " is invited to the importance of providing some adequate means of preventing attempts to obtain patents by improper means." Several cases of " attempted bribery " had occurred within the year, stated Commissioner Mason. (Executive Documents, First Session, Thirty-third Congress, 1853-54, Vol. vii, Part I: 19-20.) Every successive Commissioner of Patents called upon Congress to pass laws for the prevention of fraud, and for the better protection of the inventor, but Congress, influenced by the manufacturers, was deaf to these appeals.

of women and children eleven and twelve hours a day; owns or controls in its own selfish interest the pulpit and the press; prevents the operative classes from making themselves felt in behalf of less hours, through remorseless exercise of the power of discharge; and is rearing a population of children and youth of sickly appearance and scanty or utterly neglected schooling." . . .

As the factory system was in Massachusetts, so it was elsewhere. Any employee venturing to agitate for better conditions was instantly discharged; spies were at all times busy among the workers; and if a labor union were formed, the factory owners would obtain sneak emissaries into it, with orders to report on every move and disrupt the union if possible. The factory capitalists in Massachusetts, New York, Illinois and every other manufacturing State were determined to keep up their system unchanged, because it was profitable to work children eleven and a half hours a day in a temperature that in summer often reached 108 degrees and in an atmosphere certain to breed immorality;[18] it was profitable to compel adult men and women having families to work for an average of ninety cents a day; it was profitable to avoid spending money in equipping their factories with life-saving apparatus. Hence these factory owners, forming the aristocracy of trade, savagely fought every move or law that might expose or alter those conditions; the annals of legislative proceedings are full of evidences of bribery.

Having no illusions, and being a severely practical man,

[18] "Certain to breed immorality." See report of Carrol D. Wright, Massachusetts Bureau of Statistics of Labor, 1881. A cotton mill operative testified: "Young girls from fourteen and upward learn more wickedness in one year than they would in five out of a mill." See also the numerous recent reports of the National Child Labor Committee.

Vanderbilt well knew the pretensions of this trading class; with many a cynical remark, aptly epitomizing the point, he often made sport of their assumptions. He knew (and none knew better) that they had dived deep in bribery and fraud; they were the fine gentlemen, he well recalled, who had generally obtained patents by fraud; who had so often bribed members of Congress to vote for a high tariff; the same, too, who had bribed legislatures for charters, water rights, exemptions from taxation, the right to work employees as long as, and under whatever conditions, they wanted to. This manufacturing aristocracy professed to look down upon Vanderbilt socially as a coarse sharper; and in New York a certain ruling social element, the native aristocracy, composed of old families whose wealth, originating in fraud, had become respectable by age, took no pains to conceal their opinion of him as a parvenu, and drew about their sacred persons an amusing circle of exclusiveness into the rare precincts of which he might not enter.

Vanderbilt now proceeded to buy social and religious grace as he had bought laws. The purchase of absolution has ever been a convenient and cheap method of obtaining society's condonation of theft. In medieval centuries it took a religious form; it has become transposed to a social traffic in these superior days. Let a man steal in colossal ways and then surrender a small part of it in charitable, religious and educational donations; he at once ceases being a thief and straightway becomes a noble benefactor. Vanderbilt now shed his life-long irreverence, and gave to Deems, a minister of the Presbyterian Church, as a gift, the Church of the Strangers on Mercer street, and he donated $1,000,000 for the founding of the Vanderbilt University at Nashville, Tenn.

The press, the church and the educational world thereupon hailed him as a marvel of saintly charity and liberality.

## THE SERMONIZING OF THE " BEST CLASSES."

One section of the social organization declined to accept the views of the class above it.   This was the working class.   Superimposed upon the working class, draining the life blood of the workers to provide them with wealth, luxuries and power, were those upper strata of society known as the " best classes."   These " best classes," with a monstrous presumption, airily proclaimed their superiority and incessantly harped upon the need of elevating and regenerating the masses.

And who, it may be curiously asked, were the classes self destined or self selected to do this regenerating? The commercial and financial element, with its peculiar morals so adjusted to its interests, that it saw nothing wrong in the conditions by which it reaped its wealth — conditions that made slaves of the workers, threw them into degradation and poverty, drove multitudes of girls and women into prostitution, and made the industrial field an immense concourse of tears, agony and carnage. Hanging on to this supreme class of wealth, fawning to it, licking its very feet, were the parasites and advocates of the press, law, politics, the pulpit, and, with a few exceptions, of the professional occupations.   These were the instructors who were to teach the working class what morals were; these were the eminences under whose guidance the working class was to be uplifted!

Let us turn from this sickening picture of sordid arrogance and ignorance so historically true of all aristocracies based upon money, from the remotest time to this present day, and contemplate how the organized part of the working class regarded the morals of its " superiors."

While the commercial class, on the one hand, was determined on beating down the working class at every point, it was, on the other, unceasingly warring among itself. In business dealings there was no such recognized thing as friendship. To get the better of the other was held the quintessence of mercantile shrewdness. A flint-hard, brute spirit enveloped all business transactions. The business man who lost his fortune was generally looked upon without emotion or pity, and condemned as an incapable. For self interest, business men began to combine in corporations, but these were based purely upon mercenary aims. Not a microscopic trace was visible of that spirit of fellow kindness, sympathy, collective concern and brotherhood already far developed among the organized part of the working class.

As the supereminent magnate of his day, Vanderbilt was invested with extraordinary publicity; he was extensively interviewed and quoted; his wars upon rival capitalists were matters of engrossing public concern; his slightest illness was breathlessly followed by commercialdom and its outcome awaited. Hosts of men, women and children perished every year of disease contracted in factories, mines and slums; but Vanderbilt's least ailment was given a transcending importance, while the scourging sweep of death among the lowly and helpless was utterly ignored.

Precisely as mercantile society bestowed no attention upon the crushed and slain, except to advance roughshod over their stricken bodies while throwing out a pittance in charity here and there, so Vanderbilt embodied in himself the qualities that capitalist society in mass practiced and glorified. " It was strong men," says Croffut, "whom he liked and sympathized with, not weak ones; the self-reliant, not the helpless. He felt that the solicitor of charity was always a lazy or drunken person, trying to live by plundering the sober and industrious." This malign distrust of fellow beings, this acrid cynicism of motives, this extraordinary imputation of evil designs on the part of the penniless, was characteristic of the capitalist class as a whole. Itself practicing the lowest and most ignoble methods, governed by the basest motives, plundering in every direction, it viewed every member of its own class with suspicion and rapacity. Then it turned about, and with immense airs of superiority, attributed all of its own vices and crimes to the impoverished masses which its own system had created, whether in America or elsewhere.

The apologist may hasten forward with the explanation that the commercial class was not to be judged by Vanderbilt's methods and qualities. In truth, however, Vanderbilt was not more inhuman than many of the contemporary shining lights of the business world.

## "HONESTY AND INDUSTRY" ANALYZED.

If there is any one fortune commonly praised as having been acquired "by honesty and industry," it is the Borden millions, made from cotton factories. At the time Vanderbilt was blackmailing, the founder of this fortune, Colonel Borden, was running cotton mills in Fall River. His factory operatives worked from five o'clock in the morning to seven in the evening, with but two half hours of intermission, one for breakfast, the other for dinner. The workday of these men, women and children was thus thirteen hours; their wages were wretchedly low, their life was one of actual slavery. Insufficient nourishment, overwork, and the unsanitary and disgusting conditions in the mills, prematurely aged and debilitated them, and were a constant source of disease, killing off considerable numbers, especially the children.

In 1850, the operatives asked Borden for better wages and shorter hours. This was his reply: " I saw that mill built stone by stone; I saw the pickers, the carding engines, the spinning mules and the looms put into it, one after the other, and I would see every machine and stone crumble and fall to the floor again before I would accede to your wishes." Borden would not have been amiss had he added that every stone in that mill was cemented with human blood. His operatives went on a strike, stayed out ten months, suffered frightful hardships, and then were forced back to their tasks by hunger. Borden was inflexible, and so were all the other cotton mill owners.[19] It was not until 1874, after many further bitterly-contested strikes, that the Masachusetts Legislature was prevailed upon to pass a ten-hour law, twenty-four years after the British Parliament had passed such an enactment.

The commercial class, high and low, was impregnated with deceit and dissimulation, cynicism, selfishness and cruelty. What were the aspirations of the working class which it was to uplift? The contrast stood out with stark distinctness. While business men were frantically sapping the labor and life out of their workers, and then tricking and cheating one another to seize the proceeds of that exploitation, the labor unions were teaching the

[19] The heroism of the cotton operatives was extraordinary. Slaves themselves, they battled to exterminate negro slavery. "The spinner's union," says McNeill, "was almost dead during the [Civil] war, as most of its members had gone to shoulder the musket and to fight . . . to strike the shackles from the negro. A large number were slain in battle."—"The Labor Movement": 216-217.

nobility of brotherly coöperation   "Cultivate friendship among the great brotherhood of toil," was the advice of Uriah Stevens, master workman of the Knights of Labor, at the annual meeting of that organization on January 12, 1871.   And he went on:

> And while the toiler is thus engaged in creating the world's value. how fares his own interest and well-being?   We answer, "Badly," for he has too little time, and his faculties become too much blunted by unremitting labor to analyze his condition or devise and perfect financial schemes or reformatory measures. The hours of labor are too long, and should be shortened.   I recommend a universal movement to cease work at five o'clock Saturday afternoon, as a beginning.   There should be a greater participation in the profits of labor by the industrious and intelligent laborer.   In the present arrangements of labor and capital, the condition of the employee is simply that of wage slavery — capital dictating, labor submitting; capital superior, labor inferior.
>
> This is an artificial and man-created condition, not God's arrangement and order; for it degrades man and ennobles mere pelf.   It demeans those who live by useful labor, and, in proportion, exalts all those who eschew labor and live (no matter by what pretence or respectable cheat — for cheat it is) without productive work.

### LABOR'S PRINCIPLES IGNORED.

Such principles as these evoked so little attention that it is impossible to find them recorded in most of the newspapers of the time; and if mentioned it was merely as the object of venomous attacks.   In varying degrees, now in outright abuse and again in sneering and ridicule, the working class was held up as an ignorant, discontented, violent aggregation, led by dangerous agitators, and arrogantly seeking to upset all business by seeking to dictate to employers what wages and hours of labor should be.

And, after all, little it mattered to the capitalists what the workers thought or said, so long as the machinery of government was not in their hands.   At about the very time Master Workman Stevens was voicing the unrest of the laboring masses, and at the identical time when the panic of 1873 saw several millions of men workless, thrown upon soup kitchens and other forms of charity, and battered wantonly by policemen's clubs when they attempted to hold mass meetings of protest, an Iowa writer, D. C. Cloud, was issuing a work which showed concretely how thoroughly Government was owned by the commercial and financial classes.   This work, obscurely published and now scarcely known except to the patient delver, is nevertheless one of the few serious books on prevailing conditions written at that time, and is in marked contrast to the reams of printed nonsense then circulated.   Although Cloud was tinged greatly with the middle class point of view, and did not see that all successful business was based upon deceit and fraud, yet so far as his lights carried him, he wrote trenchantly and fearlessly, embodying series after series of facts exposing the existing system.   He observed:

. . . A measure without any merit save to advance the interest of a patentee, or contractor, or railroad company, will become a law, while measures of interest to the whole people are suffered to slumber, and die at the close of the session from sheer neglect. It is known to Congressmen that these lobbyists are paid to influence legislation by the parties interested, and that dishonest and corrupt means are resorted to for the accomplishment of the object they have undertaken. . . . Not one interest in the country nor all other interests combined are as powerful as the railroad interest. . . . With a network of roads throughout the country; with a large capital at command; with an organization perfect in all its parts, controlled by a few leading spirits like Scott, Vanderbilt, Jay Gould,

Tracy and a dozen others, the whole strength and wealth of this corporate power can be put into operation at any moment, and Congressmen are bought and sold by it like any article of merchandise.[20].

[20] " Monopolies and the People : " 155-156.

# CHAPTER VI

## THE ENTAILING OF THE VANDERBILT FORTUNE

The richer Commodore Vanderbilt grew, the more closely he clung to his old habits of intense parsimony. Occasionally he might ostentatiously give a large sum here or there for some religious or philanthropic purpose, but his general undeviating course was a consistent meanness. In him was united the petty bargaining traits of the trading element and the lavish capacities for plundering of the magnate class. While defrauding on a great scale, pocketing tens of millions of dollars at a single raid, he would never for a moment overlook the leakage of a few cents or dollars. His comprehensive plans for self-aggrandizement were carried out in true piratical style; his aims and demands were for no paltry prize, but for the largest and richest booty. Yet so ingrained by long development was his faculty of acquisition, that it far passed the line of a passion and became a monomania.

### VANDERBILT'S CHARACTERISTICS.

To such an extent did it corrode him that even when he could boast his $100,000,000 he still persisted in haggling and huckstering over every dollar, and in tricking his friends in the smallest and most underhand ways. Friends in the true sense of the word he had none; those who regarded themselves as such were of that thrifty, congealed disposition swayed largely by calculation. But if they expected to gain overmuch by their intimacy, they were generally vastly mistaken; nearly always, on the contrary, they found themselves caught in some unexpected snare, and riper in experience, but poorer in pocket, they were glad to retire prudently to a safe distance from the old man's contact. " Friends or foes," wrote an admirer immediately after his death, " were pretty much on the same level in his estimation, and if a friend undertook to get in his way he was obliged to look out for himself."

On one occasion, it is related, when a candidate for a political office solicited a contribution, Vanderbilt gave $100 for himself, and an equal sum for a friend associated with him in the management of the New York Central Railroad. A few days later Vanderbilt informed this friend of the transaction, and made a demand for the hundred dollars. The money was paid over. Not long after this, the friend in question was likewise approached for a political contribution, whereupon he handed out $100 for himself and the same amount for Vanderbilt. On being told of his debt, Vanderbilt declined to pay it, closing the matter abruptly with this laconic pronunciamento, " When I give anything, I give it myself." At another time Vanderbilt assured a friend that he would " carry " one thousand shares of New York Central stock for him. The market price rose to $115 a share and then dropped to $90. A little later, before setting out to bribe an important bill through the Legislature — a bill that Vanderbilt knew would greatly increase the value of the stock — the old magnate went to the friend and represented that since the price of the stock had fallen it would not be right to subject the friend to a loss. Vanderbilt asked for the return of the stock and got it. Once the bill became a law, the market price of the stock went up tremendously, to the utter dismay of the confiding friend who saw a profit of $80,000 thus slip out of his hands into Vanderbilt's.[1]

In his personal expenses Vanderbilt usually begrudged what he looked upon as superfluous expense. The plainest of black clothes he wore, and he never countenanced jewelry. He scanned the table bill with a hypercritical eye. Even the sheer necessities of his physical condition could not induce him to pay out money for costly prescriptions. A few days before his death his physician recommended champagne for some internal trouble. "Champagne!" exclaimed Vanderbilt with a reproachful look, "I can't afford champagne. A bottle every morning! Oh, I guess sody water'll do!"

From all accounts it would seem that he diffused about him the same forbidding environment in his own house. He is described as stern, obstinate, masterful and miserly, domineering his household like a tyrant, roaring with fiery anger whenever he was opposed, and flying into fits of fury if his moods, designs and will were contested. His wife bore him thirteen children, twelve of whom she had brought up to maturity. A woman of almost rustic simplicity of mind and of habits, she became obediently meek under the iron discipline he administered. Croffut says of her that she was "acquiescent and patient under the sway of his dominant will, and in the presence of his trying moods." He goes on: "The fact that she lived harmoniously with such an obstinate man bears strong testimony to her character."[2]

If we are to place credibility in current reports, she was forced time and time again to undergo the most

[1] These and similar anecdotes are to be found incidentally mentioned in a two-page biography, very laudatory on the whole, in the New York "Times," issue of January 5, 1877.

[2] "The Vanderbilts": 113.

violent scenes in interceding for one of their sons, Cornelius Jeremiah. For the nervous disposition and general bad health of this son the father had not much sympathy; but the inexcusable crime to him was that Cornelius showed neither inclination nor capacity to engage in a business career. If Cornelius had gambled on the stock exchange his father would have set him down as an exceedingly enterprising, respectable and promising man. But he preferred to gamble at cards. This rebellious lack of interest in business, joined with dissipation, so enraged the old man that he drove Cornelius from the house and only allowed him access during nearly a score of years at such rare times as the mother succeeded in her tears and pleadings. Worn out with her long life of drudgery, Vanderbilt's wife died in 1868; about a year later the old magnate eloped with a young cousin, Frank A. Crawford, and returning from Canada, announced his marriage, to the unbounded surprise and utter disfavor of his children.

### THE OLD MAGNATE'S DEATH.

An end, however, was soon coming to his prolonged life. A few more years of money heaping, and then, on May 10, 1876, he was taken mortally ill. For eight months he lay in bed, his powerful vitality making a vigorous battle for life; two physicians died while in the course of attendance on him; it was not until the morning of January 4, 1877, that the final symptoms of approaching death came over him. When this was seen the group about his bed emotionally sang: " Come, Ye Sinners, Poor and Needy," " Nearer, My God, To Thee," and " Show Ye Pity, Lord." He died with a conven-

tional religious end of which the world made much; all
of the proper sanctities and ceremonials were duly observed; nothing was lacking in the piety of that affect-
ing deathbed scene.  It furnished the text for many a
sermon, but while ministerial and journalistic attention
was thus eulogistically concentrated upon the loss of
America's greatest capitalist, not a reference was made
in church or newspaper to the deaths every year of
a host of the lowly, slain in the industrial vortex by injury and disease, and too often by suicide and starvation.
Except among the lowly themselves this slaughter passed
unprotested and unnoticed.

Even as Vanderbilt lay moribund, speculation was busy
as to the disposition of his fortune.  Who would inherit
his aggregation of wealth?  The probating of his will
soon disclosed that he had virtually entailed it.  About
$90,000,000 was left to his eldest son, William H., and
one-half of the remaining $15,000,000 was bequeathed
to the chief heir's four sons.[8]  A few millions were distributed among the founder's other surviving children,

[8] To Cornelius J. Vanderbilt, the Commodore's " wayward "
son, only the income derived from $200,000 was bequeathed,
upon the condition that he should forfeit even this legacy if he
contested the will.  Nevertheless, he brought a contest suit.  William H. Vanderbilt compromised the suit by giving to his brother
the income on $1,000,000.  On April 2, 1882, Cornelius J. Vander-
bilt shot and killed himself.  Croffut gives this highly enlight-
ening account of the compromising of the suit:
"At least two of the sisters had sympathized with ' Cornele's '
suit, and had given him aid and comfort, neither of them liking
the legatee, and one of them not having been for years on
speaking terms with him; but now, in addition to the bequests
made to his sisters, William H. voluntarily [sic] added $500,000
to each from his own portion.
"He drove around one evening, and distributed this splendid
largess from his carriage, he himself carrying the bonds into
each house in his arms and delivering them to each sister in

and some, comparatively small sums bequeathed to charitable and educational institutions. The Vanderbilt dynasty had begun.

## PERSONALITY OF THE CHIEF HEIR.

At this time William H. Vanderbilt was fifty-six years
old. Until 1864 he had been occupied at farming on
Staten Island; he lived at first in " a small, square, plain
two-story house facing the sea, with a lean-to on one
end for a kitchen." The explanation of why the son of a
millionaire betook himself to truck farming lay in these
facts: The old man despised leisure and luxury, and had
a correspondingly strong admiration for " self-made "
men. Knowing this, William H. Vanderbilt made a
studious policy of standing in with his father, truckling
to his every caprice and demand, and proving that he
could make an independent living. He is described as
a phlegmatic man of dull and slow mental processes, do-
mestic tastes and of kindly disposition to his children.
His father (so the chronicles tell) did not think that
he " would ever amount to anything," but by infinite
plodding, exacting the severest labor from his farm laborers, driving close bargains and turning devious tricks

turn. The donation was accompanied by two interesting incidents. In one case the husband said, 'William, I've made a
quick calculation here, and I find these bonds don't amount to
quite $500,000. They're $150 short, at the price quoted today.'
The donor smiled, and sat down and made out his check for the
sum to balance.

"In another case, a husband, after counting and receipting
for the $500,000, followed the generous visitor out of the door,
and said, 'By the way, if you conclude to give the other sisters
any more, you'll see that we fare as well as any of them, won't
you?' The donor jumped into his carriage and drove off without replying, only saying, with a laugh, to his companions,
'Well, what do you think o' that?'"—"The Vanderbilts": 151-
152.

**WILLIAM H. VANDERBILT,**
He Inherited the Bulk of His Father's Fortune and
Doubled It.

in his dealings, he gradually won the confidence and respect of the old man, who was always pleased with proofs of guile. Croffut gives a number of instances of William's craft and continues: " From his boyhood he had given instant and willing submission to the despotic will of his father, and had made boundless sacrifices to please him. Most men would have burst defiantly away from the repressive control and imperious requirements; but he doubtless thought that for the chance of becoming heir to $100,000,000 he could afford to remain long in the passive attitude of a distrusted prince." (sic.)

The old autocrat finally modified his contemptuous opinion, and put him in an executive position in the management of the New York and Harlem Railroad. Later, he elevated him to be a sort of coadjutor by installing him as vice president of the New York Central Railroad, and as an associate in the directing of other railroads. It was said to be painful to note the exhausting persistence with which William H. Vanderbilt daily struggled to get some perceptions of the details of railroad management. He did succeed in absorbing considerable knowledge. But his training at the hands of his father was not so much in the direction of learning the system of management. Men of ability could always be hired to manage the roads. What his father principally taught him was the more essential astuteness required of a railroad magnate; the manipulation of stocks and of common councils and legislatures; how to fight and overthrow competitors and extend the sphere of ownership and control; and how best to resist, and if possible to destroy, the labor unions. In brief, his education was a duplication of his father's scope of action: the methods of the sire were infused into the son.

From the situation in which he found himself, and viewing the particular traits required in the development of capitalistic institutions, it was the most appropriate training that he could have received. Book erudition and the cultivation of fine qualities would have been sadly out of place; his father's teachings were precisely what were needed to sustain and augment his possessions. On every hand he was confronted either by competitors who, if they could get the chance, would have stripped him without scruple, or by other men of his own class who would have joyfully defrauded him. But overshadowing these accustomed business practices, new and startling conditions that had to be met and fought were now appearing.

Instead of a multitude of small, detached railroads, owned and operated by independent companies, the period was now being reached of colossal railroad systems. In the East the small railroad owners had been well-nigh crushed out, and their properties joined in huge lines under the ownership of a few controlling men, while in the West, extensive systems, thousands of miles long, had recently been built. Having stamped out most of the small owners, the railroad barons now proceeded to wrangle and fight among themselves. It was a characteristic period when the railroad magnates were constantly embroiled in the bitterest quarrels, the sole object of which was to outdo, bankrupt and wreck one another and seize, if possible, the others' property.

## THE RISE OF THE FIRST TRUST.

It was these conflicts that developed the auspicious time and opportunity for a change of the most worldwide importance, and one which had a stupendous ulti-

mate purport not then realized. The wars between the
railroad magnates assumed many forms, not the least of
which was the cutting of freight rates. Each railroad
desperately sought to wrench away traffic from the others
by offering better inducements. In this cutthroat competition, a coterie of hawk-eyed young men in the oil
business, led by John D. Rockefeller, saw their fertile
chance.

The drilling and the refining of oil, although in their
comparative infancy, had already reached great proportions. Each railroad was eager to get the largest share
of the traffic of transporting oil. Rockefeller, ruminat-
ing in his small refinery at Cleveland, Ohio, had conceived the revolutionary idea of getting a monopoly of
the production and distribution of oil, obliterating the
middleman, and systematizing and centralizing the whole
business.

Then and there was the modern trust born; and from
the very inception of the Standard Oil Company Rockefeller and his associates tenaciously pursued their design
with a combined ability and unscrupulousness such as
had never before been known since the rise of capitalism.
One railroad after another was persuaded or forced into
granting them secret rates and rebates against which
it was impossible to compete. The railroad magnates —
William H. Vanderbilt, for instance — were taken in the
fold of the Standard Oil Company by being made stockholders. With these secret rates the Standard Oil Company was enabled to crush out absolutely a myriad of
competitors and middlemen, and control the petroleum
trade not only of the United States but of almost the entire world. Such fabulous profits accumulated that in the
course of forty years, after one unending career of industrial construction on the one hand, and crime on the

other, the Standard Oil Company was easily able to become owners of prodigious railroad and other systems, and completely supplant the scions of the magnates whom three or four decades before they had wheedled or browbeaten into favoring them with discriminations.

## CORPORATE WEALTH AND LABOR UNIONS.

The effects of this great industrial transition were clearly visible by 1877, so much so that two years later, Vanderbilt, more prophetically than he realized, told the Hepburn Committee that " if this thing keeps up the oil people will own the roads." But other noted industrial changes were concurrently going on. With the up-springing and growth of gigantic combinations or concentrations of capital, and the gradual disappearance of the small factors in railroad and other lines of business, workers were compelled by the newer conditions to organize on large and compact national lines.

At first each craft was purely local and disassociated from other trades unions. But comprehending the inadequacy and futility of existing separately, and of acting independently of one another, the unions had some years back begun to weld themselves into one powerful body, covering much of the United States. Each craft union still retained its organization and autonomy, but it now became part of a national organization embracing every form of trades, and centrally officered and led. It was in this way that the workers, step by step, met the organization of capital; the two forces, each representing a conflicting principle, were thus preparing for a series of great industrial battles.

Capital had the wealth, resources and tools of the country; the workers their labor power only. As it stood, it was an uneven contest, with every advantage in favor of capital. The workers could decline to work, but capital could starve them into subjection. These, however, were but the apparent differences. The real and immense difference between them was that capital was in absolute control of the political governing power of the nation, and this power, strange to say, it secured by the votes of the very working class constantly fighting it in the industrial arena. Many years were to elapse before the workers were to realize that they must organize and vote with the same political solidarity that they long had been developing in industrial matters. With political power in their hands the capitalists could, and did, use its whole weight with terrific effect to beat down the working class, and nullify most of the few concessions and laws obtained by the workers after the severest and most self-sacrificing struggles.

One of the first memorable battles between the two hostile forces came about in 1877. In their rate wars the railroad magnates had cut incisively into one another's profits. The permanent gainers were such incipient, or fairly well developed, trusts or combinations as the Standard Oil Company. Now the magnates set about asserting the old capitalist principle of recouping themselves by forcing the workers to make up their losses.

But these deficits were merely relative. Practically every railroad had issued vast amounts of bonds and watered stock, on which fixed charges and dividends had to be paid. Judged by the extent of this inflated stock, the profits of the railroads had certainly decreased. Despite, however, the prevailing cutthroat competition, and the slump in general business following the panic of 1873, the railroads were making large sums on their actual investment, so-called. Most of this investment, it will be recalled, was not private money but was public funds, which were later stolen by corrupt legislation. It was shown before the Hepburn Committee in 1879, as we have noted, that from 1869 the New York Central Railroad had been making sixteen, and perhaps more than twenty per cent., on the actual cost of the road.

Moreover, apart from the profits from ordinary traffic, the railroads were annually fattening on immense sums of public money gathered in by various fraudulent methods. One of these — and is well worth adverting to, for it exists to a greater degree than ever before — was the robbery of the people in the transportation of mails. By a fraudulent official construction, in 1873, of the postal laws, the railroads without cessation have cheated huge sums in falsifying the weight of mail carried, and since that time have charged ten times as much for mail carrying as have the express companies (the profits of which are very great) for equal haulage. But these are simply two phases of the postal plunder. In addition to the regular mail payments, the Government has long paid to the railroad companies an extra allowance of $6,250 a year for the rent of each postal car used, although official investigation has proved that the whole cost of constructing such a car averages but from $2,500 to $5,000. In rent alone, five millions a year have been paid for cars worth, all told, about four millions. From official estimates it would clearly seem that the railroads have long cheated the people out of at least $20,000,000 a year in excess rates — a total of perhaps half a billion dollars since 1873. The Vanderbilt family have been among the chief beneficiaries of this continuous looting.[4]

4 Postmaster General Vilas, Annual Report for 1887: 56. In a debate in the United States Senate on February 11, 1905, Sen-

Occasionally the postal officials have made pretences at stopping the plunder, but with no real effect.

## THE GREAT STRIKE OF 1877.

Making a loud and plaintive outcry about their declining revenues, some of the railroad systems prepared to assess their fictitious losses upon the workers by cutting down wages. They had already reduced wages to the point of the merest subsistence; and now they decreed that wages must again be curtailed ten cents on every dollar. The Baltimore and Ohio Railroad, then in the hands of the Garrett family, with a career behind it of consecutive political corruption and fraud, in some ways surpassing that of the Vanderbilts, led in reducing the wages of its workers. The Pennsylvania Railroad followed, and then the Vanderbilts gave the order for another reduction.

At once the Baltimore and Ohio Railroad employes retaliated by declaring a strike; the example was followed by the Pennsylvania men. In order to alienate the sympathy of the general public and to have a pretext for suppressing the strike with armed force, the railroads, it is quite certain, instigated riots at Martinsburg, W. Va., and at Pittsburg. Troops were called out and the so-called mobs were fired on, resulting in a number of strikers being killed and many wounded.

That the railroads deliberately destroyed their own property and then charged the culpability to the strikers, was common report. So conservative an authority as

ator Pettigrew quoted Postmaster General Wanamaker as saying that "the railroad companies see to it that the representatives in Congress in both branches take care of the interests of the railway people, and that it is practically impossible to procure legislation in the way of reducing expenses."

Carroll D. Wright, for a long time United States Commissioner of Labor, tells of the railroad agents setting a large number of old, decayed, worthless freight cars at Pittsburg on fire, and accusing the strikers of the act. He further tells of the Pennsylvania Railroad subsequently extorting millions of dollars from the public treasury on the ground that the destruction of these cars resulted from riot. Wright says that from all that he has been able to gather, he believes the reports of the railroads manufacturing riots to have been true.[5] Vanderbilt acted with greater wisdom than his fellow magnates. Adopting a conciliatory stand, he averted a strike on his lines by restoring the old rate of wages and by other mollifying measures.

He was now assailed from a different direction. The long gathering anger and enmity of the various sections of the middle class against the corporate wealth which had possessed itself of so dictatorial a power, culminated in a manner as instructive as it was ineffective.

In New York State, the Legislature was prevailed upon, in 1879, to appoint an investigating committee. Vanderbilt and other railroad owners, and a multitude of complaining traders were haled up to give testimony; the stock-jobbing transactions of Vanderbilt and Gould were fully and tediously gone into, as also were the methods of the railroads in favoring certain corporations and mercantile establishments with secret preferential freight rates.

Not in the slightest did this long-drawn investigation have any result calculated to break the power of the rail-

[5] "The Battles of Labor": 122. In all, the railroad companies secured approximately $22,000,000 from the public treasury in Pennsylvania as indemnity for property destroyed during these "riots." In a subsequent chapter, the corruption of the operation is described.

road owners, or their predominant grip upon governmental functions.

The magnate class preferred to have no official inquiries; there was always the annoying possibility that
in some State or other inconvenient laws might be passed,
or harrassing legal actions begun; and while revocation
or amendment of these laws could be put through subsequently when the popular excitement had died away,
and the suits could be in some way defeated, the ex-
posures had an inflaming effect upon a population as
yet ill-used to great one-man power of wealth. But if
the middle class insisted upon action against the railroad
magnates, there was no policy more suitable to these
magnates than that of being investigated by legislative
committees. They were not averse to their opponents
amusing themselves, and finding a vent for their wrath,
in volumes of talk which began nowhere and ended nowhere. In reply to charges, the magnates could put in
their skillful defense, and inject such a maze of argument, pettifoggery and technicalities into the proceedings, that before long the public, tired of the puzzle, was
bound to throw up its hands in sheer bewilderment, unable to get any concrete idea of what it was all about.

### FRAUD BECOMES RESPECTABLE WEALTH.

So the great investigation of 1879 passed by without
the least deterrent effect upon the constantly-spreading
power and wealth of such men as Vanderbilt and Gould.
Every new development revealed that the hard-dying
middle class was being gradually, yet surely, ground out.
But the investigation of 1879 had one significant unan-
ticipated result.

What William H. Vanderbilt now did is well worth

noting. As the owner of four hundred thousand shares of New York Central stock he had been rabidly denounced by the middle class as a plutocrat dangerous to the interests of the people. He decided that it would be wise to sell a large part of this stock; by this stroke he could advantageously exchange the forms of some of his wealth, and be able to put forward the plausible claim that the New York Central Railroad, far from being a one-man institution, was owned by a large number of investors. In November, 1879, he sold through J. Pierpont Morgan more than two hundred thousand shares to a syndicate, chiefly, however, to British aristocrats.

This sale in no way diminished his actual control of the New York Central Railroad; not only did he retain a sufficient number of shares, but he owned an immense block of the railroad's bonds. The sale of the stock brought him $35,000,000. What did he do with this sum? He at once reinvested it in United States Government bonds. Thus, the proceeds of a part of the stock obtained by outright fraud, either by his father or himself, were put into Government bonds. This surely was a very sagacious move. Stocks do not have the solid, honest air that Government bonds do; nothing is more finely and firmly respectable than a Government bondholder.

From the blackmailer, corruptionist and defrauder of one generation to the stolid Government bondholder of the next, was not a long step, but it was a sufficient one. The process of investing in Government bonds Vanderbilt continued; in a few years he owned not less than $54,000,000 worth of four per cents. In 1884 he had to sell $10,000,000 of them to make good the losses incurred by his sons on the Stock Exchange, but he later bought $10,000,000 more. Also he owned $4,000,000 in Government three and one-half per cent. bonds, many millions of State and city bonds, several millions of dollars in manufacturing stocks and mortgages, and $22,-000,000 of railroad bonds. The same Government of which his father had defrauded millions of dollars now stood as a direct guarantee behind at least $70,000,000 of his bonded wealth, and the whole population of the United States was being taxed to pay interest on bonds, the purchase of which was an outgrowth of the theft of public money committed by Cornelius Vanderbilt.

In the years following his father's death, William H. Vanderbilt found no difficulty in adding more extended railroad lines to his properties, and in increasing his wealth by tens of millions of dollars at a leap.

### MORE RAILROADS ACQUIRED.

The impact of his vast fortune was well-nigh resistless. Commanding both financial and political power, his money and resources were used with destructive effect against almost every competitor standing in his way. If he could not coerce the owners of a railroad, the possession of which he sought, to sell to him at his own price, he at once brought into action the wrecking tactics his father had so successfully used.

The West Shore Railroad, a competing line running along the west bank of the Hudson River, was bankrupted by him, and finally, in 1883, bought in under foreclosure proceedings. By lowering his freight rates he took away most of its business; through a series of years he methodically caused it to be harrassed and burdened by the exercise of his great political power; he thwarted its plans and secretly hindered it in its application for money loans or other relief.  Other means, open and covert, were employed to insure its ruination.  When at last he had driven its owners into a corner, he calmly stepped in and bought up its control cheaply, and then turned out many millions of dollars of watered stock.

He attempted to break in upon the territory traversed by the Pennsylvania Railroad by building a competing line, the South Pennsylvania Railroad.  In the construction of this road he had an agreement with the Philadelphia and Reading Railroad, an intense competitor of the Pennsylvania; and, as a precedent to building his line, he obtained a large interest in the Reading Railroad.  Out of this arrangement grew a highly important sequence which few then foresaw — the gradual assumption by the Vanderbilt family of a large share of the ownership and control of the anthracite coal mines of Pennsylvania.

Vanderbilt, aiming at sharing in the profits from the rich coal, oil and manufacturing traffic of Pennsylvania, went ahead with his building of the South Pennsylvania line.  But there was an easy way of getting millions of dollars before the road was even opened.  This was the fraudulent one, so widely practiced, of organizing a bogus construction company, and charging three and four times more than the building of the railroad actually cost.  Vanderbilt got together a dummy construction company composed of some of his clerks and brokers, and advanced the sum, about $6,500,000, to build the road.  In return, he ordered this company to issue $20,000,000 in bonds, and the same amount in stock.  Of this $40,000,000 in securities, more than $30,-000,000 was loot.[6]

---

[6] Van Oss' "American Railroads As Investments": 126.  Professor Frank Parsons, in his "Railways, the Trusts and the

If, however, Vanderbilt anticipated that the Pennsylvania Railroad would remain docile or passive while his competitive line was being built, he soon learned how sorely mistaken he was. This time he was opposing no weak, timorous or unsophisticated competitors, but a group of the most powerful and astute organizers and corruptionists. Their methods in Pennsylvania and other States were exactly the same as Vanderbilt's in New York State; their political power was as great in their chosen province as his in New York. His incursion into the territory they had apportioned to themselves for exploitation was not only resented but was fiercely resisted. Presently, overwhelmed by the crushing financial and political weapons with which they fought him, Vanderbilt found himself compelled to compromise by disposing of the line to them.

### THE SEQUEL TO A " GENTLEMEN'S AGREEMENT."

Vanderbilt's methods and his duplicity in the disposition of this project were strikingly revealed in the court proceedings instituted by the State of Pennsylvania. It appeared from the testimony that he had made a " gentlemen's agreement " with the Reading Railroad, the bitterest competitor of the Pennsylvania Railroad, for a close alliance of interests. Vanderbilt owned eighty-two thousand shares of Reading stock, much of which he had obtained on this agreement. Strangely confiding in his word, the Reading management proceeded to expend large sums of money in building terminals at Harrisburg and elsewhere to make connections with his proposed South Pennsylvania Railroad.

People," incorrectly ascribes this juggling to Commodore Vanderbilt.

The Pennsylvania Railroad, however, set about re-
taliating in various effective ways.  At this point, J.
Pierpont Morgan — whose career we shall duly describe — stepped boldly in.  Morgan was Vanderbilt's
financial agent; and it was he, according to his own testimony on October 13, 1885, before the court examiner,
who now suggested and made the arrangements between
Vanderbilt and the Pennsylvania Railroad magnates, by
which the South Pennsylvania Railroad was to become
the property of the Pennsylvania system, and the Reading Railroad magnates were to be as thoroughly thrown
over by as deft a stroke of treachery as had ever been
put through in the business world.

To their great astonishment, the Reading owners woke
up one morning to find that Vanderbilt and his associates had completely betrayed them by disposing of a
majority of the stock of the partly built South Pennsylvania line to the Pennsylvania Railroad system for
$5,600,000 in three per cent. railroad debenture bonds.
It is interesting to inquire who Vanderbilt's associates
were in this transaction.  They were John D. Rockefeller, William Rockefeller, D. O. Mills, Stephen B. Elkins, William C. Whitney and other founders of large
fortunes.  For once in his career, Vanderbilt met in the
Pennsylvania Railroad a competitor powerful enough to
force him to compromise.

Elsewhere, Vanderbilt was much more successful.
Out through the fertile wheat, corn and cattle sections of
Wisconsin, Minnesota, Iowa, Dakota and Nebraska ran
the Chicago and Northwestern Railroad, a line 4,000
miles long which had been built mostly by public funds
and land grants.  Its history was a succession of corrupt acts in legislatures and in Congress, and comprised
the usual process of stock watering and exploitation.

THE ORIGINAL VANDERBILT HOMESTEAD,
Near New Dorp, Staten Island, N. Y.

PALACES BUILT BY WILLIAM H. VANDERBILT,
And Resided in by Him and His Descendants.

By a series of manipulations ending in 1880, Vanderbilt
secured a controlling interest in this railroad, so that he
had a complete line from New York to Chicago, and
thence far into the Northwest.  During these years he
also secured control of other railroad lines.

## HE EXPANDS IN SPLENDOR.

It was at this time that he, in accord with the chrysalid
tendency manifested by most other millionaires, discarded
his long-followed sombre method of life, and invested
himself with a gaudy magnificence.  On Fifth avenue,
at Fifty-first and Fifty-second streets, he built a spacious
brown-stone mansion.  In reality it was a union of two
mansions; the southern part he planned for himself, the
northern part for his two daughters.  For a year and a
half more than six hundred artisans were employed on
the interior; sixty stoneworkers were imported from
Europe.  The capaciousness, the glitter and the clutter-
ing of splendor in the interior were regarded as of unprecedented lavishness in the United States.

All of the luxury overloading these mansions was, as
was well known, the fruit of fraud piled upon fraud; it
represented the spoliation, misery and degradation of
the many; but none could deny that Vanderbilt was fully
entitled to it by the laws of a society which decreed
that its rulers should be those who could best use and
abuse it.  And rulers must ever live imperiously and
impressively; it is not fitting that those who command
the resources, labor and Government of a nation should
issue their mandates from pinched and meager surroundings.  Mere pseudo political rulers, such as governors
and presidents, are expected to be satisfied with the plain,
unornamental official residences provided by the people;

thereby they keep up the appearance of that much-be-spoken republican simplicity which is part of the mask of political formulas.  Luckily for themselves, the financial and industrial rulers are bound by no circumscribing tradition; hence they have no set of buckramed rules to stick close to for fear of an indignant electorate.

The same populace that glowers and mutters when-ever its political officials show an inclination to pomp, regards it as perfectly natural that its financial and in-dustrial rulers should body forth all of the most obtru-sive evidences of grandeur.  Those Vanderbilt twin palaces, still occupied by the Vanderbilt family, were appropriately built and fitted, and are more truly and specifically historic as the abode of Government than official mansions; for it is the magnates who have in these modern times been the real rulers of nations; it is they who have usually been able to decide who the po-litical rulers should be; political parties have been simply their adjuncts; the halls of legislation and the courts their mouthpieces and registering bureaus.  Theirs has been the power, under cover though it has lurked, of ele-vating or destroying public officials, and of approving or cancelling legislation.  Why, indeed, should they not have their gilded palaces?

### A SUDDEN TRANSFORMATION.

The President of the United States lived in the sub-dued simplicity of the White House.  But William H. Vanderbilt ate in a great, lofty dining room, twenty-six by thirty-seven feet, wrought in Italian Renaissance, with a wainscot of golden-hued, delicately-carved Eng-lish oak around all four sides, and a ceiling with richly-painted hunting-scene panels.  When he entertained it was in a vast drawing-room, palatially equipped, its walls hung with flowing masses of pale red velvet, embroidered with foliage flowers and butterflies, and set with crystals and precious stones.

It was his art gallery, however, which flattered him most. He knew nothing of art, and underneath his pretentions cared less, for he was a complete utilitarian; but it had become fashionable to have an elaborate art gallery, and he forthwith disbursed money right and left to assemble an aggregation of paintings.

He gave orders to agents for their purchase with the same equanimity that he would contracts for railroad supplies. And, as a rule, the more generous in size the canvasses, the more satisfied he was that he was getting his money's worth; art to him meant buying by the square foot. Not a few of the paintings unloaded upon him were, despite their high-sounding reputations, essentially commonplace subjects, and flashy and hackneyed in execution; but he gloried in the celebrity that came from the high prices he was decoyed into paying for them. For one of Meissionier's paintings, "The Arrival at the Chateau," he paid $40,000, and on one of his visits to Paris he enriched Meissionier to the extent of $188,000 for seven paintings. Not until his corps of art advisers were satisfied that a painter became fashionably talked about, could Vanderbilt be prevailed upon to buy examples of his work. There was something intensely magical in the ease and cheapness with which he acquired the reputation of being a " connoisseur of art." Neither knowledge nor appreciation were required; with the expenditure of a few hundred thousand dollars he instantaneously transformed himself from a heavy-witted, uncultured money hoarder into the character of a surpassing " judge and patron of art." And his pretensions were seriously accepted by the uninformed, absorbing their opinions from the newspapers.

## "THE PUBLIC BE DAMNED."

If he had discreetly comported himself in other respects he might have passed tolerably well as an extremely public-spirited and philanthropic man. After every great fraud that he put through he would usually throw out to the public some ostentatious gift or donation. This would furnish a new ground to the sycophantic chorus for extolling his fine qualities. But he happened to inherit his father's irascibility and extreme contempt for the public whom he exploited. Unfortunately for him, he let out on one memorable occasion his real sentiments. Asked by a reporter why he did not consider public convenience in the running of his trains, he blurted out, "The public be damned!"

It was assuredly a superfluous question and answer; but expressed so sententiously, and published, as it was, throughout the length and breadth of the land, it excited deep popular resentment. He was made the target for general denunciation and execration, although unreasonably so, for he had but given candid and succinct utterance to the actuating principle of the whole capitalist class. The moral of this incident impressed itself sharply upon the minds of the masterly rich, and to this day has greatly contributed to the politic manner of their exterior conduct. They learned that however in private they might safely sneer at the mass of the people as created for their manipulation and enrichment, they must not declare so publicly. Far wiser is it, they have come to understand, to confine spoliation to action, while in outward speech affirming the most mellifluous and touching professions of solicitude for public interests.

## ADDS $100,000,000 IN SEVEN YEARS.

But William H. Vanderbilt was little affected by this outburst of public rage.  He could well afford to smile cynically at it, so long as no definite move was taken to interfere with his privileges, power and possessions. Since his father's death he had added fully $100,000,000 to his wealth, all within a short period.  It had taken Commodore Vanderbilt more than thirty years to establish the fortune of $105,000,000 he left.  With a greater population and greater resources to prey upon, William H. Vanderbilt almost doubled the amount in seven years. In January, 1883, he confided to a friend that he was worth $194,000,000.  " I am the richest man in the world," he went on.  " In England the Duke of Westminster is said to be worth $200,000,000, but it is mostly in land and houses and does not pay two per cent." [7] In the same breath that he boasted of his wealth he would bewail the ill-health condemning him to be a victim of insomnia and indigestion.

Having a clear income of $10,350,000 a year, he kept his ordinary expenses down to $200,000 a year.  Whatever an air of indifference he would assume in his grandee rôle of " art collector," yet in most other matters he was inveterately closefisted.  He had a delusion that " everybody in the world was ready to take advantage of him," and he regarded " men and women, as a rule, as a pretty bad lot." [8]  This incident — one of

[7] Related in the New York " Times," issue of December 9, 1885.
[8] " The  Vanderbilts ": 127.

many similar incidents narrated by Croffut — reveals his microscopic vigilance in detecting impositions:

When in active control of affairs at the office he followed the unwholesome habit of eating the midday lunch at his desk, the waiter bringing it in from a neighboring restaurant.

He paid his bill for this weekly, and he always scrutinized the items with proper care. "Was I here last Thursday?" he asked of a clerk at an adjoining desk.

"No, Mr. Vanderbilt; you stayed at home that day."

"So I thought," he said, and struck that day from the bill. Another time he would exclaim, sotto voce, "I didn't order coffee last Tuesday," and that item would vanish.

Up to the very last second of his life his mind was filled with a whirl of business schemes; it was while discussing railroad plans with Robert Garrett in his mansion, on December 8, 1885, that he suddenly shot forward from his chair and fell apoplectically to the floor, and in a twinkling was dead. Servants ran to and fro excitedly; messengers were dispatched to summon his sons; telegrams flashed the intelligence far and wide.

The passing away of the greatest of men could not have received a tithe of the excitement and attention caused by William H. Vanderbilt's death. The newspaper offices hotly issued page after page of description, not without sufficient reason. For he, although untitled and vested with no official power, was in actuality an autocrat; dictatorship by money bags was an established fact; and while the man died, his corporate wealth, the real director and center, to a large extent, of government functions, survived unimpaired.

He had abundantly proved his autocracy. Law after law had he violated; like his father he had corrupted and intimidated, had bought laws, ignored such as were unsuited to his interests, and had decreed his own rules and codes. Progressively bolder had the money kings become in coming out into the open in the directing of Government. Long had they prudently skulked behind forms, devices and shams; they had operated secretly through tools in office, while virtuously disclaiming any insidious connection with politics. But no observer took this pretence seriously. James Bryce, fresh from England, delving into the complexities and incongruities of American politics at about this time, wrote that " these railway kings are among the greatest men, perhaps I may say, the greatest men in America," which term, " greatest," was a ludicrously reverent way of describing their qualities. " They have power," he goes on in the same work, " more power — that is, more opportunity to make their will prevail, than perhaps any one in political life except the President or the Speaker, who, after all, hold theirs only for four years and two years, while the railroad monarch holds his for life." [9] Bryce was not well enough acquainted with the windings and depths of American political workings to know that the money kings had more power than President or Speaker, not nominally, but essentially. He further relates how when a railroad magnate traveled, his journey was like a royal progress; Governors of States and Territories bowed before him; Legislatures received him in solemn session; cities and towns sought to propitiate him, for had he not the means of making or marring a city's fortunes? " You cannot turn in any direction in American politics," wrote Richard T. Ely a little later, " without discovering the railway power. It is the power behind the throne. It is a correct popular instinct which designates the leading men in the railways, railroad magnates or kings. . . . Its power ramifies in every direction, its roots

[9] " The American Commonwealth," First Ed.: 515.

reaching counting rooms, editorial sanctums, schools and churches which it supports with a part of its revenues, as well as courts and Legislatures." . . .[10]

## HIS DEATH A NOTABLE, EVENT.

Vanderbilt's death, as that of one of the real monarchs of the day, was an event of transcendent importance, and was treated so. The vocabulary was ransacked to find adjectives glowing enough to describe his enterprise, foresight, sagacity and integrity. Much elaborated upon was the fiction that he had increased his fortune by honest, legitimate means — a fiction still disseminated by those shallow or mercenary writers whose trade is to spread orthodox belief in existing conditions. The underlying facts of his career and methods were purposely suppressed, and a nauseating sort of panegyric substituted. Who did not know that he had bribed Legislature after Legislature, and had constantly resorted to conspiracy and fraud? Not one of his eulogists was innocent of this knowledge; the record of it was too public and palpable to justify doubts of its truth. The extent of his possessions and the size of his fortune aroused wonderment, but no effort was made to contrast the immense wealth bequeathed by one man with the dire poverty on every hand, nor to connect those two conditions.

At the very time his wealth was being inventoried at $200,000,000, not less than a million wage earners were out of employment,[11] while the millions at work received

[10] "The Independent," issue of August 28, 1890.
[11] "It is probably true," said Carroll D. Wright in the United States Labor Report for 1886, "that this total (in round numbers 1,000,000) as representing the unemployed at any one time in the United States, is fairly representative."

the scantiest wages. Nearly three millions of people had been completely pauperized, and, in one way or another, had to be supported at public expense. Once in a rare while, some perceptive and unshackled public official might pierce the sophistries of the day and reveal the cause of this widespread poverty, as Ira Steward did in the fourth annual report of the Massachusetts Bureau of Statistics of Labor for 1873.

"It is the enormous profits," he pointedly wrote, "made directly upon the labor of the wage classes, and indirectly through the results of their labor, that, first, keeps them poor, and, second, furnishes the capital that is finally loaned back to them again" at high rates of interest. Unquestionably sound and true was this explanation, yet of what avail was it if the causes of their poverty were withheld from the active knowledge of the mass of the wage workers? It was the special business of the newspapers, the magazines, the pulpit and the politicians to ignore, suppress or twist every particle of information that might enlighten or arouse the mass of people; if these agencies were so obtuse or recalcitrant as not to know their expected place and duty at critical times, they were quickly reminded of them by the propertied classes. To any newspaper owner, clergyman or politician showing a tendency to radicalism, the punishment came quickly. The newspaper owner was deprived of advertisements and accommodations, the clergyman was insidiously hounded out of his pulpit by his own church associations, the funds of which came from men of wealth, and the politician was ridiculed and was summarily retired to private life by corrupt means. As for genuinely honest administrative officials (as distinguished from the *apparently* honest) who exposed prevalent conditions and sought to remedy them in their particular departments, they were eventually got rid of by a similar campaign of calumny and corrupt influences.

### HIS FRAUDS IN EVADING TAXES.

As in the larger sense all criticism of conditions was systematically smothered, so were details of the methods of the rich carefully obscured or altogether passed by in silence. At Vanderbilt's death the newspapers laved in gorgeous descriptions of his mansion. Yet apart from the proceeds of his great frauds, the amounts out of which he had cheated the city and State in taxation were alone much more than enough to have paid for his splendor of living. Like the Astors, the Goelets, Marshall Field and every other millionaire without exception, he continuously defrauded in taxes.

We have seen how the Vanderbilts seized hold of tens of millions of dollars of bonds by fraud. Certain of their railroad stocks were exempted from individual taxation, but railroad bonds ranked as taxable personal property. Year after year William H. Vanderbilt had perjured himself in swearing that his personal property did not exceed $500,000. On more than this amount he would not pay. When at his death his will revealed to the public the proportions of his estate, the New York City Commissioners of Assessments and Taxes made an apparent effort to collect some of the millions of dollars out of which he had cheated the city. It was now that the obsequious and time-serving Depew, grown gray and wrinkled in the retainership of the Vanderbilt generations, came forward with this threat: " He informed us," testified Michael Coleman, president of the commission, " that if we attempted to press too hard he would take proceedings by which most of the securities would be placed beyond our reach so that we could not tax them. The Vanderbilt family could convert everything they had into non-taxable securities, such as New York Central, Government and city bonds, Delaware and Lackawanna, and Delaware and Western Railroad stocks, and pay not a dollar provided they wished to do so." [12]

The Vanderbilt estate compromised by paying the city a mere part of the sum owed. It succeeded in keeping the greatest part of its possessions immune from taxation, in doing which it but did what the whole of the large propertied class was doing, as was disclosed in further detailed testimony before the New York Senate Committee on Cities in 1890.

### HIS WILL TRANSMITS $200,000,000.

Unlike his father, William H. Vanderbilt did not bequeath the major portion of his fortune to one son. He left $50,000,000 equally to each of his two sons, Cornelius and William K. Vanderbilt. Supplementing the fortunes they already had, these legacies swelled their individual fortunes to approximately $100,000,000 each — about the same amount as their father had himself inherited. The remaining $100,000,000 was thus disposed of in William H. Vanderbilt's will: $40,000,-000, in railroad and other securities, was set apart as a trust fund, the income of which was to be apportioned equally among each of his eight children. This provided them each with an annual income of $500,000. In turn, the principal was to descend to their children, as they should direct by will. Another $40,000,000 was shared outright among his eight children. The remaining $20,-

12 The New York Senate Committee on Cities, 1890, iii: 2355-2356.

000,000 was variously divided: the greater part to his widow; $2,000,000 as an additional gift to Cornelius; $1,000,000 to a favorite grandson; sundry items to other relatives and friends, and about $1,000,000 to charitable and public institutions.

He was buried in a mausoleum costing $300,000, which he himself had ordered to be built at New Dorp, Staten Island; and there to-day his ashes lie, splendidly interred, while millions of the living plundered and disinherited are suffered to live in the deadly congestion of miserable habitations.

# CHAPTER VII

## THE VANDERBILT FORTUNE IN THE PRESENT GENERATION

With the demise of William H. Vanderbilt the Vanderbilt fortune ceased being a one-man factor. Although apportioned among the eight children, the two who inherited by far the greater part of it — Cornelius and William K. Vanderbilt — were its rulers paramount. To them descended the sway of the extensive railroad systems appropriated by their grandfather and father, with all of the allied and collateral properties. Both of these heirs had been put through a punctilious course of training in the management of railroad affairs; all of the subtle arts and intricacies of finance, and the grand tactical and strategic strokes of railroad manipulation, had been drilled into them with extraordinary care.

Their first move upon coming into their inheritance was to surround themselves with the magnificence of imposing residences, as befitted their state and estate. A signatory stroke of the pen was the only exertion required of them; thereupon architects and a host of artisans yielded service and built palaces for them, for the one at Fifth avenue and Fifty-second street, for the other at Fifth avenue and Fifty-seventh street.

Millions were spent with prodigal lavishness. On his Fifth avenue mansion alone, Cornelius expended $5,000,000. To get the space for three beds of blossoms and a few square yards of turf, a brownstone house adjoining his mansion was torn down, and the garden created at an expense of $400,000. George, a brother of Cornelius and of William K. Vanderbilt, and a man of retiring disposition, spent $6,000,000 in building a palatial home in the heart of the North Carolina mountains. For three years three hundred stonemasons were kept busy; and he gradually added land to his surrounding estate until it embraced one hundred and eighty square miles. His game preserves were enlarged until they covered 20,000 acres. So, within thirty years from the time their grandfather, Commodore Vanderbilt, was extorting his original millions by blackmailing, did they live like princes, and in greater luxury and power than perhaps any of the titular princes of ancient or modern days. But the splendor of these abodes was intended merely for partial use. At their command spacious, majestic palaces arose at Newport, whither in the torrid season some of the Vanderbilts transferred their august seat of power and pleasure.

Hardly had they settled themselves down in the vested security of their great fortunes when an ominous situation presented itself to shake the entire propertied class into a violent state of uneasiness. Hitherto the main antagonistic movement perturbing the magnates was that of the obstreperous and still powerful middle class. Dazed and enraged at the certain prospect of their complete subjugation and eventual annihilation, these small capitalists had clamored for laws restricting the power of the great capitalists. Some of their demands were constantly being enacted into law, without, however, the expected results.

### THE GREAT LABOR MOVEMENT OF 1886.

Now, to the intense alarm of all sections of the capitalist class, a very different quality of movement reared itself upward from the deeps of the social formation.[1]

This time it was the laboring masses preparing for the most vigorous and comprehensive attack that they had ever made upon capitalism's intrenchments. Long exploited, oppressed and betrayed, starved or clubbed into intervals of apathy or submission, they were again in motion, moving forward with a set deliberation and determination which disconcerted the capitalist class. No mere local conflict of class interests was it on this occasion, but a general cohesive revolt of the workers against some of the conditions and laws under which they had to labor.

In 1884 the Federation of Trades and Labor Unions of the United States and Canada had issued a manifesto calling upon all trades to unite in the demand for an eight-hour workday. The date for a general strike was finally fixed for May 1, 1886. The year 1886, therefore, was one of general agitation throughout the United States. With rapidity and enthusiasm the movement spread. Presently it took on a radical character. Realizing it to be at basis the first national awakening of the proletariat, progressive men and women of every shade of opinion hastened forward to support it and direct it into one of opposition, not merely to a few of the evils of wage slavery, but to what they considered the fundamental cause itself — the capitalist system.

The propertied classes were not deceived. They knew

[1] It may be asked why an extended description of this movement is interposed here. Because, inasmuch as it is a part of the plan of this work to present a constant succession of contrasts, this is, perhaps, as appropriate a place as any to give an account of the highly important labor movement of 1886. Of course, it will be understood that this movement was not the result of any one capitalist fortune or process, but was a general revolt to compel all forms of capitalist control to concede better conditions to the workers.

that while this labor movement nominally confined itself
to one for a shorter workday, yet its impetus was such
that it contained the fullest potentialities for developing
into a mighty uprising against the very system by which
they were enabled to enrich themselves and enslave the
masses.

The moment this fact was discerned, both great and
small capitalists instinctively suspended hostilities. They
tacitly agreed to hold their bitter warfare for supremacy
in abeyance, and unite in the face of their common
danger. The triangular conflict between the large and
small capitalists and the trades unions now resolved into
a duel between the propertied classes of all descriptions
on the one hand, and, on the other, the workingmen's
organizations. The Farmers' Alliance, essentially a middle-class movement of the employing farmers in the
South and West, was counted upon as aligned with the
propertied classes. On the part of the capitalists there
was no unity of organization in the sense of selected
leaders or committees. It was not necessary. A
stronger bond than that of formal organization drove
them into acting in conscious unison — namely, the immediate peril involved to their property interests. Apprehension soon gave way to grim decision. This formidable labor movement had to be broken and dispersed
at any cost.

But how was the work of destruction to be done?
This was the predicament.. Vested wealth could succeed in bribing a labor leader here and there; but the
movement had bounded far beyond the elemental stage,
and had become a glowing agitation which no traitor
or set of traitors could have stopped.

One effective way of discrediting and suppressing it

there was; the ancient one of virtually outlawing it, and throwing against it the whole brute force of Government. The task of putting it down was preëminently one for the police, army and judiciary. They had been used to stifle many another protest of the workers; why not this? As the great labor movement rolled on, enlisting the ardent attachment of the masses, denouncing the injustices, corruption and robberies of the existing industrial system, the propertied classes more acutely understood that they must hasten to stamp it out by whatever means. The municipal and State governments and the National Government, completely representing their interests and ideas, and dominated by them, stood ready to use force. But there had to be some kind of pretext. The hosts of labor were acting peacefully and with remarkable self control and discipline.

### THE PROPERTIED CLASSES STRIKE BACK.

The propitious occasion soon came. It was in Chicago that the blow was struck which succeeded in discrediting the cause of the workers, stayed the progress of their movement, and covered it with a prejudice and an odium lasting for years. There, in that maddening bedlam, called a city, the acknowledged inferno of industrialism, the agitation was tensest. With its brutalities, cruelties, corruptions and industrial carnage, its hideous contrasts of dissolute riches and woe-begone poverty, its arrogant wealth lashing the working population lower and lower into squalor, pauperism and misery, Chicago was overripe for any movement seeking to elevate conditions.

In the first months of 1886, strike followed strike

throughout the United States for an eight-hour day. At McCormick's reaper works in Chicago [2] a prolonged strike of many months began in February. Determined not only to refuse shorter hours, but to force his twelve hundred wage workers to desert labor unions, McCormick drove them from his factory, hired armed mercenaries, called Pinkerton detectives, and substituted in the place of the union workers those despised irresponsibles called " scabs "— signifying laborers willing to help defeat the battles of organized labor, and, if the unions won, share in the benefits without incurring any of the responsibilities, risks or struggles. On May 1, 1886, forty thousand men and women in Chicago went on strike for an eight-hour day. Thus far, the aim of inciting violence on the part of the strikers had completely failed everywhere.

The Knights of Labor were conducting their strikes with a coolness, method and sober sense of order, giving no opportunity for the exercise of force. On May 2, a great demonstration of the McCormick workers was held near that company's factories to protest against the employment of armed Pinkertons. The Pinkerton detective bureau was a private establishment, founded during the Civil War; in the ensuing contests between labor and capital it was alleged to have made a profitable business of supplying spies and armed men to capitalists under the pretense of safeguarding property. These armed bands really constituted private armies; recruited often from the most debased and worthless part of the

[2] The McCormick fortune was the outgrowth, to a large extent, of a variety of frauds and corruptions. Later on in this work, the facts are given as to how Cyrus H. McCormick, the founder of the fortune, bribed Congress, in 1854, to give him a time extension of his patent rights.

population, as well as from the needy and shifty, they
were, it was charged, composed largely of men who
would perjure themselves, fabricate evidence, provoke
trouble, and slaughter without scruple for pay. Some,
as was well established, were ex-convicts, others thugs,
and still others were driven to the ignoble employment
by necessity.[3] During the course of the meeting in the
afternoon the factory bell rung, and the " scabs " were
seen leaving. Some boys in the audience began throwing stones and there was hooting. Fully aware of the
combustible accounts wanted by their offices, the reporters immediately telephoned exaggerated, inflammatory
stories of a riot being under way; the police on the spot
likewise notified headquarters.[4] Police in large numbers
soon arrived; the boys kept throwing stones; and suddenly, without warning, the police drew their revolvers
and indiscriminately opened a general fire upon the men,

[3] The prevailing view of the working class toward the Pinkerton detectives was thus expressed at the time in a chapter on
the mine workers by John McBride, one of the trade union leaders: " They have awakened," he wrote, " the hatred and detesta-
tion of the workingmen of the United States; and this hatred is
due, not only to the fact that they protect the men who are
stealing the bread from the mouths of the families of strikers,
but to the fact that as a class they seem rather to invite trouble
than to allay it. . . . They are employed to terrorize the
workingmen, and to create in the minds of the public the idea
that the miners are a dangerous class of citizens that have to be
kept down by armed force. These men had an interest in keeping up and creating troubles which gave employers opportunity to
demand protection from the State militia at the expense of
the State, and which the State has too readily granted."— " The
Labor Movement ": 264-265.
[4] In a statement published in the Chicago " Daily News," issue
of May 10, 1889, Captain Ebersold, chief of police in 1886,
charged that Captain Schaack, who had been the police official
most active in proceeding against the labor leaders and causing
them to be executed and imprisoned, had deliberately set about
concocting " anarchist " conspiracies in order to get the credit
for discovering and breaking them up.

women and children in the crowd, killing four and
wounding many. Terror stricken and in horror the
crowd fled.

There was a group of radical spirits in Chicago, popularly branded as anarchists, but in reality men of advanced ideas who, while differing from one another in
economic views, agreed in denouncing the existing system as the prolific cause of bitter wrongs and rooted
injustices. Sincere, self-sacrificing, intellectual, out-
spoken, absolutely devoted to their convictions, burn-
ing with compassion and noble ideals for suffering
humanity, they had stepped forward and had greatly
assisted in arousing the militant spirit in the working
class in Chicago. At all of the meetings they had spoken
with an ardor and ability that put them in the front
ranks of the proletarian leaders; and in two newspapers
published by them, the " Alarm," in English, and the
" Arbeiter Zeitung," in German, they unceasingly advocated the interests of the working class. These men
were Albert R. Parsons, a printer, editor of the
" Alarm;" August Spies, an upholsterer by trade, and
editor of the " Arbeiter Zeitung;" Adolph Fischer, a
printer; Louis Lingg, a carpenter; Samuel Fielden, the
son of a British factory owner; George Engel, a painter;
Oscar Neebe, a well-to-do business man, and Michael
Schwab, a bookbinder. All of them were more or less
deep students of economics and sociology; they had become convinced that the fundamental cause of the prevalent inequalities of opportunity and of the widespread
misery was the capitalist system itself. Hence they opposed it uncompromisingly.[5]

[5] The utterances of these leaders revealed the reasons why
they were so greatly feared by the capitalist class. Fischer, for
instance, said: " I perceive that the diligent, never-resting hu-

The newspapers, voicing the interests and demands of the intrenched classes, denounced these radicals with a sinister emphasis as destructionists. But it was not ignorance which led them to do this; it was intended as a deliberate poisoning and inflaming of public opinion. Themselves bribing, corrupting, intimidating, violating laws and slaying for profit everywhere, the propertied classes ever assumed, as has so often been pointed out, the pose of being the staunch conservers of law and order. To fasten upon the advanced leaders of the labor movement the stigma of being sowers of disorder, and then judicially get rid of them, and crush the spirit and movement of the aroused proletariat — this was the plan determined upon. Labor leaders who confined their programme to the industrial arena were not feared so much; but Parsons, Spies and their comrades were not only pointing out to the masses truths extremely unpalatable to the capitalists, but were urging, although in a crude way, a definite political movement to overthrow capitalism. With the finest perception, fully alert to their danger, the propertied classes were intent upon exterminating this portentous movement by striking down its leaders and terrifying their followers.

### THE HAYMARKET TRAGEDY.

Fired with indignation at the slaughter at the McCormick meeting, Spies and others of his group issued a

---

man working bees, who create all wealth and fill the magazines with provisions, fuel and clothing, enjoy only a minor part of this product, while the drones, the idlers, keep the warehouses locked up, and revel in luxury and voluptuousness." Engel said: "The history of all times teaches us that the oppressing always maintain their tyrannies by force and violence. Some day the war will break out; therefore all workingmen should unite and prepare for the last war, the outcome of which will be the end forever of all war, and bring peace and happiness to mankind."

call for a meeting on the night of May 4, at the Haymarket, to protest against the police assaults. Spies opened the meeting, and was followed by Fielden. Observers agreed that the meeting was proceeding in perfect quiet, so quietly that the Mayor of Chicago, who was present to suppress it if necessary, went home — when suddenly one hundred and eighty policemen, with arms in readiness, appeared and peremptorily ordered the meeting to disperse.' It seems that without pausing for a reply they immediately charged, and began clubbing and mauling the few hundred persons present. At this juncture a small bomb, thrown by someone, exploded in the ranks of the police, felling sixty and killing one. The police instantly began firing into the crowd.

No one has ever been able to find out definitely who threw the bomb. Suspicions were not lacking that it was done by a mercenary of corporate wealth. At Pittsburg, in 1877, as we have seen, the Pennsylvania railroad hirelings deliberately destroyed property and incited riot in order to charge the strikers with crime. In the coal mining regions of Pennsylvania, subsidized detectives had provoked trouble during the strikes, and by means of bogus evidence and packed juries had hung some labor leaders and imprisoned others.

The hurling of the bomb, whether done by a secret emissary, or by a sympathizer with labor, proved the lever which the propertied classes had been feverishly awaiting. Spies, Fielding and their comrades were at once cast into jail; the newspapers invented wild yarns of conspiracies and midnight plots, and raucously demanded the hanging of the leaders. The trifling formality of waiting until their guilt had been proved was not considered. The most significant event, however, was the secret meeting of about three hundred leading American capitalists to plan the suppression of "anarchy." Very horrified they professed themselves to be at violent outrages and destruction of property and life. Their views were given wide circulation and commendation; they were the finest types of commercial success and prestige. They were the owners of railroads that slaughtered thousands of human beings every year, because of the demands of profit; of factories which sucked the very life out of their toilers, and which filled the hospitals, slums, brothels and graveyards with an ever-increasing assemblage; every man in that conclave, as a beneficiary of the existing system, had drained his fortune from the sweat, sorrow, miseries and death agonies of a multitude of workers.[6] These were the men who came forth to form the "Citizens' Association," and within a few hours subscribed $100,000 as a fighting fund.

### JUDICIAL MURDER OF LABOR'S LEADERS.

The details of the trial will not be gone into here. The trial itself is now everywhere recognized as having been a tragic farce. The jury, it is clear, was purposely drawn from the employing class, or their dependents; of a thousand talesmen summoned, only five or six belonged

[6] This seems a very sweeping and extraordinarily prejudicial statement. It should be remembered, however, that these capitalists, both individually and collectively, had contested the passage of every proposed law, the aim of which was to improve conditions for the workers on the railroads and in mines and factories. Time after time they succeeded in defeating or ignoring this legislation. Although the number of workers killed or injured in accidents every year was enormous, and although the number slain by diseases contracted in workshops or dwellings was even greater, the capitalists insisted that the law had no right to interfere with the conduct of their "private business."

to the working class. The malignant class nature of
the trial was revealed by the questions asked of the
talesmen; nearly all declared that they had a prejudice
against Socialists, Anarchists and Communists. Soon
the blindest could see that the conviction of the group
was determined upon in advance, and that it was but
the visible evidence of a huge conspiracy to terrorize the
whole working class.

The theory upon which the group was prosecuted was
that they were actively engaged in a conspiracy against
the existing authorities, and that they advocated violence and bloodshed. No jurist would now presume to
contend that the slightest evidence was adduced to prove
this. But all were rushed to conviction: Spies, Parsons,
Fischer, and Engel were hanged on November 11, 1887,
after fruitless appeals to the higher courts; Lingg committed suicide in prison, and Fielden, Neebe and Schwab
were sentenced to long terms in prison. The four executed leaders met their death with the heroic calmness
of martyrdom. " Let the voice of the people be heard! "
were Parsons' last words. Fielden, Neebe and Schwab
might have rotted away in prison, were it not that one
of the noblest-minded and most maligned men of his
time, in the person of John P. Altgeld, was Governor
of Illinois in 1893. Governor Altgeld pardoned them
on these grounds, which he undoubtedly proved in an
exhaustive review: (1) The jury was a packed one selected to convict; (2) the jurors were prejudiced; (3)
no guilt was proved; (4) the State's attorney had admitted no case against Neebe, yet he had been imprisoned; (5) the trial judge (Gary) was either so prejudiced or subservient to class influence that he did not
or could not give a fair trial. Even many of those who

denounced Altgeld for his action, now admit that his grounds were justified.

## THE LABOR UPRISING IN NEW YORK.

In the meanwhile, between the time of the Haymarket episode and the hanging and imprisonment of the Chicago group, the labor movement in New York City had assumed so strong a political form that the ruling class was seized with consternation. The Knights of Labor, then at the summit of organization and solidarity, were ripe for independent political action; the effects of the years of active propaganda carried on in their ranks by the Socialists and Single-Tax advocates now began to show fruit. At the critical time, when the labor unions were wavering in the decision as to whether they ought to strike out politically or not, the ruling class supplied the necessary vital impulsion. While in Chicago the courts were being used to condemn the labor leaders to death or prison, in the East they were used to paralyze the weapons of offense and defence by which the unions were able to carry on their industrial warfare.

The conviction, in New York City, of certain members of a union for declaring a boycott, proved the one compelling force needed to mass all of the unions and radical societies and individuals into a mighty movement resulting in an independent labor party. To meet this exigency an effort was made by the politicians to buy off Henry George, the distinguished Single-Tax advocate, who was recognized as the leader of the labor party. But this flanking attempt at bribing an incorruptible man failed; the labor unions proceeded to nominate George for Mayor, and a campaign was begun of an ardor, vigor and enthusiasm such as had not been known since the Workingmen's party movement in 1829.

The election was for local officers of the foremost city in the United States — a point of vantage worth contending for, since the moral effect of such a victory of the working class would be incalculable, even if short-lived. To the ruling classes the triumph of the labor unions, while restricted to one city, would unmistakably denote the glimmerings of the beginning of the end of their regime. Such rebellious movements are highly contagious; from the confines of one municipality they sweep on to other sections, stimulating action and inspiring emulation. The New York labor campaign of 1886 was an intrinsic part and result of the general labor movement throughout the United States. And it was the most significant manifestation of the onward march of the workers; elsewhere the labor unions had not gone beyond the stage of agitation and industrial warfare; but in New York, with the most acute perception of the real road it must traverse, the labor movement had plunged boldly into political action. It realized that it must get hold of the governmental powers. Its antagonists, the capitalists, had long had a rigid grip on them, and had used them almost wholly as they willed.

But the capitalist class was even more doggedly determined upon retaining and intensifying those powers. Government was an essential requisite to its plans and development. The small capitalists bitterly fought the great; but both agreed that Government with its legislators, laws, precedents, and the habits of thought it created, must be capitalistic. Both saw in the uprising of labor a prospective overturning of conditions.

From this identity of interest a singular concrete alliance resulted. The great capitalists, whom the middle-class had denounced as pirates, now became the decorous and orthodox "saviors of society," with the small capitalists trailing behind their leadership, and shouting their praises as the upholders of law and the conservators of order. In Chicago the same men who had bribed legislators and common councils to give them public franchises, and who had hugely swindled and stolen under guise of law, had been the principals in calling for the execution and imprisonment of the group of labor leaders, and this they had decreed in the name of law. In New York City a pretext for dealing similarly with the labor leaders was entirely lacking, but another method was found effective in the subjugation and dispersion of the movement.

### CAPITALIST TRIUMPH BY FRAUD.

This was the familiar one of corruption and fraud. It was a method in the exercise of which the capitalists as a class had proved themselves adepts; they now summoned to their aid all of the ignoble and subterranean devices of criminal politics.

In the New York City election of 1886 three parties contested, the Labor party, Tammany Hall and the Republican party. Steeped in decades of the most loathsome corruption, Tammany Hall was chosen as the medium by which the Labor party was to be defrauded and effaced. Pretending to be the "champion of the people's rights," and boasting that it stood for democracy against aristocracy, Tammany Hall had long deceived the mass of the people to plunder them. It was a powerful, splendidly-organized body of mercenaries and self-seekers which, by trading on the principles of democracy, had been able to count on the partisan votes of a predominating element of the wage-working class. In reality, however, it was absolutely directed by a leader or "boss," who, with his confederates, made a regular traffic of selling legislation to the capitalists, on the one hand, and who, on the other, enriched themselves by a colossal system of blackmail. They sold immunity to pickpockets, confidence men and burglars, compelled the saloonkeepers to pay for protection, and even extorted from the wretched women of the street and brothels. This was the organization that the ruling class, with its fine assumptions of respectability, now depended upon to do its work of breaking up the political labor revolt.

The candidate of Tammany Hall was the ultra-respectable Abram S. Hewitt, a millionaire capitalist. The Republican party nominated a verbose, pushful, self-glorifying young man, who, by a combination of fortuitous circumstances, later attained the position of President of the United States. This was Theodore Roosevelt, the scion of a moderately rich New York family, and a remarkable character whose pugnacious disposition, indifference to political conventionalities, capacity for exhortation, and bold political shrewdness were mistaken for greatness of personality. The phenomenal success to which he subsequently rose was characteristic of the prevailing turgidity and confusion of the popular mind. Both Hewitt and Roosevelt were, of course, acceptable to the capitalist class. As, however, New York was normally a city of Democratic politics, and as Hewitt stood the greater chance of winning, the support of those opposed to the labor movement was concentrated upon him.

Intrenched respectability, for the most part, came forth to join sanctimony with Tammany scoundrelism. It was an edifying union, yet did not comprise all of the forces

linked in that historic coalition.   The Church, as an institution, cast into it the whole weight of its influence and
power.   Soaked with the materialist spirit while dogmat-
ically preaching the spiritual, dominated and pervaded by
capitalist influences, the Church, of all creeds and de-
nominations, lost no time in subtly aligning itself in its
expected place.   And woe to the minister or priest who
defied the attitude of his church!   Father McGlynn, for
example, was excommunicated by the Pope, ostensibly for
heretical utterances, but in actuality for espousing the
cause of the labor movement.

Despite every legitimate argument coupled with venomous ridicule and coercive and corrupt influence that
wealth, press and church could bring to bear, the labor
unions stood solidly together.   On election day groups
of Tammany repeaters, composed of dissolutes, profli-
gates, thugs and criminals, systematically, under directions from above, filled the ballot boxes with fraudulent
votes.   The same rich class that declaimed with such
superior indignation against rule by the "mob" had
poured in funds which were distributed by the politicians
for these frauds.   But the vote of the labor forces was
so overwhelming, that even piles of fraudulent votes
could not suffice to overcome it.   One final resource was
left.   This was to count out Henry George by grossly
tampering with the election returns and misrepresenting
them.   And this is precisely what was done, if the testimony of numerous eye-witnesses is to be believed.   The
Labor party, it is quite clear, was deliberately cheated
out of an election won in the teeth of the severest and
most corrupt opposition.   This result it had to accept;
the entire elaborate machinery of elections was in the full
control of the Labor party's opponents; and had it instituted a contest in the courts, the Labor party would

have found its efforts completely fruitless in the face of an adverse judiciary.

## THE LABOR PARTY EVAPORATES.

By the end of the year 1887 the political phase of the labor movement had shrunk to insignificant proportions, and soon thereafter collapsed. The capitalist interests had followed up their onslaught in hanging and imprisoning some of the foremost leaders, and in corruption and fraud at the polls, by the repetition of other tactics that they had long so successfully used.

Acting through the old political parties they further insured the disintegration of the Labor party by bribing a sufficient number of its influential men. This bribery took the form of giving them sinecurist offices under either Democratic or Republican local, State or National administrations. Many of the most conspicuous organizers of the labor movement were thus won over, by the proffer of well-paying political posts, to betray the cause in the furtherance of which they had shown such energy. Deprived of some of its leaders, deserted by others, the labor political movement sank into a state of disorganization, and finally reverted to its old servile position of dividing its vote between the two capitalist parties.

From now on, for many years, the labor movement existed purely as an industrial one, disclaiming all connection with politics. Voting into power either of the old political parties, it then humbly begged a few crumbs of legislation from them, only to have a few sops thrown to it, or to receive contemptuous kicks and humiliations, and, if it grew too importunate or aggressive, insults backed with the strong might of judicial, police and military power.

When it was jubilantly seen by the coalesced propertied classes that the much-dreaded labor movement had been thrust aside and shorn, they resumed their interrupted conflict.

The small capitalist evinced a fierce energy in seeking to hinder in every possible way the development of the great. It was in these years that a multitude of middle-class laws were enacted both by Congress and by the State legislatures; the representatives of that class from the North and East joined with those of the Farmers' Alliance from the West and South. Laws were passed declaring combinations conspiracies in restraint of trade and prohibiting the granting of secret discriminative rates by the railroads. In 1889 no fewer than eighteen States passed anti-trust laws; five more followed the next year. Every one of these laws was apparently of the most explicit character, and carried with it drastic penal provisions. " Now," exulted the small capitalists in high spirits of elation, " we have the upper hand. We have laws enough to throttle the monopolists and preserve our righteous system of competition. They don't dare violate them, with the prospects of long terms in prison staring them in the face."

## THE SMALL CAPITALISTS' LOSING FIGHT.

The great capitalists both dared and did. If specific statutes were against them, the impelling forces of economic development and the power of might were wholly on their side. The competitive system was already doomed; the middle class was too blind to realize that what seemed to be victory was the rattle of the slow death struggle. At first, the great capitalists made no attempt to have these laws altered or repealed. They adopted a slyer and more circuitous mode of warfare. They simply evaded them. As fast as one trust was dissolved by court decision, it nominally complied, as did, for instance, the Standard Oil Trust and the Sugar Trust, and then furtively caused itself to be reborn into a new combination so cunningly sheltered within the technicalities of the law that it was fairly safe from judicial overthrow.

But the great capitalists were too wise to stake their existence upon the thin refuge of technicalities. With their huge funds they now systematically struck out to control the machinery of the two main political parties; they used the ponderous weight of their influence to secure the appointment of men favorable to them as Attorneys General of the United States, and of the States, and they carried on a definite plan of bringing about the appointment or election of judges upon whose decisions they could depend. The laws passed by the middle class remained ornamental encumbrances on the statute books; the great capitalists, although harassed continually by futile attacks, triumphantly swept forward, gradually in their consecutive progress strangling the middle class beyond resurrection.

Such was the integral impotence of the warfare of the small against the great capitalists that, during this convulsive period, the existing magnates increased their wealth and power on every hand, and their ranks were increased by the accession of new members. From the chaos of middle-class industrial institutions, one trust after another sprang full-armed, until presently there was a whole array of them. The trust system had proved itself immensely superior in every respect to the competitive, and by its own superiority it was bound to supplant the other.

Where William H. Vanderbilt had thought himself compelled to temporize with the middle class agitation by making a show of dividing the stock ownership of the New York Central Railroad, his sons Cornelius and William ignored or defied it. Utterly disdainful of the bitter feeling, especially in the West, against the consolidation of railroads in the hands of the powerful few, they tranquilly went ahead to gather more railroads in their ownership. The Cleveland, Cincinnati, Chicago and St. Louis Railroad (popularly dubbed the " Big Four ") acquired by them in 1890 was one of these. It would be tiresome, however, to enter into a narrative of the complex, tortuous methods by which they possessed themselves of these railroads. By the beginning of the year 1893 the Vanderbilt system embraced at least 12,000 miles of railways, with a capitalized value of several hundred million dollars, and a total gross earning power of more than $60,000,000 a year. " All of the best railroad territory," says John Moody in his sketch entitled " The Romance of the Railways," " outside of New England, Pennsylvania and New Jersey was penetrated by the Vanderbilt lines, and no other railroad system in the country, with the single notable exception of the Pennsylvania Railroad, covered anything like the same amount of rich and settled territory, or reached so many towns and cities of importance. New York, Buffalo, Chicago, Cleveland, St. Louis, Cincinnati, Detroit, Indianapolis, Omaha — these were a few of the great marts which were embraced in the Vanderbilt preserves." So impregnably rich and powerful were the Vanderbilts, so profitable their railroads, and their command of resources, financial institutions and legislation so great, that the panic of 1893 instead of impairing their fortunes gave them extraordinary opportunities for getting hold of the properties of weaker railroads.

It was now, acting jointly with other puissant interests, that they saw their chance to get control of a large part of the fabulously rich coal mines of Pennsylvania. These coal mines had originally been owned by separate companies or operators, each independent of the other. But by about the year 1867 the railroads penetrating the coal regions had conceived the plan of owning the mines themselves. Why continue to act as middlemen in transporting the coal? Why not vest in themselves the ownership of these vast areas of coal lands, and secure all the profits instead of those from merely handling the coal?

The plan ingratiated itself as a capital one; it could be easily carried out with little expenditure. All that was necessary for the railroad to do was to burden down the operators with exorbitant charges, and hamper and beleaguer them in a variety of compressing ways.[7] As was proved in subsequent lawsuits, the railroads frequently declined to carry coal for this or that mine, on the pretext that they had no cars available. Every means was used to crush the independent operators and depreciate the selling value of their property. It was a campaign of ruination; in law it stood as criminal conspiracy; but the railroads persisted in it without any further molestation than prolix civil suits, and they finally forced a number of the well-nigh bankrupted independent op-

[7] See testimony before the committee to investigate the Philadelphia and Reading Railroad Company, and the Philadelphia and Reading Coal and Iron Company, Pennsylvania Legislative Docs. 1876, Vol. v, Doc. No. 2. This investigation fully revealed how the railroads detained the cars of the "independent" operators, and otherwise used oppressive methods.

erators to sell out to them for comparatively trifling sums.[8]

By these methods such railroads as the Philadelphia and Reading, the Delaware, Lackawana and Western, the Central Railroad of New Jersey, the Lehigh Valley and others gradually succeeded, in the course of years, in extending an ownership over the coal mines. The more powerful independent operators struck back early at them by getting a constitutional provision passed in Pennsylvania, in 1873, prohibiting railroads from owning and operating coal mines. The railroads evaded this law with facility by an illegal system of leasing, and by organizing nominally separate and independent companies the stock of which, in reality, was owned by them.

To the men who did the actual labor of working in the mines — the coal miners — this change of ownership was not regarded with alarm. Indeed, they at first cherished the pathetic hope that it might benefit their condition, which had been desperate and intolerable enough under the old company system. The small coal-owning capitalists, who had emitted such wailings at their own oppression by the railroads, had long relentlessly exploited their tens of thousands of workers. One abuse had been piled upon another. The miners were paid by the ton; the companies had fraudulently increased the size of the ton, so that the miners had to perform much more labor while wages remained stationary or were reduced.

But one of the most serious grievances was that against what were called " company or truck stores." Ingenious contrivances for getting back the miserable wages paid out, these were company-owned merchandise stores in

[8] Spahr quotes an independent operator in 1900 as saying that the railroads charged the independents three times as much for handling hard coal as they charged for handling soft coal from the West —" America's Working People ": 122-223.

which the miners were compelled to buy their supplies..
In many collieries the mine worker was not paid in
money but was given an order on the company store,
where he was forced to purchase inferior goods at exorbitant prices.

To blast in the mines powder was necessary; the miner
had to buy it at his own expense, and was charged $2.75
a keg, although its selling value was not more than $1.10
or 90 cents. In every direction the mine worker was
defrauded and plundered. "Often," says John Mitchell,
long the leader of the miners, and a compromiser whose
career proves that he cannot be charged with any deep-
seated antagonism to capitalist interests, " a man together
with his children would work for months without receiving a dollar of money, and not infrequently he would
find at the end of the month nothing in his envelope but
a statement that his indebtedness to the company had increased so many dollars." [9]   Mitchell adds that the Legislature of Pennsylvania passed anti-truck store laws, " but
the operators who have always cried out loudest against
illegal action by miners openly and unhesitatingly violated the act and subsequently evaded it by various devices." [10]   The wretched houses the miners occupied
" also," says Mitchell, " served as a means of extortion,
and, in other instances, as a weapon to be used against the
miners." In case they complained or struck, the miners
were evicted under the most cruel circumstances. Many
other media of extortion were common. In the entire
year the miners averaged only one hundred and ninety

[9] " Organized Labor ": 359. Mitchell's comments were fully
supported by the vast mass of testimony taken by the United
States Anthracite Coal Commission in 1902. Mitchell is, at this
writing (1909), in the employ of the Civic Federation, an organization financed by capitalists. Its alleged purpose is to bring
about " harmony " between capital and labor.
[10] Ibid.

working days of ten hours each, and, of course, were paid
for working time only. According to Spahr 350,000
miners drudged for an average wage of $350 a year.[11]

### SEIZING RAILROADS AND COAL MINES.

This system of abject slavery was in full force when
the railroads ousted many of the small operators, and
largely by pressure of power took possession of the mines.
In vain did the miners' unions implore the railroad magnates for redress of some kind. The magnates abruptly
refused, and went on extending and intrenching their
authority. The Vanderbilts manipulated themselves
into being important factors in the Delaware and Hudson Railroad, and in the Delaware, Lackawana and Western Railroad, which had deviously obtained title to some
of the richest coal deposits in Wyoming County, and
they also became prominent in the directing of the Lehigh Valley Railroad.

The most important coal-owning railroad, however,
which they and other magnates coveted was the Philadelphia and Reading Railroad. At least one-half of the
anthracite coal supply of Pennsylvania was owned or
controlled by this railroad. The ownership of the Reading Railroad, with its subordinate lines, was the pivotal
requisite towards getting a complete monopoly of the anthracite coal deposits. William H. Vanderbilt had acquired an interest in it years before, but the actual controlling ownership at this time was held by a group of
Philadelphia capitalists of the second rank with their
three hundred thousand shares.

Unfortunately for this group, the Philadelphia and
Reading Railroad was afflicted with a president, one

11 " The Present Distribution of Wealth in the United States ":
110-111.

Arthur A. McLeod, who was not only too recklessly ambitious, but who was temerarious enough to cross the path of the really powerful magnates. With immense confidence in his plans and in his ability to carry them out, he set out to monopolize the anthracite coal supply and to make the Reading Railroad a great trunk line. To perfect this monopoly he leased some coal-carrying railroads and made " a gentlemen's agreement " with others; and in line with his policy of raising the importance of the road, he borrowed large sums of money for the construction of new terminals and approaches and for equipment.

Now, all of these plans interfered seriously with the aims and ambition of magnates far greater than he. These magnates quickly saw the stupendous possibilities of a monopoly of the coal supply — the hundreds of millions of dollars of profits it held out — and decided that it was precisely what they themselves should control and nobody else. Second, in his aim to have his own railroad connections with the rich manufacturing and heavily-populated New England districts, McLeod had arranged with various small railroads a complete line from the coal fields of Pennsylvania into the heart of New England. In doing this he overreached his mark. He was soon taught the folly of presuming to run counter to the interests of the big magnates.

### AND THE WAY IN WHICH IT WAS DONE.

The two powers controlling the large railroads traversing most of the New England States were the Vanderbilts and J. Pierpont Morgan. The one owned the New York Central, the other dominated the New York, New Haven and Hartford Railroad. The Pennsylvania

Railroad likewise had no intention of allowing such a
powerful competitor in its own province.  These magnates viewed with intense amazement the effrontery of
what they regarded as an upstart interloper.  Although
they had been constantly fighting one another for supremacy, these three interests now made common cause.

They adroitly prepared to crush McLeod and bankrupt the railroad of which he was the head.  By this
process they would accomplish three highly important
objects; one the wresting of the Philadelphia and Reading Railroad into their own divisible ownership; second,
the securing of their personal hold on the connecting
railroads that McLeod had leased; and, finally, the obtaining of undisputed sovereignty over a great part of
the anthracite coal mines.  The warfare now began
without those fanciful ceremonials, heralds or proclama-
tions considered so necessary by Governments as a pre-
lude to slaughter.  These formalities are dispensed with
by business combatants.

First, the Morgan-Vanderbilt interests caused the publication of terrifying reports that grave legislation hostile to the coal combination was imminent.  The price
of Reading stock on the Stock Exchange immediately
declined.  Then, following up their advantage, this dual
alliance inspired even more ruinous reports.  The credit
of the Philadelphia and Reading Railroad was represented as being in a very bad state.  As the railroad had
borrowed immense sums of money both to finance its
coal combination and to build extensive terminals and
other equipment, large payments to creditors were due
from time to time.  To pay these creditors the railroad
had to borrow more; but when the credit of the railroad was assailed, it found that its sources of borrowing
were suddenly shut off.  The group of Philadelphia cap-

italists had already borrowed large sums of money, giv
ing Reading shares as collateral. When the market price
of the stock kept going down they were called upon to
pay back their loans. Declining or unable to do so,
their fifty thousand shares of pledged stock were sold.
This sale still more depressed the price of Reading stock.

In this group of Philadelphia capitalists were men
who were reckoned as very astute business lights —
George M. Pullman, Thomas Dolan, one of the street
railway syndicate whose briberies of legislatures and common councils, and whose manipulation of street railways
in Philadelphia and other cities were so notorious a scandal; John Wanamaker, combining piety and sharp business; — these were three of them. But they were no
match for the much more powerful and wily Vanderbilt-
Morgan forces. They were compelled under resistless
pressure to throw over their Reading stock at a great
loss to themselves. Most of it was promptly bought up
by J. P. Morgan and Company and the Vanderbilts, who
then leisurely arranged a division of the spoils between
themselves.

This transaction (strict interpreters of the law would
have styled it a conspiracy) opened a facile way for a
number of extremely important changes. The Vanderbilts and the Morgan interests apportioned between them
much of the ownership of the Philadelphia and Reading
Railroad with its vast ownership of coal deposits and
its coal carrying traffic.[12] The New York, New Haven
and Hartford Railroad grasped the New York and New

---

[12] An investigation, in 1905, showed that the " Baltimore and
Ohio Railroad and the New York Central and Hudson River
Railroad owned about 43.3 per cent. of the entire capital stock
of the Philadelphia and Reading Railroad Company." " Report
on Discriminations and Monopolies in Coal and Oil, Interstate
Commerce Commission, January 25, 1907 ": 46.

England Railroad from the Reading's broken hold, and there were further far-reaching changes militating to increase the railroad, and other, possessions of both parties.[18]  It was but another of the many instances of the supreme capitalists driving out the smaller fry and seizing the property which they had previously seized by fraud.[14]

[13] A good account of this expropriating transaction is that of Wolcott Drew, " The Reading Crash in 1903 " in " Moody's Magazine " (a leading financial periodical), issue of January, 1907.

[14] One of the particularly indisputable examples of the glaring fraud by which immense areas of coal fields were originally obtained was that of the disposition of the estate of John Nicholson.

Dying in December, 1800, Nicholson left an estate embracing land, the extent of which was variously estimated at from three to five million acres.  Some of the Pennsylvania legislative documents place the area at from three to four million acres, while others, notably a report in 1842, by the judiciary committee of the Pennsylvania House of Representatives, state that it was 5,000,000 acres.  Nicholson was a leading figure in the Pennsylvania Land Company which had obtained most of its vast land possessions by fraud.  Some of Nicholson's landed estate lay in Virginia, Kentucky, North Carolina, South Carolina, Georgia and other States, but the bulk of it was in Pennsylvania, and included extensive regions containing the very richest coal deposits.

The State of Pennsylvania held a lien upon Nicholson's estate for unpaid taxes amounting to $300,000.  Notwithstanding this lien, different individuals and corporations contrived to get hold of practically the whole of the estate in dispute.  How they did it is told in many legislative documents; the fraud and theft connected with it were a great scandal in Pennsylvania for forty-five years.  We will quote only one of these documents. Writing on January 24, 1842, to William Elwell, chairman of the Judiciary Committee of the Pennsylvania House of Representatives, Judge J. B. Anthony, of the Nicholson Court (a court especially established to pass upon questions arising from the disposition of the estate), said: .

"On the 11th of April, 1825, an act passed the Governor to appoint agents to discover and sell the Nicholson lands at auction, for which they were allowed *twenty-five per cent.*  A Special Board of Property was also formed to compromise and settle with claimants.  From what has come to my knowledge in relation to this Act, I am satisfied that the commonwealth was seriously injured by the manner in which it was carried out by

The Vanderbilts' ownership of a large part of the shares of railroads, which, in turn, own and control the coal mines, may be summed up as follows: Through the Lake Shore Railroad, which they have owned almost absolutely, they own, or until recently did own, $30,000,000 of shares in the Philadelphia and Reading Railroad with its stupendous anthracite coal deposits, and they owned, for a long time, large amounts of stock in the Lehigh Valley Railroad with its unmined coal deposits of 400,-000,000 tons. In 1908 they disposed of their Lehigh Valley Railroad ownings, receiving an equivalent in either money or some other form of property. The ownership of the Delaware, Lackawana and Western Railroad with its equally large unmined coal deposits is divided between the Vanderbilt family and the Standard Oil interests. The Vanderbilts, according to the latest official reports, also own heavy interests in the Delaware and Hudson Railroad, the New York, Ontario and Western Railroad, $12,500,000 of stock in the Chesapeake and Ohio Railroad, and large amounts of stock in other coal mining and coal carrying railroads.[15]

Here, then, is another important step in the acquisition of a large part of the country's resources by the Vanderbilts. A recapitulation will not be out of place. His

some of the agents. It was made use of principally for the benefit of land speculators; and the very small sums received by the State treasurer for large and valuable tracts sold and compromised, show that the cunning and astute land jobbers could easily overreach the Board of Property at Harrisburg. . . . Many instances of gross fraud might be enumerated, but it would serve no useful purpose." Judge Anthony further said that "very many of the most influential, astute and intelligent inhabitants" and "gentlemen of high standing" were participants in the frauds.— Pennsylvania House Journal, 1842, Vol. ii, Doc. No. 127: 700-704.

[15] See Special Report No. 1 of the Interstate Commerce Commission on Intercorporate Relationship of Railroads: 39. Also Carl Snyder's "American Railways as Investments": 473.

first millions obtained by blackmailing, Commodore Vanderbilt then uses those millions to buy a railroad. By further fraudulent methods, based upon bribery of law-making bodies, he obtains more railroads and more wealth. His son, following his methods, adds other railroads to the inventory, and converts tens of millions of fraudulently-acquired millions into interest-bearing Government, State, city and other bonds. The third generation (in point of order from the founder) continues the methods of the father and grandfather, gets hold of still more railroads, and emerges as one of the powers owning the great coal deposits of Pennsylvania.

### THE DICTATION OF THE COAL FIELDS.

The Vanderbilt and the Morgan interests at once increased the price of anthracite coal, adding to it $1.25 to $1.35 a ton. In 1900 they appeared in the open with a new and gigantic plan of consolidation by which they were able to control almost absolutely the production and prices. That the Vanderbilt family and the Morgan interests were the main parties to this combination was well established.[16] Already high, a still heavier increase of price at once was put on the 40,000,000 tons of anthracite then produced, and the price was successively raised until consumers were taxed seven times the cost of production and transportation.

The population was completely at the mercy of a few magnates; each year, as the winter drew on, the Coal Trust increased its price. In the needs and suffering of millions of people it found a ready means of laying on fresher and heavier tribute. By the mandate of the

[16] Final Report of the U. S. Industrial Commission, 1902, xix: 462–463.

Coal Trust, housekeepers were taxed $70,000,000 in extra impositions a year, in addition to the $40,000,000 annually extorted by the exorbitant prices of previous years. At a stroke the magnates were able to confiscate by successive grabs the labor of the people of the United States at will. Neither was there any redress; for those same magnates controlled all of the ramifications of Government.

What, however, of the workers in the mines? While the combination was high-handedly forcing the consumer to pay enormous prices, how was it acting toward them? The question is almost superfluous. The railroads made little concealment of their hostility to the trades unions, and refused to grant reforms or concessions. Consequently a strike was declared in 1900 by which the mine workers obtained a ten per cent increase in wages and the promise of semi-monthly wages in cash. But they had not resumed work before they discovered the hollowness of these concessions. Two years of futile application for better conditions passed, and then, in 1902, 150,000 men and boys went on strike. This strike lasted one hundred and sixty-three days. The magnates were generally regarded as arrogant and defiant; they contended that they had nothing to arbitrate; [17] and only yielded to an arbitration board when President Roosevelt threatened them with the full punitive force of Government action.

By the decision of this board the miners secured an increase of wages (which was assessed on the consumer

[17] It was on this occasion that George F. Baer, president of the Philadelphia and Reading Railroad, in scoring the public sympathy for the strikers, justified the attitude of the railroads in his celebrated utterance in which he spoke " of the Christian men and women to whom God in His infinite wisdom has intrusted the property interests of the country," which alleged divine sanction he was never able to prove.

in the form of higher prices) and several minor concessions. Yet at best, their lot is excessively hard. Writing a few years later, Dr. Peter Roberts, who, if anything, is not partial to the working class, stated that the wages of the contract miners were (in 1907) about $600 a year, while adults in other classes of mine workers, who formed more than sixty per cent. of the labor forces, did not receive an annual wage of $450. Yet Roberts quotes the Massachusetts Bureau of Statistics as saying that " a family of five persons requires $754 a year to live on." The average number in the family of a mine worker is five or six. " This small income," Roberts observes, " drives many of our people to live in cheap and rickety houses, where the sense of shame and decency is blunted in early youth, and where men cannot find such home comforts as will counteract the attractions of the saloon." Hundreds of company houses, according to Roberts, are unfit for habitation, and " in the houses of mine employees, of all nationalities, is an appalling infant mortality." [18]

### THE BITUMINOUS COAL MINES ALSO.

The sway of the Vanderbilts, however, extends not only over the anthracite, but over a great extent of the bituminous coal fields in Pennsylvania, Maryland, West Virginia, Ohio and other States. By their control of the New York Central Railroad, they own various ostensibly independent bituminous coal mining companies. The Clearfield Corporation, the Pennsylvania Coal and Coke Co., and the West Branch Coal Company are some of these. By their great holdings in other railroads traversing the soft coal regions, the Vanderbilts control

[18] " The Anthracite Coal Communities " : 346-347.

about one-half of the bituminous coal supply in the Eastern, and most of the Middle-Western, States.

According to the Interstate Commerce Commission's report, in 1907, the New York Central Railroad and the Pennsylvania Railroad owned in that year about forty-five per cent. of the stock of the Chesapeake and Ohio Railroad, and the New York Central owned large amounts of stock in other railroads. " The Commission, therefore, reaches the conclusion," the report reads on after going into the question of ownership in detail, " that, as a matter of fact, the Baltimore and Ohio Railroad Company, the Norfolk and Western Railroad Company, and the Philadelphia and Reading Railway Company were practically controlled by the Pennsylvania Railroad Company and the New York Central and Hudson River Railroad Company, and that the result was to practically abolish substantial competition between the carriers of coal in the territories under consideration." Although the Standard Oil oligarchy now owns considerable stock in the Vanderbilt railroads, it is an undoubted fact that the Vanderbilts share to a great extent the mastery of both hard and soft coal fields.

It is not possible here to present even in condensed form the outline, much less the full narrative, of the labyrinth of tricks, conspiracies and frauds which the railroad magnates have resorted to, and still practice, in the throttling of the small capitalists, and in guaranteeing themselves a monopoly. A great array of facts are to be found in the reports of the exhaustive investigations made by the United States Industrial Commission in 1901-1902, and by the Interstate Commerce Commission in 1907.

Thousands of times was the law glaringly violated, yet the magnates were at all times safe from prosecution.

Periodically the Government would make a pretense of subjecting them to an inquiry, but in no serious sense were they interfered with. These investigations all have shown that the railroads first crushed out the small operators by a conspiracy of rates, blockades and reprisals, and then by a juggling process of stocks and bonds, bought in the mines with the expenditure of scarcely any actual money. Having done this they formed a monopoly and raised prices which, in law, was a criminal conspiracy. The same weapons destructively used against the small coal operators years ago are still being employed against the few independent companies remaining in the coal fields, as was disclosed, in 1908, in the suit of the Government to dissolve the workings of the various railroad companies in the anthracite coal combination.[19]

### THE HUGE PROFITS FROM THE COAL MINES.

No one knows or can ascertain the exact profits of the Vanderbilts and of other railroad owners from their control of both the anthracite, and largely the bituminous, coal mines. As has been noted, the railroad magnates cloud their trail by operating through subsidiary companies. That their extortions reach hundreds of millions of dollars every year is a patent enough fact. Some of the accompaniments of this process of extortion have been referred to; — the confiscation, on the one hand, of the labor of the whole consuming population by taxing from them more and more of the products of their labor

[19] See testimony brought out before Charles H. Guilbert, Examiner appointed by the United States District Court in Philadelphia. The Government's petition charged the defendants with entering into a conspiracy contrary to the letter and the spirit of the Sherman act.

by repeated increases in the price of coal, and, on the other, the confiscation of the labor of the several hundred thousand miners who are compelled to work for the most precarious wages, and in conditions worse, in some respects, than chattel slavery.

But not alone is labor confiscated. Life is also immolated. The yearly sacrifice of life in the coal mines of the United States is steadily growing. The report for 1908 of the United States Geological Survey showed that 3,125 coal miners were killed by accidents in the current year, and that 5,316 were injured. The number of fatalities was 1,033 more than in 1906. " These figures," the report explains, " do not represent the full extent of the disasters, as reports were not received from certain States having no mine inspectors." Side by side with these appalling figures must be again brought out the fact adverted to already: that the owners of the coal mines have at all times violently opposed the passage of laws drafted to afford greater safeguard for life in the working of the mines. Being the owners, at the same time, of the railroads, their opposition in that field to life-saving improvements has been as consistent.

Improvements are expensive; human life is contemptibly cheap; so long as there is a surplus of labor it is held to be commercial folly to go to the unnecessary expense of protecting an article of merchandise which can be had so cheaply. Human tragedies do not enter into the making of profit and loss accounts; outlays for mechanical appliances do. Assuredly this is a business age wherein profits must take precedence over every other consideration, which principle has been most elaborately enunciated and established by a long list of exalted court decisions. Yea, and the very magnates whose power rests on force and fraud are precisely those who insidiously dictate what men shall be appointed to these omniscient courts, before whose edicts all men are expected to bow in speechless reverence.[20]

[20] This is far from being a rhetorical figure of speech. Witness the dictating of the appointment and nominations of judges by the Standard Oil Company (which now owns immense railroad systems and industrial plants) as revealed by certain authentic correspondence of that trust made public in the Presidential campaign of 1908.

# CHAPTER VIII

## FURTHER ASPECTS OF THE VANDERBILT FORTUNE

The juggling of railroads and the virtual seizure of coal mines were by no means the only accomplishments of the Vanderbilt family in the years under consideration. Colorless as was the third generation, undistinguished by any marked characteristic, extremely commonplace in its conventions, it yet proved itself a worthy successor of Commodore Vanderbilt. The lessons he had taught of how to appropriate wealth were duly followed by his descendants, and all of the ancestral methods were closely adhered to by the third generation. Whatever might be its pretensions to a certain integrity and to a profound respectability, there was really no difference between its methods and those of the Commodore. Times had changed; that was all. What had once been regarded as outright theft and piracy were now cloaked under high-sounding phrases as "corporate extension" and "high finance" and other catchwords calculated to lull public suspicion and resentment. A refinement of phraseology had set in; and it served its purpose.

Concomitantly, while executing the transactions already described, the Vanderbilts of the third generation put through many others, both large and small, which were converted into further heaps of wealth. An enumeration of all of these diverse frauds would necessitate a tiresome presentation. A few examples will suffice.

The small frauds were but lesser in relation to the

larger. At this period of the economic development of the country, when immense thefts were being consummated, a fraud had to rise to the dignity of at least fifty million dollars to be regarded a large one. The law, it is true, proscribed any theft involving more than $25 as grand larceny, but it was law applying to the poor only, and operative on them exclusively. The inordinately rich were beyond all law, seeing that they could either manufacture it, or its interpretation, at will. Among the conspicuous, audacious capitalists the fraud of a few paltry millions shrank to the modesty of a small, cursory, off-hand operation. Yet, in the aggregate, these petty frauds constituted great results, and for that reason were valued accordingly.

## AN $8,000,000 AREA CONFISCATED.

Such a slight fraud was, for instance, the Vanderbilts' confiscation of an entire section of New York City. In 1887 they decided that they had urgent and particular need for railroad yard purposes of a sweep of streets from Sixtieth street to Seventy-second street along the Hudson River Railroad division. What if this property had been bought, laid out and graded by the city at considerable expense? The Vanderbilts resolved to have it and get it for nothing. Under special forms of law dictated by them they thereupon took it. The method was absurdly easy.

Ever compliant to their interests, and composed as usual of men retained by them or responsive to their influences, the Legislature of 1887 passed an act compelling the city authorities to close up the required area of streets. Then the city officials, fully as accommodating, turned the property over to the exclusive, and practically perpetual, use of the New York Central and Hudson River Railroad. With the profusest expressions of regard for the public interests, the railroad officials did not in the slightest demur at signing an agreement with the municipal authorities. In this paper they pledged themselves to coöperate with the city in conferring upon the Board of Street Openings the right to reopen any of the streets at any time. This agreement was but a decoy for immediate popular effect. No such reopening ordinance was ever passed; the streets remained closed to the public which, theoretically at least, was left with the title. In fact, the memorandum of the agreement strangely disappeared from the Corporation Counsel's office, and did not turn up until twenty years later, when it was accidentally and most mysteriously discovered in the Lenox Library. Whence came it to this curious repository? The query remains unanswered.

For seventeen and a half acres of this confiscated land, comprising about three hundred and fifty city lots, now valued at a round $8,000,000, the New York Central and Hudson River Railroad has not paid a cent in rental or taxes since the act of 1887 was passed. On the island of Manhattan alone 70,000 poor families are every year evicted for inability to pay rent — a continuous and horribly tragic event well worth comparing with the preposterous facility with which the great possessing classes everywhere either buy or defy law, and confiscate when it suits them. So cunningly drafted was the act of 1887 that while New York City was obliged to give the exclusive use of this large stretch of property to the company, yet the title to the property — the empty name — remained vested in the city. This being so, a corporation counsel complaisantly decided that the railroad company could not be taxed so long as the city owned the title.[1]

Another of what may be called — for purposes of distinction — the numerous small frauds at this time, was that foisting upon New York City the cost of replacing the New York Central's masonry viaduct approaches with a fine steel elevated system. This fraud cost the public treasury about $1,200,000, quite a sizable sum, it will be admitted, but one nevertheless of pitiful proportions in comparison with previous and later transactions of the Vanderbilt family.

We have seen how, in 1872, Commodore Vanderbilt put through the Legislature an act forcing New York City to pay $4,000,000 for improving the railroad's roadway on Park avenue. His grandsons now repeated his method. In 1892 the United States Government was engaged in dredging a ship canal through the Harlem River. The Secretary of War, having jurisdiction of all navigable waters, issued a mandate to the New York Central to raise its bridge to a given height, so as to permit the passing under of large vessels.

To comply with this order it was necessary to raise the track structure both north and south of the Harlem River. Had an ordinary citizen, upon receiving an order from the authorities to make improvements or alterations in his property, attempted to compel the city to pay all or any part of the cost, he would have been laughed at or summarily dealt with. The Vanderbilts were not ordinary property holders. Having the power

---

[1] Minutes of the New York City Board of Estimate and Apportionment — Financial and Franchise Matters, 1907 : 1071-1085. " It will thus be seen," reported Harry P. Nichols, Engineer-in-Charge of the Franchise Bureau, " that the railroad is at present, and has been for twenty years, occupying more than three hundred city lots, or something less than twenty acres, without compensation to the city."

to order legislatures to do their bidding, they now proceeded to imitate their grandfather, and compel the city
to pay the greater portion of the cost of supplying them
with a splendid steel elevated structure.

### PUBLIC TAXATION TO SUPPLY PRIVATE CAPITAL.

The Legislature of 1892 was thoroughly responsive.
This was a Legislature which was not merely corrupt,
but brazenly and frankly so, as was proved by the scandalous openness with which various spoliative measures
were rushed through.

An act was passed compelling New York City to pay
one-half of the cost of the projected elevated approaches
up to the sum of $1,600,000. New York City was thus
forced to pay $800,000 for constructing that portion
south of the Harlem River. If, so the law read on,
the cost exceeded the estimate of $800,000, then the New
York Central was to pay the difference. Additional
provision was made for the compelling of New York
City to pay for the building of the section north of the
Harlem River. But who did the work of contracting
and building, and who determined what the cost was?
The railroad company itself. It charged what it pleased
for material and work, and had complete control of the
disbursing of the appropriations. The city's supervising
commissions had, perforce, to accept its arbitrary demands, and lacked all power to question, or even scruti-
nize, its reports of expenditures. Apart from the New
York Central's officials, no one to-day knows what the
actual cost has been, except as stated by the company.

South of the Harlem River this reported cost has been
$800,000, north of the Harlem River $400,000. At practically no expense to themselves, the Vanderbilts ob-

**CORNELIUS VANDERBILT,**
Grandson of Commodore Vanderbilt.

tained a massive four-track elevated structure, running
for miles over the city streets.  The people of the city
of New York were forced to bear a compulsory taxation
of $1,200,000 without getting the slightest equivalent for
it.  The Vanderbilts own these elevated approaches absolutely; not a cent's worth of claim or title have the
people in them.  Together with the $4,000,000 of public
money extorted by Commodore Vanderbilt in 1872, this
sum of $1,200,000 makes a total amount of $5,200,000
plucked from the public treasury under form of law to
make improvements in which the people who have footed
the bill have not a moiety of ownership.[2]  The Vanderbilts have capitalized these terminal approaches as though
they had been built with private money.[3]

At this point a significant note may be made in passing.
While these and other huge frauds were going on, Cornelius Vanderbilt was conspicuously presenting himself
as a most ardent " reformer " in politics.  He was, for
instance, a distinguished member of the Committee of
Seventy, organized in 1894, to combat and overthrow
Tammany corruption!  Such, as we have repeatedly
observed, is the quality of the men who compose the
bourgeois reform movements.  For the most part great
rogues, they win applause and respectability by virtu-

[2] The facts as to the expenses incurred under the act of 1892
were stated to the author by Ernest Harvier, a member of the
Change of Grade Commission representing New York City
in supervising the work.

[3] The New York Central has long compelled the New York,
New Haven and Hartford Railroad to pay seven cents toll for
every passenger transported south of Woodlawn, and also one-
third of the maintenance cost, including interest, of the terminal.
In reporting an effort of the New York, New Haven and Hartford Railroad to have these terms modified, the New York
" Times " stated in its financial columns, issue of December 25,
1908: " As matters now stand the New Haven, without its
consent, is forced to bear one-third of the charge arising from
*the increased capital invested in the Central's terminal.*"

ously denouncing petty, vulgar political corruption which they themselves often instigate, and thus they divert attention from their own extensive rascality.

## A MULTITUDE OF ACQUISITIONS.

Why tempt exhaustion by lingering upon a multitude of other frauds which went to increase the wealth and possessions of the Vanderbilt family? One after another — often several simultaneously — they were put through, sometimes surreptitiously, again with overt effrontery. Legislative measures in New York and many other States were drafted with such skill that sly provisions allowing the greatest frauds were concealed in the enactments; and the first knowledge that the plundered public frequently had of them was after they had already been accomplished. These frauds comprised corrupt laws that gave, in circumstances of notorious scandal, tracts of land in the Adirondack Mountains to railroad companies now included in the Vanderbilt system. They embraced laws, and still more laws, exempting this or that stock or property from taxation, and laws making presents of valuable franchises and allowing further consolidations. Laws were enacted in New York State the effects of which were to destroy the Erie Canal (which has cost the people of New York State $100,000,000) as a competitor of the New York Central Railroad. All of these and many other measures will be skimmed over by a simple reference, and attention focussed on a particularly large and notable transaction by which William K. Vanderbilt in 1898 added about $50,000,000 to his fortune at one superb swoop.

The Vanderbilt ownership of various railroad systems has been of an intricate, roundabout nature. A group of railroads, the majority of the stock of which was actually owned by the Vanderbilt family, were nominally put under the ownership of different, and apparently distinct, railroad companies. This devious arrangement was intended to conceal the real ownership, and to have a plausible claim in counteracting the charge that many railroads were concentrated in one ownership, and were combined in monopoly in restraint of trade. The plan ran thus: The Vanderbilts owned the New York Central and Hudson River Railroad. In turn this railroad, as a corporation, owned the greater part of the $50,000,-000 stock of the Lake Shore Railroad. The Lake Shore, in turn, owned the control, or a chief share of the control, of other railroads, and thus on.

In 1897, William K. Vanderbilt began clandestinely campaigning to combine the New York Central and the Lake Shore under one definite, centralized management. This plan was one in strict harmony with the trend of the times, and it had the undoubted advantage of promising to save large sums in managing expenses. But this anticipated retrenchment was not the main incentive. A dazzling opportunity was presented of checking in an immense amount in loot. The grandson again followed his eminent grandfather's teachings; his plan was nothing more than a repetition of what the old Commodore had done in his consolidations.

During the summer and fall of 1897 the market gymnastics of Lake Shore stock were cleverly manipulated. By the declaration of a seven per cent. dividend the market price of the stock was run up from 115 to about 200. The object of this manipulation was to have a justification for issuing $100,000,000 in three and one-half per cent. New York Central bonds to buy $50,000,-000 of Lake Shore seven per cent. capital stock. By his personal manipulation, William K. Vanderbilt at the same time ballooned the price of New York Central stock.

The purpose was kept a secret until shortly before the plan was consummated on February 4, 1898. On that day William K. Vanderbilt and his subservient directors of the New York Central gathered their corpulent and corporate persons about one table and voted to buy the Lake Shore stock. With due formalities they then adjourned, and moving over to another table, declared themselves in meeting as directors of the Lake Shore Railroad, and solemnly voted to accept the offer.

Presently, however, an awkward and slightly annoying defect was discovered. It turned out that the Stock Corporation law of New York State specifically prohibited the bonded indebtedness of any corporation being more than the value of the capital stock. This discovery was not disconcerting; the obstacle could be easily overcome with some well-distributed generosity. A bill was quickly drawn up to remedy the situation, and hurried to the Legislature then in session at Albany. The Assembly balked and ostentatiously refused to pass it. But after the lapse of a short time the Assembly saw a great new light, and rushed it through on March 3, on which same day it passed the Senate. It was at this precise time that a certain noted lobbyist at Albany somehow showed up, it was alleged, with a fund of $500,000, and members of the Assembly and Senate suddenly revealed evidences of being unusually flush with money.[4]

---

[4] The author is so informed by an official who represented New York City's legal interests at this session and successive Legislative sessions, and who was thoroughly conversant with every move. See Chapter 80, Laws of 1898, Laws of New York, 1898, ii: 142. The amendment declared that Section 24 of the Stock Corporation Law did not apply to a railroad corporation.

A very illuminating transaction, surely, and well deserving of philosophic comment. This, however, will be eschewed, and attention next turned to the manner in which the Vanderbilts, in 1899, obtained control of the Boston and Albany Railroad.

## THE BOSTON AND ALBANY RAILROAD BECOMES THEIRS.

To a great extent this railroad had been built with public funds raised by enforced taxation, the city of Albany contributing $1,000,000, and the State of Massachusetts $4,300,000 of public funds. Originally it looked as if the public interests were fully conserved. But gradually, little by little, predatory corporate interests got in their delicate work, and induced successive legislatures and State officials to betray the public interests. The public holdings of stock were entirely subordinated, so that in time a private corporation secured the practical ownership.

Finally, in 1899, the Legislature of Massachusetts effaced the last vestige of State ownership by giving the Vanderbilts a perpetual lease of this richly profitable railroad for a scant two million dollars' payment a year. During the debate over this act Representative Dean charged in the Legislature that " it is common rumor in the State House that members are receiving $300 apiece for their votes." The acquisition of this railroad enabled the New York Central to make direct connection with Boston, and with much of the New England coast, and added about four hundred miles to the Vanderbilt system. Most of the remainder of the New England territory is subservient to the Boston and Maine Railroad system in which the American Express Company, controlled by the Vanderbilts, owns 30,000 shares.

To pay interest and dividends on the hundreds of millions of dollars of inflated bonds and stock which three generations of the Vanderbilts had issued, and to maintain and enhance their value, it was necessary to keep on increasingly extorting revenues.  The sources of the profits were palpable.  Time after time freight rates were raised, as was more than sufficiently proved in various official investigations, despite denials.  Conjunctively with this process, another method of extortion was the ceaseless one of beating down the wages of the workers to the very lowest point at which they could be hired.  While the Vanderbilts and other magnates were manufacturing law at will, and boldly appropriating, under color of law, colossal possessions in real and personal property, how was the law, as embodied in legislatures, officials and courts acting toward the working class?

### THE GOVERNMENT AN ENGINE OF TYRANNY.

The grievances and protests of the workers aroused no response save the ever-active one of contumely, coercion and violent reprisals.  The treasury of Nation, States and cities, raised by a compulsory taxation falling heavily upon the workers, was at all times at the complete disposal of the propertied interests, who emptied it as fast as it was filled.  The propertiless and jobless were left to starve; to them no helping arm was outstretched, and if they complained, no quarter given.  The State as an institution, while supported by the toil of the producers, was wholly a capitalist State with the capitalists in complete supremacy to fashion and use it as they chose.  They used the State political machinery to plunder the masses, and then, at the slightest tendency on the part of the workers to resist these crushing injustices and burdens, called upon the State to hurry out its armed forces to repress this dangerous discontent.

In Buffalo, in 1890-1891, thirty-one in every hundred destitutes were impoverished because of unemployment, and in New York City twenty-nine in every hundred.[5] Hundreds of millions of dollars of public funds were given outright to the capitalists, but not a cent appropriated to provide work for the unemployed. In the panic of 1893, when millions of men, women and children were out of work, the machinery of government, National, State and municipal, proffered not the least aid, but, on the contrary, sought to suppress agitation and prohibit meetings by flinging the leaders into jail. Basing his conclusions upon the (Aldrich) United States Senate Report of 1893 — a report highly favorable to capitalist interests, and not unexpectedly so, since Senator Aldrich was the recognized Senatorial mouthpiece of the great vested interests — Spahr found that the highest daily wage for all earners, taken in a mass, was $2.04.[6]

More than three-quarters of all the railroad employees in the United States received less than two dollars a day. Large numbers of railroad employees were forced to work from twelve to fourteen hours a day, and their efficiency and stamina thus lowered. Periodically many were laid off in enforced idleness; and appalling numbers were maimed or killed in the course of duty.[7] Injured

[5] "Encyclopedia of Social Reform," Edition of 1897: 1073.
[6] "The Present Distribution of Wealth in The United States."
[7] The report of the Wisconsin Railway Commissioners for 1894, Vol. xiii., says: "In a recent year more railway employees were killed in this country than three times the number of Union men slain at the battle of Lookout Mountain, Missionary Ridge and Orchard Knob combined. . . . In the bloody Crimean War, the British lost 21,000 in killed and wounded — not as many as are slain, maimed and mangled among the railroad men

or slain largely because the railroad corporations refused to expend money in the introduction of improved automatic coupling devices, these workers or their heirs were next confronted by what? The unjust and oppressive provisions of worthless employers' liability laws drafted by corporation attorneys in such a form that the worker or his family generally had almost no claim. The very judges deciding these suits were, as a rule, put on the bench by the railroad corporations.

## MACHINE GUNS FOR THE OVERWORKED.

These deadly conditions prevailed on the Vanderbilt railroads even more than on any others; it was notorious that the Vanderbilt system was not only managed in semi-antiquated ways so far as the operation was concerned, but also that its trainmen were terribly underpaid and overworked.[8] In reply to a continued agitation for better hours on the part of the Vanderbilt employees, the New York Legislature passed an act, in 1892, which apparently limited the working hours of railroad employees to ten a day. There was a gleam of sunshine, but lo! when the act was critically examined after it had become a law, it was found that a "little joker" had been sneaked into its mass of lawyers' terminology. The surreptitious clause ran to this effect: That railroad companies were permitted to exact from their employees overtime work for extra compensation. This practically made the whole law a negation.

of the country in a single year." Various reports of the Interstate Commerce Commission state the same facts.

[8] "Semi-antiquated ways." Only recently the "Railway Age Gazette," issue of January, 1909, styled the New York Central's directors as mostly "concentrated absurdities, physically incompetent, mentally unfit, or largely unresident and inattentive."

So it turned out; for in August, 1892, the switchmen employed by various railroad lines converging at Buffalo struck for shorter hours and more pay. The strike spread, and was meeting with tactical success; the strikers easily persuaded men who had been hired to fill their jobs to quit. What did the Vanderbilts and their allies now do? They fell back upon the old ruse of invoking armed force to suppress what they proclaimed to be violence. They who had bought law and had violated the law incessantly now represented that their property interests were endangered by " mob violence," and prated of the need of soldiers to " restore law and order." It was a serviceable pretext, and was immediately acted upon.

The Governor of New York State obediently ordered out the entire State militia, a force of 8,000, and dispatched it to Buffalo. The strikers were now confronted with bayonets and machine guns. The soldiery summarily stopped the strikers from picketing, that is to say, from attempting to persuade strikebreakers to refrain from taking their places. Against such odds the strike was lost.

If, however, the Vanderbilts could not afford to pay their workers a few cents more in wages a day, they could afford to pay millions of dollars for matrimonial alliances with foreign titles. These excursions into the realm of high-caste European nobility have thus far cost the Vanderbilt family about $15,000,000 or $20,000,000. When impecunious counts, lords, dukes and princes, having wasted the inheritance originally obtained by robbery, and perpetuated by robbery, are on the anxious lookout for marriages with great fortunes, and the American money magnates, satiated with vulgar wealth, aspire to titled connections, the arrangement becomes easy.[9]  Romance can be dispensed with, and the lawyers depended upon to settle the preliminaries.

### TEN MILLIONS FOR A DUKEDOM.

The announcement was made in 1895 that " a marriage had been arranged " between Consuelo, a young daughter of William K. Vanderbilt, and the Duke of Marlborough.  The wedding ceremony was one of showy splendor; millions of dollars in gifts were lavished upon the couple.  Other millions in cash, wrenched also from the labor of the American working population, went to rehabilitate and maintain Blenheim House, with its prodigal cost of reconstruction, its retinue of two hundred servants, and its annual expense roll of $100,000.  Millions more flowed out from the Vanderbilt exchequer in defraying the cost of yachts and of innumerable appurtenances and luxuries.  Not less than $2,500,000 was spent in building Sutherland House in London.  Great as was this expense, it was not so serious as to perturb the duchess' father; his $50,000,000 feat of financial legerdemain, in 1898, alone far more than made up for these extravagant outlays.  The Marlborough title was an expensive one; it turned out to be a better thing to retain than the man who bore it; after a thirteen years' compact, the couple decided to separate for " good and sufficient reasons," into which it is not our business to inquire.  All told, the Marlborough dukedom had cost William K. Vanderbilt, it was said, fully $10,000,000.

Undeterred by Cousin Consuelo's experience, Gladys

[9] More than 500 American women have married titled foreigners.  The sum of about $220,000,000, it is estimated (1909), has followed them to Europe.

THE DUCHESS OF MARLBOROUGH,
Daughter of William K. Vanderbilt.

Vanderbilt, a daughter of Cornelius, likewise allied herself with a title by marrying, in 1908, Count Laslo Szechenyi, a sprig of the Hungarian feudal nobility. "The wedding," naively reported a scribe, " was characterized by elegant simplicity, and was witnessed by only three hundred relatives and intimate friends of the bride and bridegroom." The " elegant simplicity " consisted of gifts, the value of which was estimated at fully a million dollars, and a costly ceremony. If the bride had beauty, and the bridegroom wit, no mention of them was made; the one fact conspicuously emphasized was the all-important one of the bride having a fortune " in her own right " of about $12,000,000.

The precise sum which made the Count eager to share his title, no one knew except the parties to the transaction. Her father had died, in 1899, leaving a fortune nominally reaching about $100,000,000. Its actual proportions were much greater. It had long been customary on the part of the very rich, as the New York State Board of Tax Commissioners pointed out, in 1903, to evade the inheritance tax in advance by various fraudulent devices. One of these was to inclose stocks or money in envelopes and apportion them among the heirs, either at the death bed, or by subsequent secret delivery.[10]

Like his father, Cornelius Vanderbilt had died of apoplexy. In his will he had cut off his eldest son, Cornelius, with but a puny million dollars. And the reason for this parental sternness? He had disapproved of Cornelius' choice in marriage. To his son, Alfred, the unrelenting multimillionaire left the most of his fortune, with a showering of many millions upon his widow, upon Reginald, another son, and upon his two daughters.

[10] See Annual Report of the New York State Board of Tax Commissioners, New York Senate Document, No. 5, 1903: 10.

Cornelius objected to the injustice and hardship of being
left a beggar with but a scanty million, and threatened
a legal contest, whereupon Alfred, pitying the dire straits
to which Brother Cornelius had been reduced, presented
him with six or seven millions with which to ease the
biting pangs of want.

Marriages with titled foreigners have proved a drain
upon the Vanderbilt fortune, although, thanks to their
large share in the control of laws and industrial institutions, the Vanderbilts possess at all times the power of
recouping themeselves at volition.  The American marriages, on the other hand, contracted by this family, have
interlinked other great fortunes with theirs.

One of the Vanderbilt buds married Harry Payne
Whitney, whose father, William C. Whitney, left a large
fortune, partly drawn from the Standard Oil Company,
and in part from an industrious career of corruption and
theft.  The elder Whitney, according to facts revealed
in many official investigations and lawsuits, debauched
legislatures and common councils into giving him and
his associates public franchises for street railways and
for other public utilities, and he stole outright tens of
millions of dollars in the manipulation of the street railways in various cities.  His crimes, and those of his
associates, were of such boldness and magnitude that
even the cynical business classes were moved to astonishment.[11]  Cornelius Vanderbilt, jr., married a daughter
of R. T. Wilson, a multimillionaire, whose fortune came
to a great extent from the public franchises of Detroit.
The initial and continued history of the securing and
exploitation of the street railway and other franchises
of that city has constituted a solid chapter of the most

[11] For a detailed account see that part of this work, "Great
Fortunes from Public Franchises."

**CORNELIUS VANDERBILT,**
Great-Grandson of Commodore Vanderbilt.

flagrant fraud. William K. Vanderbilt, jr., married a daughter of the multimillionaire Senator Fair, of California, whose fortune, dug from mines, bought him a seat in the United States Senate. Thus, various multimillionaire fortunes have been interconnected by these American marriages.

## DIVERSITY OF THE VANDERBILT POSSESSIONS.

The fortune of the Vanderbilt family, at the present writing, is represented by the most extensive and different forms of property. Railroads, street railways, electric lighting systems, mines, industrial plants, express companies, land, and Government, State and municipal bonds — these are some of the forms. From one industrial plant alone — the Pullman Company — the Vanderbilts draw millions in revenue yearly. Formerly they owned their own palace car company, the Wagner, but it was merged with the Pullman. The frauds and extortions of the Pullman Company have been sufficiently dealt with in the particular chapter on Marshall Field. In the far-away Philippine Islands the Vanderbilts are engaged, with other magnates, in the exploitation of both the United States Government and the native population. The Visayan Railroad numbers one of the Vanderbilts among its directors. This railroad has already received a Government subsidy of $500,000, in addition to the free gift of a perpetual franchise, on the ground that " the railroad was necessary to the development of the archipelago."

But the Vanderbilts' principal property consists of the New York Central Railroad system. The Union Pacific Railroad, controlled by the Harriman-Standard Oil interests, now owns $14,000,000 of stock in the New York

Central system, and has directors on the governing board.
The probabilities are that the voting power of the New
York Central, the Lake Shore and other Vanderbilt lines
is passing into the hands of the Standard Oil interests,
of which Harriman was both a part and an ally.  This
signifies that it is only a question of a short time when
all or most of the railroads of the United States will be
directed by one all-powerful and all-embracing trust.

But this does not by any means denote that the Vanderbilts have been stripped of their wealth.  However
much they may part with their stock, which gives the
voting power, it will be found that, like William H. Vanderbilt, they hold a stupendous amount in railroad, and
other kinds of, bonds.  As the Astors and other rich families were perfectly willing, in 1867, to allow Commodore
Vanderbilt to assume the management of the New York
Central on the ground that under his bold direction
their profits and loot would be greater, so the lackadaisical
Vanderbilts of the present generation perhaps likewise
looked upon Harriman, who proved his ability to accomplish vast fraudulent stock-watering operations and consolidations, and to oust lesser magnates.  The New York
Central, at this writing, still remains a Vanderbilt property, not so distinctively so as it was twenty years ago,
yet strongly enough under the Vanderbilt domination.
According to Moody, this railroad's net annual income
in 1907 was $34,000,000.[12]  In alluringly describing its
present and prospective advantages and value Moody
went on:

" To begin with, it has entry into the heart of New
York City, with extensive passenger and freight terminals, all of which are bound to be of steadily increasing

[12] " Moody's Magazine," issue of August, 1908.

worth as the years go by, as New York continues to
grow in population and wealth. It has, in addition, a
practically 'water grade' line all the way from New
York to Chicago, and, therefore, for all time must necessarily have a great advantage over lines like the Erie,
the Lackawanna and others with heavy grades, many
curves, etc. It has a myriad of small feeders and
branches in growing and populous parts of the State of
New York, as well as in the sections further to the west.
It touches the Great Lakes at various points, operates
water transportation for freight to all parts of the lakes;
enters Chicago over its own tracks and competes aggressively with the Pennsylvania for all traffic to and
from all parts of the Mississippi Valley and the West
and Southwest. It is in no danger from disastrous competition in its own chosen territory, therefore, and constantly receives income of vast importance through a network of feeders which penetrate the territory of some of
the largest of its rivals."

## THE SORT OF ABILITY DISPLAYED.

The particular kind of ability by which one man, followed by his descendants, obtained the controlling ownership of this great railroad system, and of other properties, has been herein adequately set forth. Long has it
been the custom to attribute to Commodore Vanderbilt
and successive generations of Vanderbilts an almost su-
pernatural "constructive genius," and to explain by that
glib phrase their success in getting hold of their colossal
wealth. This explanation is clumsy fiction that at once
falls to pieces under historical scrutiny. The moment a
genuine investigation is begun into the facts, the glamour

of superior ability and respectability evaporates, and the Vanderbilt fortune stands out, like all other fortunes, as the product of a continuous chain of frauds.

Just as fifty years ago Commodore Vanderbilt was blackmailing his original millions without molestation by law, so to-day the Vanderbilts are pursuing methods outside the pale of law. Not all of the facts have been given, by any means; only the most important have been included in these chapters. For one thing, no mention has been made of their repeated violations of a law prohibiting the granting of rebates — a law which was stripped of its imprisonment clause by the railroad magnates, and made punishable by fine only. Time and time again in recent years has the New York Central been proved guilty in the courts of violating even this emasculated law. From the very inception of the Vanderbilt fortune the chronicle is the same, and ever the same — legalized theft by purchase of law, and lawlessness by evasion or defiance of law. With fraud it began, by fraud it has been increased and extended and perpetuated, and by fraud it is held.

# CHAPTER IX

## THE RISE OF THE GOULD FORTUNE

The greater part of this commanding fortune was originally heaped up, as was that of Commodore Vanderbilt, in about fifteen years, and at approximately the same time. One of the most powerful fortunes in the United States, it now controls, or has exercised a dominant share of the control, over more than 18,000 miles of railway, the total ownership of which is represented by considerably more than a billion dollars in stocks and bonds. The Gould fortune is also either openly or covertly paramount in many telegraph, transatlantic cable, mining, land and industrial corporations.

Its precise proportions no one knows except the Gould family itself. That it reaches many hundreds of millions of dollars is fairly obvious, although what is its exact figure is a matter not to be easily ascertained. In the flux of present economic conditions, which, so far as the control of the resources of the United States is concerned, have simmered down to desperate combats between individual magnates, or contesting sets of magnates, the proportions of great fortunes, especially those based upon railroads and industries, constantly tend to vary.

In the years 1908 and 1909 the Gould fortune, if report be true, was somewhat diminished by the onslaughts of that catapultic railroad baron, E. H. Harriman, who unceremoniously seized a share of the voting control of some of the railroad systems long controlled by the Goulds. Despite this reported loss, the Gould fortune is an active, aggressive and immense one, vested with the most extensive power, and embracing hundreds of millions of dollars in cash, land, palaces, or profit-producing property in the form of bonds and stocks. Its influence and ramifications, like those of the Vanderbilt and of other huge fortunes, penetrate directly or indirectly into every inhabited part of the United States, and into Mexico and other foreign countries.

### JAY GOULD'S BOYHOOD.

The founder of this fortune was Jay Gould, father of the present holding generation. He was the son of a farmer in Delaware County, New York, and was born in 1836. As a child his lot was to do various chores on his father's farm. In driving the cows he had to go barefoot, perforce, by reason of poverty, and often thistles bruised his feet — a trial which seems to have left such a poignant and indelible impression upon his mind that when testifying before a United States Senate investigating committee forty years later he pathetically spoke of it with a reminiscent quivering. His father was, indeed, so poor that he could not afford to let him go to the public school. The lad, however, made an arrangement with a blacksmith by which he received board in return for certain clerical services. These did not interfere with his attending school. When fifteen, he became a clerk in a country store, a task which, he related, kept him at work from six o'clock in the morning until ten o'clock at night. It is further related that by getting up at three o'clock in the morning and studying mathematics for three years, he learned the rudiments of surveying.

According to Gould's own story, an engineer who was making a map of Ulster County hired him as an assistant at "twenty dollars a month and found." This engagement somehow (we are not informed how) turned out unsatisfactorily. Gould was forced to support himself by making "noon marks" for the farmers. To two other young men who had worked with him upon the map of Ulster County, Gould (as narrated by himself) sold his interest for $500, and with this sum as capital he proceeded to make maps of Albany and Delaware counties. These maps, if we may believe his own statement, he sold for $5,000.

## HE GOES INTO THE TANNING BUSINESS.

Subsequently Gould went into the tanning business in Pennsylvania with Zadoc Pratt, a New York merchant, politician and Congressman of a certain degree of note at the time.[1]  Pratt, it seems, was impressed by young Gould's energy, skill and smooth talk, and supplied the necessary capital of $120,000. Gould, as the phrase goes, was an excellent bluff; and so dexterously did he manipulate and hoodwink the old man that it was quite some time before Pratt realized what was being done. Finally, becoming suspicious of where the profits from the Gouldsboro tannery (named after Gould) were

[1] Pratt was regarded as one of the leading agricultural experts of his day. His farm of three hundred and sixty-five acres, at Prattsville, New York, was reputed to be a model. A paper of his, descriptive of his farm, and containing woodcut engravings, may be found in U. S. Senate Documents, Second Session, Thirty-seventh Congress, 1861-62, v: 411-415.

going, Pratt determined upon some overhauling and investigating.

Gould was alert in forestalling this move. During his visits to New York City, he had become acquainted with Charles M. Leupp, a rich leather merchant. Gould prevailed upon Leupp to buy out Pratt's interest. When Gould returned to the tannery, he found that Pratt had been analyzing the ledger. A scene followed, and Pratt demanded that Gould buy or sell the plant. Gould was ready, and offered him $60,000, which was accepted. Immediately Gould drew upon Leupp for the money. Leupp likewise became suspicious after a time, and from the ascertained facts, had the best of grounds for becoming so. The sequel was a tragic one. One night, in the panic of 1857, Leupp shot and killed himself in his fine mansion at Madison avenue and Twenty-fifth street. His suicide caused a considerable stir in New York City.[2]

### HE BUYS RAILROAD BONDS WITH HIS STEALINGS.

Three years later, in 1860, Gould set up as a leather merchant in New York City; the New York directory for that year contains this entry: " Jay Gould, leather merchant, 39 Spruce street; house Newark." For several years after this his name did not appear in the directory.

He had been, however, edging his way into the railroad

[2] Although later in Gould's career it was freely charged that he had been the cause of Leupp's suicide, no facts were *officially* brought out to prove the charge. The coroner's jury found that Leupp had been suffering from melancholia, superinduced, doubtless, by business reverses.

Even Houghton, however, in his flamboyantly laudatory work describes Gould's cheating of Pratt and Leupp, and Leupp's suicide. According to Houghton, Leupp's friends ascribed the cause of the act to Gould's treachery. See " Kings of Fortune," 265-266.

business with the sums that he had stolen from Pratt and Leupp. At the very time that Leupp committed suicide, Gould was buying the first mortgage bonds of the Rutland and Washington Railroad — a small line, sixty-two miles long, running from Troy, New York, to Rutland, Vermont. These bonds, which he purchased for ten cents on the dollar, gave him control of this bankrupt railroad. He hired men of managerial ability, had them improve the railroad, and he then consolidated it with other small railroads, the stock of which he had bought in.

With the passing of the panic of 1857, and with the incoming of the stupendous corruption of the Civil War period, Gould was able to manipulate his bonds and stock until they reached a high figure. With a part of his profits from his speculation in the bonds of the Rutland and Washington Railroad, he bought enough stock of the Cleveland and Pittsburg Railroad to give him control of that line. This he manipulated until its price greatly rose, when he sold the line to the Pennsylvania Railroad Company. In these transactions there were tortuous substrata of methods, of which little to-day can be learned, except for the most part what Gould himself testified to in 1883, which testimony he took pains to make as favorable to his past as possible.

His career from 1867 onward stood out in the fullest prominence; a multitude of official reports and investigations and court records contribute a translucent record. He became invested with a sinister distinction as the most cold-blooded corruptionist, spoliator, and financial pirate of his time; and so thoroughly did he earn this reputation that to the end of his days it confronted him at every step, and survived to become the standing reproach and terror of his descendants. For nearly a half century the very name of Jay Gould has been a persisting jeer and by-word, an object of popular contumely and hatred, the signification of every foul and base crime by which greed triumphs.

## WHY THIS BIASED VIEW OF GOULD'S CAREER?

Yet, it may well be asked now, even if for the first time, why has Jay Gould been plucked out as a special object of opprobrium? What curious, erratic, unstable judgment is this that selects this one man as the scapegoat of commercial society, while deferentially allowing his business contemporaries the fullest measure of integrity and respectability?

Monotonous echoes of one another, devoid of understanding, writer has followed writer in harping undiscriminatingly upon Jay Gould's crimes. His career has been presented in the most forbidding colors; and in order to show that he was an abnormal exception, and not a familiar type, his methods have been darkly contrasted with those of such illustrious capitalists as the Astors, the Vanderbilts, and others.

Thus, has the misinformed thing called public opinion been shaped by these scribbling purveyors of fables; and this public opinion has been taught to look upon Jay Gould's career as an exotic, "horrible example," having nothing in common with the careers of other founders of large fortunes. The same generation habitually addicted to cursing the memory of Jay Gould, and taunting his children and grandchildren with the reminders of his thefts, speaks with traditional respect of the wealth of such families as the Astors and the Vanderbilts. Yet the cold truth is, as has been copiously proved, John Jacob Astor was proportionately as notorious a swindler in his day as Gould was in his; and as for Commodore Vander-

bilt, he had already made blackmailing on a large scale
a safe art before Gould was out of his teens.

Gould has been impeached as one of the most audacious
and successful buccaneers of modern times.  Without
doubt he was so; a freebooter who, if he could not appropriate millions, would filch thousands; a pitiless
human carnivore, glutting on the blood of his numberless
victims; a gambler destitute of the usual gambler's code
of fairness in abiding by the rules; an incarnate fiend of
a Machiavelli in his calculations, his schemes and am-
bushes, his plots and counterplots.

But it was only in degree, and not at all in kind, that
he differed from the general run of successful wealth
builders.  The Vanderbilts committed thefts of as great
an enormity as he, but they gradually managed to weave
around themselves an exterior of protective respectability.
All sections of the capitalist class, in so fiercely reviling
Gould, reminded one of the thief, who, to divert attention
from himself, joins with the pursuing crowd in loudly
shouting, " Stop thief! "   We shall presently see whether
this comparison is an exaggerated one or not.


## THE TEACHINGS OF HIS ENVIRONMENT.

To understand the incentives and methods of Gould's
career, it is necessary to know the endemic environment
in which he grew up and flourished, and its standards
and spirit.  He, like others of his stamp, were, in a great
measure, but products of the times; and it is not the man
so much as the times that are of paramount interest, for
it is they which supply the explanatory key.   In preceding
chapters repeated insights have been given into the
methods not merely of one phase, but of all phases, of
capitalist formulas and processes.  At the outset, how-

ever, in order to approach impartially this narrative of the Gould fortune, and to get a clear perception of the dominant forces of his generation, a further presentation of the business-class methods of that day will be given.

As a young man what did Jay Gould see? He saw, in the first place, that society, as it was organized, had neither patience nor compassion for the very poverty its grotesque system created. Prate its higher classes might of the blessings of poverty; and they might spread broadcast their prolix homilies on the virtues of a useful life, "rounded by an honorable poverty." But all of these teachings were, in one sense, chatter and nonsense; the very classes which so unctuously preached them were those who most strained themselves to acquire all of the wealth that they possibly could. In another sense, these teachings proved an effective agency in the infusing into the minds of the masses of established habits of thought calculated to render them easy and unresisting victims to the rapacity of their despoilers.

From these "upper classes" proceeded the dictation of laws; and the laws showed (as they do now) what the real, unvarnished attitude of these fine, exhorting moralists was towards the poor. Poverty was virtually prescribed as a crime. The impoverished were regarded in law as paupers, and so repugnant a term of odium was that of pauper, so humilating its significance and treatment, that great numbers of the destitute preferred to suffer and die in want and silence rather than avail themselves of the scanty and mortifying public aid obtainable only by acknowledging themselves paupers.

Sickness, disability, old age, and even normal life, in poverty were a terrifying prospect. The one sure way of escaping it was to get and hold wealth. The only guarantee of security was wealth, provided its possessor could keep it intact against the maraudings of his own class. Every influence conspired to drive men into making desperate attempts to break away from the stigma and thraldom of poverty, and gain economic independence and social prestige by the ownership of wealth.

But how was this wealth to be obtained? Here another set of influences combined with the first set to suppress or shatter whatever doubts, reluctance or scruples the aspirant might have. The acquisitive young man soon saw that toiling for the profit of others brought nothing but poverty to himself; perhaps at the most, some small savings that were constantly endangered. To get wealth he must not only exploit his fellow men, he found, but he must not be squeamish in his methods. This lesson was powerfully and energetically taught on every hand by the whole capitalist class.

Conventional writers have descanted with a show of great indignation upon Gould's bribing of legislative bodies and upon his cheatings and swindlings. Without adverting again to the corruption, reaching far back into the centuries, existing before his time, we shall simply describe some of the conditions that as a young man he witnessed or which were prevalent synchronously with his youth.

Whatever sphere of business was investigated, there it was at once discovered that wealth was being amassed, not only by fraudulent methods, but by methods often a positive peril to human life itself. Whether large or small trader, these methods were the same, varying only in degree.

### ALL BUSINESS REEKED WITH FRAUD.

A Congressional committee, probing, in 1847-48, into frauds in the sale of drugs found that there was scarcely a wholesale or retail druggist who was not consciously selling spurious drugs which were a menace to human life.   Dr. M. J. Bailey, United States Examiner of Drugs at the New York Custom House, was one of the many expert witnesses who testified.   " More than one-half of many of the most important chemical and medicinal preparations," Dr. Bailey stated, " together with large quantities of crude drugs, come to us so much adulterated as to render them not only worthless as a medicine, but often dangerous."   These drugs were sold throughout the United States at high prices.[3]   There is not a single record of any criminal action pressed against those who profited from selling this poisonous stuff.

The manufacture and sale of patent medicines were attended with the grossest frauds.   At that time, to a much greater extent than now, the newspapers profited more (comparatively) from the publication of patent medicine advertisements; and even after a Congressional committee had fully investigated and exposed the nature of these nostrums, the newspapers continued publishing the alluring and fraudulent advertisements.

After showing at great length the deceptive and dangerous ingredients used in a large number of patent medicines, the Committee on the Judiciary of the House of Representatives went on in its report of February 6, 1849: " The public prints, without exception, published these promises and commendations.   The annual [advertising] fee for publishing Brandeth's pills has amounted to $100,000.   Morrison paid more than twice as much for the advertisement of his never-dying hygiene."   The com-

[3] Report of Select Committee on the Importation of Drugs. House Reports, Thirtieth Congress, First Session, 1847–48, Report No. 664 : 9.   In a previous chapter, other extracts from this report have been given showing in detail what many of these fraudulent practices were.

mittee described how Morrison's nostrums often contained powerful poisons, and then continued: " Morrison is forgotten, and Brandeth is on the high road to the same distinction.  T. W. Conway, from the lowest obscurity, became worth millions from the sale of his nostrums, and rode in triumph through the streets of Boston in his coach and six.  A stable boy in New York was enrolled among the wealthiest in Philadelphia by the sale of a panacea which contains both mercury and arsenic.  Innumerable similar cases can be adduced."[4]  Not a few multimillionaire families of to-day derive their wealth from the enormous profits made by their fathers and grandfathers from the manufacture and sale of these poisonous medicines.

### SUCCESS AS GOULD LEARNED IT.

The frauds among merchants and manufacturers reached far more comprehensive and permeating proportions.  In periods of peace these fraudulent methods were nauseating enough, but in times of war they were inexpressibly repellant and ghastly.  During the Mexican War the Northern shoe manufacturers dumped upon the army shoes which were of so inferior a make that they could not be sold in the private market, and these shoes were found to be so absolutely worthless that it is on record that the American army in Mexico threw them away upon the sands in disgust.  But it was during the Civil War that Northern capitalists of every kind coined fortunes from the national disasters, and from the blood of the very armies fighting for their interests.

In the chapters on the Vanderbilt fortune, it has been

[4] Report No. 52.  Reports of Committees, Thirtieth Congress, Second Sess., 1: 31.

shown how Commodore Vanderbilt and other shipping merchants fraudulently sold or leased to the Government for exorbitant sums, ships for the transportation of soldiers — ships so decayed or otherwise unseaworthy, that they had to be condemned.  In those chapters such facts were given as applied mainly to Vanderbilt; in truth, however, they constituted but a mere part of the gory narrative.  While Vanderbilt, as the Government agent, was leasing or buying rotten ships, and making millions of dollars in loot by collusion, the most conspicuous and respectable shipping merchants of the time were unloading their old hulks upon the Government at extortionate prices.

One of the most ultra-respectable merchants of the time, ranked of high commercial standing and austere social prestige, was, for instance, Marshall O. Roberts.  This was the identical Roberts so deeply involved in the great mail-subsidy frauds.  This was also the same sanctimonious Roberts, who, as has been brought out in the chapters on the Astor fortune, joined with John Jacob Astor and others in signing a testimonial certifying to the honesty of the Tweed Regime.  A select Congressional committee, inquiring into Government contracts in 1862-63, brought forth volumes of facts that amazed and sickened a committee accustomed to ordinary political corruption.  Here is a sample of the testimony:  Samuel Churchman, a Government vessel expert engaged by Welles, Secretary of the Navy, told in detail how Roberts and other merchants and capitalists had contrived to palm off rotten ships on the Government; and, in his further examination on January 3, 1863, Churchman was asked:

Q. Did Roberts sell or charter any other boats to the Government?

A. Yes, sir. He sold the Winfield Scott and the Union to the Government.

Q. For how much?

A. One hundred thousand dollars each, and one was totally lost and the other condemned a few days after they went to sea.[5]

In the course of later inquiries in the same examination, Churchman testified that the Government had been cheated out of at least $25,000,000 in the chartering and purchase of vessels, and that he based his judgment upon " the chartered and purchased vessels I am acquainted with, and the enormous sums wasted there to my certain knowledge." [6]   This $25,000,000 swindled from the Government in that one item of ships alone formed the basis of many a present plutocratic fortune.

### FRAUD UNDERLIES RESPECTABILITY.

But this was not by any means the only schooling Gould received from the respectable business element. It can be said advisedly that there was not a single avenue of business in which the most shameless frauds were not committed upon both Government and people. The importers and manufacturers of arms scoured Europe to buy up worthless arms, and then cheated the Government out of millions of dollars in supplying those guns and other ordnance, all notoriously unfit for use. " A large proportion of our troops," reported a Congressional Commission in 1862, " are armed with guns of very inferior quality, and tens of thousands of the refuse arms of Europe are at this moment in our arsenals, and thou-

[5] Report of Select Committee to Inquire into Government Contracts, House Reports, Thirty-seventh Congress, Third Session, 1862-63, Report No. 49 : 95.

[6] Ibid., 95-97.

sands more are still to arrive, all unfit." [7]    A Congressional committee appointed, in 1862, to inquire into the
connection between Government employees on the one
hand, and banks and contractors on the other, established
the fact conclusively, that the contractors regularly bribed
Government inspectors in order to have their spurious
wares accepted. [8]

In fact, the ramifications of the prevalent frauds were
so extensive that a number of Congressional committees
had to be appointed at the same time to carry on an
adequate investigation; and even after long inquiries, it
was admitted that but the surface had been scratched.

During the Civil War, prominent merchants, with

[7] House Reports of Committees, Thirty-seventh Congress,
Second Session, 1861-62, vol. ii, Report No. 2: lxxix.

[8] House Reports, Thirty-seventh Congress, Second Session,
1862-63, Report No. 64. The Chairman of this committee, Representative C. H. Van Wyck, of New York, in reporting to the
House of Representatives on February 23, 1863, made these
opening remarks:

"In the early history of the war it was claimed that frauds
and peculations were unavoidable; that the cupidity of the ava-
ricious would take advantage of the necessities of the nation,
and for a time must revel and grow rich amidst the groans and
griefs of the people; that pressing wants must yield to the extortion of the base; that when the capital was threatened, railroad communication cut off, the most exorbitant prices could
safely be demanded for steam and sailing vessels; that when our
arsenals had been robbed of arms, gold could not be weighed
against cannon and muskets; that the Government must be excused if it suffered itself to be overreached. Yet, after the
lapse of two years, we find the same system of extortion prevailing, and robbery has grown more unblushing in its exactions
as it feels secure in its immunity from punishment, and that
species of fraud which shocked the nation in the spring of 1861
has been increasing. The fitting out of each expedition by water
as well as land is but a refinement upon the extortion and immense profits which preceded it. The freedom from punishment by which the first greedy and rapacious horde were suffered to run at large with ill-gotten gains seems to have demor-
alized too many of those who deal with the Government."— Appendix to The Congressional Globe, Third Session, Thirty-seventh Congress, 1862-63, Part ii: 117.

eloquent outbursts of patriotism, formed union defense committees in various Northern cities, and solicited contributions of money and commodities to carry on the war.   It was disclosed before the Congressional investigating committees that not only did the leading members of these union defense committees turn their patriotism to thrifty account in getting contracts, but that they engaged in great swindles upon the Government in the process.

Thus, Marcellus Hartley, a conspicuous dealer in military goods, and the founder of a multimillionaire fortune,[9] admitted that he had sold a large consignment of Hall's carbines to a member of the New York Union Defense Committee.   In a sudden burst of contrition he went on, " I think the worst thing this Government has been swindled upon has been these confounded Hall's carbines ; they have been elevated in price to $22.50, I think." [10] He could have accurately added that these carbines were absolutely dangerous ; it was found that their mechanism was so faulty that they would shoot off the thumbs of the very soldiers using them.   Hartley was one of the importers who brought over the refuse arms of Europe, and sold them to the Government at extortionate prices. He owned up to having contracts with various of the States (as distinguished from the National Government) for $600,000 worth of these worthless arms.[11]   That corruscating patriot and philanthropic multimillionaire of these present times, J. Pierpont Morgan, was, as we shall

[9] When Marcellus Hartley died in 1902, his personal property alone was appraised at $11,000,000.  His entire fortune was said to approximate $50,000,000.  His chief heir, Marcellus Hartley Dodge, a grandson, married, in 1907, Edith Geraldine Rockefeller, one of the richest heiresses in the world.  Hartley was the principal owner of large cartridge, gun and other factories.
[10] House Report No. 2, etc., 1861-62, vol. ii : 200-204.
[11] Ibid.

see, profiting during the Civil War from the sale of Hall's carbines to the Government.

One of the Congressional committees, investigating contracts for other army material and provisions, found the fullest evidences of gigantic frauds. Exorbitant prices were extorted for tents " which were valueless "; these tents, it appeared, were made from cheap or old " farmers' " drill, regarded by the trade as " truck." Soldiers testified that they " could better keep dry out of them than under." [12] Great frauds were perpetrated in passing goods into the arsenals. One manufacturer in particular, Charles C. Roberts, was awarded a contract for 50,000 haversacks and 50,000 knapsacks. " Every one of these," an expert testified, " was a fraud upon the Government, for they were not linen; they were shoddy." [18] A Congressional committee found that the provisions supplied by contractors were either deleterious or useless. Captain Beckwith, a commissary of subsistence, testified that the coffee was " absolutely good for nothing and is worthless. It is of no use to the Government."

Q. Is the coffee at all merchantable?
A. It is not.
Q. Describe that coffee as nearly as you can.
A. It seems to be a compound of roasted peas, of licorice, and a variety of other substances, with just coffee enough to give it a taste and aroma of coffee.[14]

This committee extracted much further evidence showing how all other varieties of provisions were of the very worst quality, and how " rotten and condemned blankets " in enormous quantities were passed into the army by

[12] House Report No. 64, etc., 1862-63:6.
[18] Ibid.
[14] House Report No. 2, etc., 1861-62, ii: 1459.

bribing the inspectors. It disclosed, at great length, how the railroads in their schedule of freight rates were extorting from the Government fifty per cent. more than from private parties.[15]  Don Cameron, leader of the corrupt Pennsylvania political machine, and a railroad manipulator,[16] was at that time Secretary of War. Whom did he appoint as the supreme official in charge of railroad transportation?  None other than Thomas A. Scott, the vice-president of the Pennsylvania Railroad. Scott, it may be said, was another capitalist whose work has so often been fulsomely described as being that of "a remarkable constructive ability."  The ability he displayed during the Civil War was unmistakable.  With his collusion the railroads extorted right and left.  The committee described how the profits of the railroads after his appointment rose fully fifty per cent. in one year, and how quartermasters and others were bribed to obtain the transportation of regiments.  "This," stated the committee, "illustrates the immense and unnecessary profits which was spirited from the Government and secured to the railroads by the schedule fixed by the vice-president of the Pennsylvania Central under the auspices of Mr. Cameron."[17]

These many millions of dollars extorted in frauds "came," reported the committee, "out of the impoverished and depleted Treasury of the United States, at a time when her every energy and resources were taxed to the utmost to maintain the war."[18]

[15] House Report No. 2, etc., 1861–62, xxix.
[16] He had been involved in at least one scandal investigated by a Pennsylvania Legislative Committee, and also in several dubious railroad transactions in Maryland.
[17] House Report No. 2, etc., 1861–62, xix.  The Pennsylvania Railroad, for example, made in 1862 the sum of $1,350,237.79 more in profits than it did in the preceding year.
[18] Ibid., 4.

These are but a few facts of the glaring fraud and corruption prevailing in every line of mercantile and financial business. Great and audacious as Gould's thefts were later, they could not be put on the same indescribably low plane as those committed during the Civil War by men most of whom succeeded in becoming noted for their fine respectability and " solid fortunes." So many momentous events were taking place during the Civil War, that amid all the preparations, the battles and excitement, those frauds did not arouse that general gravity of public attention which, at any other time, would have inevitably resulted. Consequently, the men who perpetrated them contrived to hide under cover of the more absorbing great events of those years. Gould committed his thefts at a period when the public had little else to preoccupy its attention; hence they loomed up in the popular mind as correspondingly large and important.

### A SPECIMEN OF GOULD'S TUITION.

At the very dawn of his career in 1857, as a railroad owner, Gould had the opportunity of securing valuable and gratuitous instruction in the ways by which railroad projects and land grants were being bribed through Congress. He was then only twenty-one years old, ready to learn, but, of course, without experience in dealing with legislative bodies. But the older capitalists, veterans at bribing, who for years had been corrupting Congress and the Legislatures, supplied him with the necessary information.

Not voluntarily did they do it; their greatest ally was concealment; but one crowd of them had too baldly bribed Congress to vote for an act giving an enormous land grant in Iowa, Minnesota and other states, to the Des

Moines Navigation and Railroad Company.  The facts unearthed must have been a lasting lesson to Gould as to how things were done in the exalted halls of Congress. The charges made an ugly stir throughout the United States, and the House of Representatives, in self defense, had to appoint a special committee to investigate itself.

This committee made a remarkable and unusual report. Ordinarily in charges of corruption, investigating committees were accustomed to reporting innocently that while it might have been true that corruption was used, yet they could find no evidence that members had received bribes; almost invariably such committees put the blame, and the full measure of their futile excoriations, on "the iniquitous lobbyists." But this particular committee, surprisingly enough, handed in no such flaccid, whitewashing report.  It found conclusively that corrupt combinations of members of Congress did exist; and it recommended the expulsion of four members whom it decreed guilty of receiving either money or land in exchange for their votes.  One of these four expelled members, Orasmus B. Matteson, it appeared, was a leader of a corrupt combination; the committee branded him as having arranged with the railroad capitalists to use "a large sum of money [$100,000] and other valuable considerations corruptly." [19]

But it was essentially during the Civil War that Gould received his completest tuition in the great art of seizing property and privileges by bribing legislative bodies. While many sections of the capitalist class were, as we have seen, swindling manifold hundreds of millions of dollars from a hard-pressed country, and reaping fortunes

[19] Reports of Committees, House of Representatives, Thirty-fourth Congress, Third Session, 1856-57.  Report No. 243, Vol. iii.    In subsequent chapters many further details are given of the corruption during this period.

by exploiting the lives of the very defenders of their interests, other sections, equally mouthy with patriotism, were sneaking through Congress and the Legislatures act after act, further legalizing stupendous thefts.

### PATRIOTISM AT FIFTY PER CENT.

Some of these acts, demanded by the banking interests, made the people of the United States pay an almost unbelievable usurious interest for loans. These banking statutes were so worded that nominally the interest did not appear high; in reality, however, by various devices, the bankers, both national and international, were often able to extort from twenty to fifty, and often one hundred per cent., in interest, and this on money which had at some time or somehow been squeezed out of exploited peoples in the United States or elsewhere.

By these laws the bankers were allowed to get an annual payment from the Government of six per cent. interest in gold on the Government bonds that they bought. They could then deposit those same bonds with the Government, and issue their own bank notes against ninety per cent. of the bonds deposited. They drew interest from the Government on the deposited bonds, and at the time charged borrowers an exorbitant rate of interest for the use of the bank notes, which passed as currency.

It was by this system of double interest that they were able to sweep into their coffers hundreds upon hundreds of millions of dollars, not a dollar of which did they earn, and all of which were sweated out of the adversities of the people of the United States. From 1863 to 1878 alone the Government paid out to national banks as interest on bonds the enormous sum of $252,837,-

556.77.[20] On the other hand, the banks were entirely relieved from paying taxes; they secured the passage of a law exempting Government bonds from taxation. Armies were being slaughtered and legions of homes desolated, but it was a rich and safe time for the bankers; a very common occurrence was it for banks to declare dividends of twenty, forty, and sometimes one hundred, per cent.

It was also during the stress of this Civil War period, when the working and professional population of the nation was fighting on the battlefield, or being taxed heavily to support their brothers in arms, that the capitalists who later turned up as owners of various Pacific railroad lines were bribing through Congress acts giving them the most comprehensive perpetual privileges and great grants of money and of land.

Gould saw how all of the others of the wealth seekers were getting their fortunes; and the methods that he now plunged into use were but in keeping with theirs, a little bolder and more brutally frank, perhaps, but nevertheless nothing more than a repetition of what had long been going on in the entire sphere of capitalism.

[20] House Documents, Forty-fifth Congress, Second Session, Ex. Document No. 34, Vol. xiv., containing the reply of Secretary of the Treasury Sherman, in answer to a resolution of the House of Representatives.

# CHAPTER X

## THE SECOND STAGE OF THE GOULD FORTUNE

The first medium by which Jay Gould transferred
many millions of dollars to his ownership was by his
looting and wrecking of the Erie Railroad. If physical
appearance were to be accepted as a gauge of capacity,
none would suspect that Gould contained the elements
of one of the boldest and ablest financial marauders
that the system in force had as yet produced. About
five feet six inches in height and of slender figure, he
gave the random impression of being a mild, meek
man, characterized by excessive timidity. His complex-
ion was swarthy and partly hidden by closely-trimmed
black whiskers; his eyes were dark, vulpine and acutely
piercing; his forehead was high. His voice was very
low, soft and insinuating.

### PRIVATE CONFISCATION OF THE ERIE RAILROAD.

The Erie Railroad, running from New York City to
Buffalo and thence westward to Chicago, was started in
1832. In New York State alone, irrespective of gifts
in other States, it received what was virtually a gift of
$3,000,000 of State funds, and $3,217,000 interest, making $6,217,000 in all. Counties, municipalities and
towns through which it passed were prevailed upon
to contribute freely donations of money, lands and
rights. From private proprietors in New York State

it obtained presents of land then valued at from $400,-
000 to $500,000,[1] but now worth tens of millions of
dollars. In addition, an extraordinary series of special
privileges and franchises was given to it. This process
was manifolded in every State through which the railroad passed. The cost of construction and equipment
came almost wholly from the grants of public funds.[2]

Confiding in the fair promises of its projectors, the
people credulously supposed that their interests would
be safeguarded. But from time to time, Legislature
after Legislature was corrupted or induced to enact
stealthy acts by which the railroad was permitted to
pass without restriction into the possession of a small
clique of exploiters and speculators. Not only were
the people cheated out of funds raised by public taxation and advanced to build the road — a common occurrence in the case of most railroads — but this very
money was claimed by the capitalist owners as private
capital, large amounts of bonds and stocks were issued
against it, and the producers were assessed in the form
of high freight and passenger rates to pay the necessary
interest and dividends on those spurious issues.

### THE SPECULATOR, DREW, GETS CONTROL.

Not satisfied with the thefts of public funds, the
successive cliques in control of the Erie Railroad con-

---

[1] Report on the New York and Erie Railroad Company, New
York State Assembly Document, No. 50, 1842. See also, Investigation of the Railroads of the State of New York, 1879, 1 : 100.

[2] "The Erie Railway was built by the citizens of this State
with money furnished by its people. The State in its sovereign
capacity gave the corporation $3,000,000. The line was subse-
quently captured, or we may say stolen, by the fraudulent issue
of more than $50,000,000 of stock." . . . "An Analysis of
the Erie Reorganization bill, etc., submitted to the Legislature
by John Livingston, Esq., counsel for the Erie Railway Share-
holders, 1876."

tinually plundered its treasury, and defrauded its stockholders. So little attention was given to efficient management that shocking catastrophies resulted at frequent intervals. A time came, however, when the old locomotives, cars and rails were in such a state of decay, that the replacing of them could no longer be postponed. To do this money was needed, and the treasury of the company had been continuously emptied by looting.

The directors finally found a money loaner in Daniel Drew, an uncouth usurer. He had graduated from being a drover and tavern keeper to being owner of a line of steamboats plying between New York and Albany. He then, finally, had become a Wall street banker and broker. For his loans Drew exacted the usual required security. By 1855 he had advanced nearly two million dollars — five hundred thousand in money, the remainder in endorsements. The Erie directors could not pay up, and the control of the railroad passed into his hands. As ignorant of railroad management as he was of books, he took no pains to learn; during the next decade he used the Erie railroad simply as a gambling means to manipulate the price of its stocks on the Stock Exchange. In this way he fleeced a large number of dupes decoyed into speculation out of an aggregate of millions of dollars.

Old Cornelius Vanderbilt looked on with impatience. He foresaw the immense profits which would accrue to him if he could get control of the Erie Railroad; how he could give the road a much greater value by bettering its equipment and service, and how he could put through the same stock-watering operations that he did in his other transactions. Tens of millions of dollars would be his, if he could only secure control. Moreover, the Erie was likely at any time to become a dangerous competitor of his railroads. Vanderbilt secretly began buying stock; by 1866 he had obtained enough to get control. Drew and his dummy directors were ejected, Vanderbilt superseding them with his own.

## VANDERBILT OUSTS DREW, THEN RESTORES HIM.

The change was worked with Vanderbilt's habitual brusque rapidity. Drew apparently was crushed. He had, however, one final resource, and this he now used with histrionic effect. In tears he went to Vanderbilt and begged him not to turn out and ruin an old, self-made man like himself. The appeal struck home. Had the implorer been anyone else, Vanderbilt would have scoffed. But, at heart, he had a fondness for the old illiterate drover whose career in so many respects resembled his own. Tears and pleadings prevailed; in a moment of sentimental weakness — a weakness which turned out to be costly — Vanderbilt relented. A bargain was agreed upon by which Drew was to resume directorship and represent Vanderbilt's interests and purposes.

Reinstated in the Erie board, Drew successfully pretended for a time that he was fully subservient. Ostensibly to carry out Vanderbilt's plans he persuaded that magnate to allow him to bring in as directors two men whose pliancy, he said, could be depended upon. These were Jay Gould, demure and ingratiating, and James Fisk, Jr., a portly, tawdry, pompous voluptuary. In early life Fisk had been a peddler in Vermont, and afterwards had managed an itinerant circus. Then he had become a Wall street broker. Keen and suspicious as old Vanderbilt was, and innately distrustful of both of them, he nevertheless, for some inexplicable reason, allowed Drew to install Gould and Fisk as directors. He knew Gould's record, and probably supposed him, as well as Fisk, handy tools (as was charged) to do his " dirty work " without question. He put Drew, Gould and Fisk on Erie's executive committee. In that capacity they could issue stock and bonds, vote improvements, and generally exercise full authority.

### DREW, GOULD AND FISK BETRAY VANDERBILT.

At first, they gave every appearance of responding obediently to Vanderbilt's directions. Believing it to his interest to buy as much Erie stock as he could, both as a surer guarantee of control, and to put his own price upon it, Vanderbilt continued purchasing. The trio, however, had quietly banded to mature a plot by which they would wrest away Vanderbilt's control.

This was to be done by flooding the market with an extra issue of bonds which could be converted into stock, and then by running down the price, and buying in the control themselves. It was a trick that Drew had successfully worked several years before. At a certain juncture he was apparently " caught short " in the Stock Exchange, and seemed ruined. But at the critical moment he had appeared in Wall street with fifty-eight thousand shares of stock, the existence of which no one had suspected. These shares had been converted from bonds containing an obscure clause allowing the conversion. The projection of this large number of shares into the stock market caused an immediate and violent decline in the price. By selling " short "— a Wall street process which we have described elsewhere

—Drew had taken in large sums as speculative winnings.

The same ruse Drew, Gould and Fisk now proceeded to execute on Vanderbilt. Apparently to provide funds for improving the railroad, they voted to issue a mass of bonds. Large quantities of these they turned over to themselves as security for pretended advances of moneys. These bonds were secretly converted into shares of stock, and then distributed among brokerage houses of which the three were members. Vanderbilt, intent upon getting in as much as he could, bought the stock in unsuspectingly. Then came revelations of the treachery of the three men, and reports of their intentions to issue more stock.

Vanderbilt did not hesitate a moment. He hurried to invoke the judicial assistance of Judge George C. Barnard, of the New York State Supreme Court. He knew that he could count on Barnard, whom at this time he corruptly controlled. This judge was an unconcealed tool of corporate interests and of the plundering Tweed political "ring"; for his many crimes on the bench he was subsequently impeached.[8] Barnard promptly issued a writ enjoining the Erie directors from issuing further stock, and ordered them to return to the Erie treasury one-fourth of that already issued. Furthermore, he prohibited any more conversion of bonds into stock on the ground that it was fraudulent.

So pronounced a victory was this considered for Vanderbilt, that the market price of Erie stock went up thirty points. But the plotters had a cunning trick in reserve. Pretending to obey Barnard's order, they had

[8] At his death $1,000,000 in bonds and cash were found among his effects.

Fisk wrench away the books of stock from a messenger boy summoned ostensibly to carry them to a deposit place on Pine street. They innocently disclaimed any knowledge of who the thief was; as for the messenger boy, he "did not know." These one hundred thousand shares of stock Drew, Gould and Fisk instantly threw upon the stock market. No one else had the slightest suspicion that the court order was being disobeyed. Consequently, Vanderbilt's brokers were busily buying in this load of stock in million-dollar bunches; other persons were likewise purchasing. As fast as the checks came in, Drew and his partners converted them into cash.

## GOULD AND HIS PARTNERS FLEE WITH MILLIONS.

It was not until the day's activity was over that Vanderbilt, amazed and furious, realized that he had been gouged out of $7,000,000. Other buyers were also cheated out of millions. The old man had been caught napping; it was this fact which stung him most. However, after the first paroxysm of frenzied swearing, he hit upon a plan of action. The very next morning warrants were sworn out for the arrest of Drew, Fisk and Gould. A hint quickly reached them; they thereupon fled to Jersey City out of Barnard's jurisdiction, taking their cargo of loot with them. According to Charles Francis Adams, in his "Chapters of Erie," one of them bore away in a hackney coach bales containing $6,000,000 in greenbacks.[4] The other two fugitives were loaded down with valises crammed with bonds and stocks.

Here in more than one sense was an instructive and

[4] "Chapters of Erie": 30.

significant situation. Vanderbilt, the foremost black-mailer of his time, the plunderer of the National Treasury during the Civil War, the arch briber and corruptionist, virtuously invoking the aid of the law on the ground that he had been swindled! Drew, Gould and Fisk sardonically jested over it. But joke as they well might over their having outwitted a man whose own specialty was fraud, they knew that their position was perilous. Barnard's order had declared their sales of stock to be fraudulent, and hence outlawed; and, moreover, if they dared venture back to New York, they were certain, as matters stood, of instant arrest with the threatened alternative of either disgorging or of a criminal trial and possibly prison. To themselves they extenuated their thefts with the comforting and self-sufficient explanation that they had done to Vanderbilt precisely what he had done to others, and would have done to them. But it was not with themselves that the squaring had to be done, but with the machinery of law; Vanderbilt was exerting every effort to have them imprisoned.

How was this alarming exigency to be met? They speedily found a way out. While Vanderbilt was thundering in rage, shouting out streaks of profanity, they calmly went ahead to put into practice a lesson that he himself had thoroughly taught. He controlled a sufficient number of judges; why should not they buy up the Legislature, as he had often done? The strategic plan was suggested of getting the New York Legislature to pass an act legalizing their fraudulent stock issues. Had not Vanderbilt and other capitalists often bought up Congress and Legislatures and common councils? Why not now do the same? They well knew the approved method of procedure in such matters; an onslaught of bribing legislators, they reckoned, would bring the desired result.

### GOULD BRIBES THE LEGISLATURE WITH $500,000.

Stuffing $500,000 in his satchel, Gould surreptitiously hurried to Albany. Detected there and arrested, he was released under heavy bail which a confederate supplied. He appeared in court in New York City a few days later, but obtained a postponement of the action. No time was lost by him. "He assiduously cultivated," says Adams, "a thorough understanding between himself and the Legislature." In the face of sinister charges of corruption, the bill legalizing the fraudulent stock issues was passed. Ineffectually did Vanderbilt bribe the legislators to defeat it; as fast as they took and kept his money, Gould debauched them with greater sums. One Senator in particular, as we have seen, accepted $75,000 from Vanderbilt, and $100,000 from Gould, and pocketed both amounts.

A brisk scandal naturally ensued. The usual effervescent expedient of appointing an investigating committee was adopted by the New York State Senate on April 10, 1868. This committee did not have to investigate to learn the basic facts; it already knew them. But it was a customary part of the farce of these investigating bodies to proceed with a childlike assumption of entire innocence.

Many witnesses were summoned, and much evidence was taken. The committee reported that, according to Drew's testimony, $500,000 had been drawn out of the Erie railroad's treasury, ostensibly for purposes of litigation, and that it was clear "that large sums of money did come from the treasury of the Erie Railroad Company, which were expended for some purpose in Albany, for which no vouchers seem to have been filed in the offices of the company." The committee further found that " large sums of money were expended for corrupt purposes by parties interested in legislation concerning railways during the session of 1868."

But who specifically did the bribing? And who were the legislators bribed? These facts the committee declared that it did not know. This investigating sham resulted, as almost always happened in the case of similar inquisitions, in the culpability being thrown upon certain lobbyists " who were enriched." These lobbyists were men whose trade it was to act as go-betweens in corrupting legislators. Gould and Thompson — the latter an accomplice — testified that they had paid " Lou " Payn, a lobbyist who subsequently became a powerful Republican politician, $10,000 " for a few days' services in Albany in advocating the Erie bill "; and it was further brought out that $100,000 had been given to the lobbyists Luther Caldwell and Russell F. Hicks, to influence legislation and also to shape public opinion through the press. Caldwell, it appeared, received liberal sums from both Vanderbilt and Gould.[5] A subsequent investigating committee appointed, in 1873, to inquire into other charges, reported that in the one year of 1868 the Erie railroad directors, comprising Drew, Gould, Fisk and their associates, had spent more than a million dollars for " extra and legal services," and that it was " their custom from year to year to spend large sums to control elections and to influence legislation." [6]

[5] Report of the Select Committee of the New York Senate, appointed April 10, 1868, in Relation to Members Receiving Money from Railway Companies. Senate Document No. 52, 1869: 3-12, and 137, 140-146.
[6] Report of the Select Committee of the Assembly, Assembly Documents, 1873, Doc. No. 98: xix.

**Vanderbilt** later succeeded in compelling the Erie Railroad to reimburse him for the sums that he thus corruptly spent in fighting Drew, Gould and Fisk.[7]

Their huge thefts having been legalized, Drew, Gould and Fisk returned to Jersey City. But their path was not yet clear. Vanderbilt had various civil suits in New York against them; moreover they were adjudged in contempt of court. Parleying now began. With the severest threats of what the courts would do if they refused, Vanderbilt demanded that they buy back the shares of stock that they had unloaded upon him.

Drew was the first to compromise; Gould and Fisk shortly afterward followed. They collectively paid Vanderbilt $2,500,000 in cash, $1,250,000 in securities for fifty thousand Erie shares, and another million dollars for the privilege of calling upon him for the remaining fifty thousand shares at any time within four months. Although this settlement left Vanderbilt out of pocket to the extent of almost two million dollars, he consented to abandon his suits. The three now left their lair in Jersey City and transferred the Erie offices to the Grand Opera House, at Eighth avenue and Twenty-third street, New York City. In this collision with Vanderbilt, Gould learned a sharp lesson he thereafter never overlooked; namely, that it was not sufficient to bribe common councils and legislatures; he, too, must own his

"What the Erie has done," the Committee reported, "other great corporations are doubtless doing from year to year. Combined as they are, the power of the great moneyed corporations of this country is a standing menace to the liberties of the people.

"The railroad lobby flaunts its ill-gotten gains in the faces of our legislatures, and in all our politics the debasing effect of its influence is felt" (p. 18).

[7] Railroad Investigation of the State of New York, 1879, ii: 1654.

judges.  Events showed that he at once began negotia-
tions.

## GOULD AND FISK THROW OVER DREW.

The next development was characteristic.  Having
no longer any need for their old accomplice, Gould and
Fisk, by tactics of duplicity, gradually sheared Drew
and turned him out of the management to degenerate
into a financial derelict.  It was Drew's odd habit,
whenever his plans were crossed, or he was depressed,
to rush off to his bed, hide himself under the coverlets
and seek solace in sighs and self-compassion, or in
prayer — for with all his unscrupulousness he had an
orthodox religious streak.  When Drew realized that he
had been plundered and betrayed, as he had so often
acted to others, he sought his bed and there long remained in despair under the blankets.  The whimsical
old extortionist never regained his wealth or standing.
Upon Drew's effacement Gould caused himself to be
made president and treasurer of the Erie Railroad, and
Fisk vice-president and controller.

When Gould and Fisk began to turn out more watered
stock various defrauded malcontent stockholders resolved to take an intervening hand.  This was a new
obstacle, but it was coolly met.  Gould and Fisk brought
in gangs of armed thugs to prevent these stockholders
from getting physical possession of the books of the
company.  Then the New York Legislature was again
corrupted.

A bill called the Classification Act, drafted to insure
Gould and Fisk's legal control, was enacted.  This bill
provided that only one-fifth of the board of directors
should be retired in any year.  By this means, although

the majority of stockholders might be opposed to the Gould-Fisk management, it would be impossible for them to get possession of the road for at least three years, and full possession for not less than five years.

But to prevent the defrauded large stockholders from getting possession of the railroad through the courts, another act was passed. This provided that no judgment to oust the board of directors could be rendered by any court unless the suit was brought by the Attorney-General of the State. It was thus only necessary for Gould and Fisk to own the Attorney-General entirely (which they took pains, of course, to do) in order to close the courts to the defrauded stockholders. On a trumped-up suit, and by an order of one of the Tweed judges, a receiver was appointed for the stock owned by foreign stockholders; and when any of it was presented for record in the transfer book of the Erie railroad, the receiver seized it. In this way Gould and Fisk secured practical possession of $6,000,000 of the $50,-000,000 of stock held abroad.

### ALLIANCE WITH CORRUPT POLITICS AND JUDICIARY.

From 1868 to 1872 Gould, abetted by subservient directors, issued two hundred and thirty-five thousand more shares of stock.[8] The frauds were made uncommonly easy by having the Tweed machine as an auxiliary; in turn, Tweed, up to 1871, controlled the New York City and State dominant political machine, including the Legislature and many of the judges. To insure Tweed's connivance, they made him a director of the Erie Railroad, besides heavily bribing him.[9] With Tweed as an

[8] Fisk was murdered by a rival in 1872 in a feud over Fisk's mistress. His death did not interrupt Gould's plans.

[9] "Did you ever receive any money from either Fisk or Gould

associate they were able to command the judges who owed their elevation to him. Barnard, one of Tweed's servile tools, was sold over to Gould and Fisk, and so thoroughly did this judge prostitute his office at their behest that once, late at night, at Fisk's order, he sportively held court in the apartment of Josie Mansfield, Fisk's mistress.[10]  When the English stockholders sent over a large number of shares to be voted in for a new management, it was Barnard who allowed this stock to be voted by Gould and Fisk. At another time Gould and Fisk called at Barnard's house and obtained an injunction while he was eating breakfast.

It was largely by means of his corrupt alliance with the Tweed "ring" that Gould was able to put through his gigantic frauds from 1868 to 1872.

Gould was, indeed, the unquestioned master mind in these transactions; Fisk and the others merely executed his directions. The various fraudulent devices were of

to be used in bribing the Legislature?" Tweed was asked by an aldermanic committee in 1877, after his downfall.

A. "I did sir! They were of frequent occurrence. Not only did I receive money but I find by an examination of the papers that everybody else who received money from the Erie railroad charged it to me."—Documents of the Board of Aldermen, 1877, Part II, No. 8:49.

[10] The occasion grew out of an attempt of Gould and Fisk in 1869 to get control of the Albany and Susquehanna Railroad. Two parties contested—the Gould and the "Ramsey," headed by J. Pierpont Morgan. Each claimed the election of its officers and board of directors. One night, at half-past ten o'clock, Fisk summoned Barnard from Poughkeepsie to open chambers in Josie Mansfield's rooms. Barnard hurried there, and issued an order ousting Ramsey from the presidency. Judge Smith at Rochester subsequently found that Ramsey was legally elected, and severely denounced Gould and Fisk.—"Letters of General Francis C. Barlow, Albany": 1871.

The records of this suit (as set forth in Lansing's Reports, New York Supreme Court, 1:308, etc.) show that each of the contesting parties accused the other of gross fraud, and that the final decision was favorable to the "Ramsey" party. See the chapters on J. Pierpont Morgan in Vol. III of this work.

Gould's origination. A biographer of Fisk casually wrote at the time: "Jay Gould and Fisk took William M. Tweed into their board, and the State Legislature, Tammany Hall and the Erie 'ring' were fused together and have contrived to serve each other faithfully." [11] Gould admitted before a New York State Assembly investigating committee in 1873 that, in the three years prior to 1873, he had paid large sums to Tweed and to others, and that he had also disbursed large sums "which might have been used to influence legislation or elections." These sums were facetiously charged on the Erie books to "India Rubber Account" — whatever that meant.

Gould cynically gave more information. He could distinctly recall, he said, "that he had been in the habit of sending money into various districts throughout the State," either to control nominations or elections for Senators or members of the Assembly. He considered "that, as a rule, such investments paid better than to wait until the men got to Albany." Significantly he added that it would be as impossible to specify the numerous instances "as it would be to recall the number of freight cars sent over the Erie Railroad from day to day." His corrupt operations, he indifferently testified, extended into four different States. "In a Republican district I was a Republican; in a Democratic district, a Democrat; in a doubtful district I was doubtful; but I was always for Erie." [21] The funds that he thus used in widespread corruption came obviously from the proceeds of his great thefts; and he might have added, with equal truth, that with this stolen money he was able to

[11] "A Life of James Fisk, Jr.," New York, 1871.
[12] Report of, and Testimony Before, the Select Assembly Committee, 1873, Assembly Documents, Doc. No. 98:xx, etc.

employ some of the most eminent lawyers of the day,
and purchase judges.

## GOULD'S TRADING CLASS SUPPORT.

Those writers who are content with surface facts, or
who lack understanding of popular currents, either state,
or leave the inference, that it was solely by bribing
and trickery that Gould was able to consummate his
frauds. Such assertions are altogether incorrect. To
do what he did required the support, or at least toler-
ance, of a considerable section of public opinion. This
he obtained. And how? By posing as a zealous anti-
monopolist.

The cry of anti-monopoly was the great fetich of the
entire middle class; this class viewed with fear the growing concentration of wealth; and as its interests were
reflected by a large number of organs of public opinion,
it succeeded in shaping the thoughts of no small a section of the working class.

While secretly bribing, Gould constantly gave out
for public consumption a plausible string of arguments,
in which act, by the way, he was always fertile. He
represented himself as the champion of the middle and
working classes in seeking to prevent Vanderbilt from
getting a monopoly of many railroads. He played
adroitly upon the fears, the envy and the powerful main-
springs of the self interest of the middle class by pointing out how greatly it would be at the mercy of Vanderbilt should Vanderbilt succeed in adding the Erie Railroad and other railroads to his already formidable list.

It was a time of all times when such arguments were
bound to have an immense effect; and that they did
was shown by the readiness with which the trading class

excused his corruption and frauds on the ground that he seemed to be the only man who proved that he could prevent Vanderbilt from gobbling up all of the railroads leading from New York City. With a great fatuousness the middle class supposed that he was fighting for its cause.

The bitterness of large numbers of the manufacturing, jobbing and agricultural classes against Commodore Vanderbilt was deep-seated. By an illegal system of preferential freight rates to certain manufacturers, Vanderbilt put these favorites easily in a position where they could undersell competitors. Thus, A. T. Stewart, one of the noted millionaire manufacturers and merchants of the day, instead of owing his success to his great ability, as has been set forth, really derived it, to a great extent, from the secret preferential freight rates that he had on the Vanderbilt railroads. A variety of other coercive methods were used by Vanderbilt. Special freight trains were purposely delayed and run at snail's pace in order to force shippers to pay the extraordinary rates demanded for shipping over the Merchant's Dispatch, a fast freight line owned by the Vanderbilt family.

These were but a few of the many schemes for their private graft that the Vanderbilts put in force. The agricultural class was taxed heavily on every commodity shipped; for the transportation of milk, for example, the farmer was taxed one-half of what he himself received for milk. These taxes, of course, eventually fell upon the consumer, but the manufacturer and the farmer realized that if the extortions were less, their sales and profits would be greater. They were in a rebellious mood and gladly welcomed a man such as Gould who thwarted Vanderbilt at every turn. Gould well knew of this bitter feeling against Vanderbilt; he used it, and thrust himself forward constantly in the guise of the great deliverer.

As for the small stockholders of the Erie railroad, Gould easily pacified them by holding out the bait of a larger dividend than they had been getting under the former regime. This he managed by the common and fraudulent expedient of issuing bonds, and paying dividends out of proceeds. So long as the profits of these small stockholders were slightly better than they had been getting before, they were complacently satisfied to let Gould continue his frauds. This acquiscence in theft has been one of the most pronounced characteristics of the capitalistic investors, both large and small. Numberless instances have shown that they raise no objections to plundering management provided that under it their money returns are increased.

The end of Gould's looting of the Erie railroad was now in sight. However the small stockholders might assent, the large English stockholders, some of whom had invidious schemes of their own in the way of which Gould stood, were determined to gain control themselves.

### GOULD'S DIRECTORS BRIBED TO RESIGN.

They made no further attempt to resort to the law. A fund of $300,000 was sent over by them to their American agents with which to bribe a number of Gould's directors to resign. As Gould had used these directors as catspaws, they were aggrieved because he had kept all of the loot himself. If he had even partly divided, their sentiments would have been quite different. The

$300,000 bribery fund was distributed among them, and they cárried out their part of the bargain by resigning.[18] The Assembly Investigating Committee of 1873 referred carelessly to the English stockholders as being "impatient at the law's delay" and therefore taking matters into their own hands.  If a poor man or a trade union had become "impatient at the law's delay" and sought an illegal remedy, the judiciary would have quickly pronounced condign punishment and voided the whole proceeding.  The boasted "majesty of law" was a majesty to which the underdogs only were expected to look up to in fear and trepidation.

When the English stockholders elected their own board Gould obtained an injunction from the courts. This writ was absolutely disregarded, and the anti-Gould faction on March 11, 1872, seized possession of the offices and books of the company by physical force. Did the courts punish these men for criminal contempt? No effort was made to.  Many a worker or labor union leader had been sent to jail (and has been since), for "contempt of court," but the courts evidently have been willing enough to stomach all of the contempt profusely shown for them by the puissant rich.  The propertyless owned nothing, not to speak of a judge, but the capitalists owned whole strings of judges, and those whom they did not own or corrupt were generally influenced to their side by association or environment. "All of this," reported the Assembly Investigating Committee of 1873, speaking of the means employed to overthrow Gould, "has been done without authority

[18] Assembly Document No. 98, 1873: xii and xiii.  The English stockholders took no chances on this occasion.  The committee reported that not until the directors had resigned did they "receive their price."

of law." But no law was invoked by the officials to make the participants account for their illegal acts.

## THE LEGISLATURE BRIBED AGAIN.

It seems that the entire amount, including the large fees paid to agents and lawyers, corruptly expended by the English capitalists in ousting Gould, was $750,000. Did they foot this bill out of their own pockets? By no means. They arranged the reimbursements by voting this sum to themselves out of the Erie Railroad treasury; [14] that is to say, they compelled the public to shoulder it by adding to the bonded burdens on which the people were taxed to pay interest.

To complete their control they bribed the New York Legislature to repeal the Classification Act. . As has been shown, the Legislature of 1872 was considered a " reform " body, and it also has been brought out how Vanderbilt bribed it to give him invaluable public franchises and large grants of public money. In fact, other railroad magnates as well as he systematically bribed; and it is clear that they contributed jointly a pool of money both to buy laws and to prevent the passage of objectionable acts. "It appears conclusive," reported the Assembly Investigating Committee of 1873, "that a large amount — reported by one witness at $100,000 — was appropriated for legislative purposes by the railroad interest in 1872, and that this [$30,000] was Erie's proportion." [15] One of the lobbyists, James D. Barber, " a ruling spirit in the Republican party," admitted receiving $50,000 from the Vanderbilts. [16] While uniting to

14 Assembly Document No. 98, 1873: xii and xvi.
15 Ibid., xvii.
16 Ibid., 633.

suppress bills feared by them all, each of the magnates bribed to foil the others' purposes.

### GOULD'S DIRECT ERIE THEFTS WERE $12,000,000.

What did Gould's plunder amount to? His direct thefts, by reason of his Erie frauds, seem to have reached more than twelve million dollars, all, or nearly all, of which he personally kept.

That sum, considering the falling prices of commodities after the panic of 1873, and comparable with current standards of cost and living, was equivalent to perhaps double the amount at present. Various approximations of his thefts were made. After a minute examination of the Erie railroad's books, Augustus Stein, an expert accountant, testified before the " Hepburn Committee " (the New York Assembly Investigating Committee of 1879) that Gould had himself pocketed twelve or thirteen million dollars.[17]

This, however, was only one aspect. Between 1868 and 1873 Gould and his accomplices had issued $64,000,-000 of watered stock. Gould, so the Erie books revealed, had charged $12,000,000 as representing the outlay for construction and equipment, yet not a new rail had been laid, nor a new engine put in use, nor a new station built. These twelve millions or more were what he and his immediate accomplices had stolen outright from the Erie Railroad treasury. Considerable sums

[17] Q.— Do you think that you could remember the aggregate amount of wrong-doing on the part of Mr. Gould that you have discovered?
A.— I could give an estimate throwing off a couple of millions here and there; I could say that it amounted to — that is, what we discovered — amounted to about twelve or thirteen million dollars.— Railroad Investigation of the State of New York, 1879, ii : 1765.

were, of course, paid corruptly to politicians, but Gould got them all back, as well as the plunder of his associates, by personally manipulating Erie stock so as to compel them to sell at a great loss to themselves, and a great profit to himself.   Furthermore, in these manipulations of stock, he scooped in more millions from other sources.

Had it not been for his intense greed and his constitutional inability to remain true to his confederates, Gould might have been allowed to retain the proceeds of his thefts.   His treachery to one of them, Henry N. Smith, who had been his partner in the brokerage firm of Smith, Gould and Martin, resulted in trouble.   Gould cornered the stock of the Chicago and Northwestern Railroad; to put it more plainly, he bought up the outstanding available supply of shares, and then ran the price up from 75 to 250.   Smith was one of a number of Wall Street men badly mulcted in this operation, as Gould intended.   Seeking revenge, Smith gave over the firm's books, which were in his possession, to General Barlow, counsel for the Erie Railroad's protesting stockholders.[18]   Evidence of great thefts was quickly discovered, and an action was started to compel Gould to disgorge about $12,000,000.   A criminal proceeding was also brought, and Gould was arrested and placed under heavy bonds.

## AN EXTRAORDINARY " RESTITUTION."

Apparently Gould was trapped.   But a wonderful and unexpected development happened which filled the Wall Street legion with admiration for his craft and audacity. He planned to make his very restitution the basis for

[18] Railroad Investigation, etc., v : 531.

taking in many more millions by speculation; he knew
that when it was announced that he had concluded to
disgorge, the market value of the stock would instantly
go up and numerous buyers would appear.

Secretly he bought up as much Erie stock as he could.
Then he ostentatiously and with the widest publicity
declared his intention to make restitution. Such a cack-
ling sensation it made! The price of Erie stock at once
bounded up, and his brokers sold quantities of it to his
great accruing profit. The pursuing stockholders as-
sented to his offer to surrender his control of the Erie
Railroad, and to accept real estate and stocks seemingly
worth $6,000,000. But after the stockholders had with-
drawn their suits, they found that they had been tricked
again. The property that Gould had turned over to them
did not have a market value of more than $200,000.[19]

[19] Railroad Investigation, etc., 1879, iii : 2503.
One of the very rare instances in which any of Gould's victims was able to compel him to disgorge, was that described in
the following anecdote, which went the rounds of the press:
"An old friend had gone to Gould, telling him that he had
managed to save up some $20,000, and asking his advice as to
how he should invest it in such a manner as to be absolutely
safe, for the benefit of his family. Gould told him to invest
it in a certain stock, and assured him that the investment would
be absolutely safe as to income, and, besides, its market value
would shortly be greatly enhanced.
"The man did as advised by Gould, and the stock promptly
started to go down. Lower and lower it went, and seeing the
steady depreciation in the price of the stock, and hearing stories
to the effect that the dividends were to be passed, the man
wrote to Gould asking if the investment was still good. Gould
replied to his friend's letter, assuring him that the stories had
no foundation in fact and were being circulated purely for
market effect.
"But still the stock declined. Each day the price went to
new lower figures on the Stock Exchange, and finally the rumors became fact, and the Directors passed the dividend. The
man had seen the savings of years vanish in a few months
and realized that he was a ruined man.
"Goaded to an almost insane frenzy, he rushed into Gould's
office the afternoon the Directors announced the passing of the

Gould's thefts from the Erie railroad were, however, only one of his looting transactions during those busy years. At the same time, he was using these stolen millions to corner the gold supply. In this " Black Friday " conspiracy (for so it was styled) he fraudulently reaped another eleven million dollars to the accompaniment of a financial panic, with a long train of failures, suicides and much disturbance and distress.

dividend, and told Gould that he had been deliberately and grossly deceived and that he was ruined. He wound up by announcing his intention of shooting Gould then and there.

"Gould heard his quondam friend through. There could be no mistaking the man's intent. He was evidently half crazed and possessed of an insane desire to carry out his threat. Gould turned to him and said: 'My dear Mr. —' calling him by name, 'you are laboring under a most serious misapprehension. Your money is not lost. If you will go down to my bank to-morrow morning, you will find there a balance of $25,000 to your credit. I sold out your stock some time ago, but had neglected to notify you.' The man looked at him in amazement and, half doubting, left the office.

"As soon as he had left the office Gould sent word to his bank to place $25,000 to this man's credit. The man spent a sleepless night, torn by doubts and fears. When the bank opened for business he was the first man in line, and was nearly overcome when the cashier handed him the sum that Gould had named the previous afternoon.

"Gould had evidently decided in his own mind that the man was determined to kill him, and that the only way to save his life and his name was to pay the man the sum he had lost plus a profit, in the manner he did. But as a sidelight on the absolutely cold-blooded self-possession of the man, it is interesting."

# CHAPTER XI

## THE GOULD FORTUNE BOUNDS FORWARD

The " gold conspiracy " as plotted and consummated by Gould was in its day denounced as one of the most disgraceful events in American history. To adjudge it so was a typical exaggeration and perversion of a society caring only about what was passing in its upper spheres. The spectacular nature of this episode, and the ruin it wrought in the ranks of the money dealers and of the traders, caused its importance to be grossly misrepresented and overdrawn.

### THE ABUSE OF GOULD OVERDONE.

It was not nearly as discreditable as the gigantic and repulsive swindles that traders and bankers had carried on during the dark years of the Civil War. The very traders and financiers who beslimed Gould for his " gold conspiracy " were those who had built their fortunes on blood-soaked army contracts. Nor could the worst aspects of Gould's conspiracy, bad as they were, begin to vie in disastrous results with the open and insidious abominations of the factory and landlord system. To repeat, it was a system in which incredible numbers of working men, women and children were killed off by the perils of their trades, by disease superinduced and aggravated by the wretchedness of their work, and by the misery of their lot and habitations. Millions more died prematurely because of causes directly traceable to the withering influences of poverty.

But this unending havoc, taking place silently in the routine departments of industry, and in obscure alleyways, called forth little or no notice. What if they did suffer and perish? Society covered their wrongs and injustices and mortal throes with an inhibitive silence, for it was expected that they, being lowly, should not complain, obtrude grievances, or in any way make unpleasant demonstrations. Yet, if the prominent of society were disgruntled, or if a few capitalists were caught in the snare of ruin which they had laid for others, they at once bestirred themselves and made the whole nation ring with their outcries and lamentations. Their merest whispers became thunderous reverberations. The press, the pulpit, legislative chambers and the courts became their strident voices, and in all the influential avenues for directing public opinion ready advocates sprang forth to champion their plaints, and concentrate attention upon them. So it was in the " gold conspiracy."

### GOULD EMBARKS ON HIS CONSPIRACY.

After the opening of the Civil War, gold was exceedingly scarce, and commanded a high premium. The supply of this metal, this yellow dross, which to a considerable degree regulated the world's relative values of wages and commodities, was monopolized by the powerful banking interests. In 1869 but fifteen million dollars of gold was in actual circulation in the United States.

Notwithstanding the increase of industrial productive power, the continuous displacement of obsolete methods by the introduction of labor-saving machinery, and the consecutive discovery of new means for the production of wealth, the task of the worker was not lightened. He had, for the most part, after great struggles, secured a shorter workday, but if the hours were shorter the work was more tense and racking than in the days before steam-driven machinery supplanted the hand tool. The mass of the workers were in a state of dependence and poverty. The land, industrial and financial system, operating in the three-fold form of rent, interest and profit, tore away from the producer nearly the whole of what he produced. Even those factory-owning capitalists exercising a personal and direct supervision over their plants, were often at the mercy of the clique of bankers who controlled the money marts.

Had the supply of money been proportionate to the growth of population and of business, this process of expropriation would have been less rapid. As it was, the associated monopolies, the international and national banking interests, and the income classes in general, constricted the volume of money into as narrow a compress as possible. As they were the very class which controlled the law-making power of Government, this was not difficult.

The resulting scarcity of money produced high rates of interest. These, on the one hand, facilitated usury, and, on the other, exacted more labor and produce for the privilege of using that money. Staggering under burdensome rates of interest, factory owners, business men in general, farmers operating on a large scale, and landowners with tenants, shunted the load on to the worker. The producing population had to foot the additional bill by accepting wages which had a falling buying power, and by having to pay more rent and greater prices for necessities.  Such conditions were certain to accelerate the growth of poverty and the centralization of wealth.

Gould's plan was to get control of the outstanding fifteen millions of dollars of gold, and fix his own price upon them.  Not only from what was regarded as legitimate commerce would he exact tribute, but he would squeeze to the bone the whole tribe of gold speculators — for at that time gold was extensively speculated in to an intensive degree.

With the funds stolen from the Erie Railroad treasury, he began to buy in gold.  To accommodate the crowd of speculators in this metal, the Stock Exchange had set apart a " Gold Room," devoted entirely to the speculative purchase and sale of gold.  Gould was confident that his plan would not miscarry if the Government would not put in circulation any part of the ninety-five million dollars in gold hoarded as a reserve in the National Treasury.  The urgent and all-important point was to ascertain whether the Government intended to keep this sum entirely shut out from circulation.

### HE BRIBES GOVERNMENT OFFICIALS.

To get this inside information he succeeded in corruptly winning over to his interests A. R. Corbin, a brother-in-law of President Grant.  The consideration was Gould's buying two million dollars' worth of gold bonds, without requiring margin or security, for Corbin's account.[1]  Thus Gould thought he had surely secured an intimate spy within the authoritative precincts

[1] Gold Panic Investigation, House Report No. 31, Forty-first Congress, Second Session, 1870: 157.  Corbin's venality in lobbying for corrupt bills was notorious; he admitted his complicity before a Congressional Investigating Committee in 1857.

of the White House. As the premium on gold constantly rose, these bonds yielded Corbin as much sometimes as $25,000 a week in profits. To insure the further success of his plan, Gould subsidized General Butterfield, whose appointment as sub-treasurer at New York Corbin claimed to have brought about. Gould testified in 1870 that he had made a private loan to Butterfield, and that he had carried speculatively $1,500,-000 for Butterfield's benefit. These statements Butterfield denied.[2]

Through Corbin, Gould attempted to pry out Grant's policies, and with Fisk as an interlocutor, Gould personally attempted to draw out the President. To their consternation they found that Grant was not disposed to favor their arguments. The prospect looked very black for them. Gould met the situation with matchless audacity. By spreading subtle rumors, and by inspiring press reports through venal writers, he deceived not only the whole of Wall Street, but even his own associates, into believing that high Government officials were in collusion with him. The report was assiduously disseminated that the Government did not intend to release any of its hoard of gold for circulation. The premium, accordingly, shot up to 146. Soon after this, certain financial quarters suspected that Gould was bluffing. The impression spreading that he could not depend upon the Government's support, the rate of the premium declined, and Gould's own array of brokers turned against him and sold gold.

### GOULD BETRAYS HIS PARTNERS.

Entrapped, Gould realized that something had to be done, and done quickly, if he were to escape complete

---

[2] Gold Panic Investigation, etc., 160.

ruin, holding as he did the large amount of gold that he had bought at steep prices. By plausible fabrications he convinced Fisk that Grant was really an ally. Gould had bought a controlling interest in the Tenth National Bank. This institution Gould and Fisk now used as a fraudulent manufactory of certified checks. These they turned out to the amount of tens of millions of dollars. With the spurious checks they bought from thirty to forty millions in gold.[3] Such an amount of gold did not, of course, exist in circulation. But the law permitted gambling in it as though it really existed. Ordinary card gamblers, playing for actual money, were under the ban of the law; but the speculative gamblers of the Stock Exchange who bought and sold goods which frequently did not exist, carried on their huge fraudulent operations with the full sanction of the law. Gould's plan was not intricate. Extensive purchases of gold naturally—as the laws of trade went—were bound to increase constantly its price.

By September, 1869, Gould and his partners not only held all of the available gold in circulation, but they held contracts by which they could call upon bankers, manufacturers, merchants, brokers and speculators for about seventy millions of dollars more of the metal. To the banking, manufacturing and importing interests gold, as the standard, was urgently required for various kinds of interfluent business transactions: to pay international debts, interest on bonds, customs dues or to move the crops. They were forced to borrow it at Gould's own price. This price was added to the cost of operation, manufacture and sale, to be eventually assessed upon the consumer. Gould publicly announced that he would show no mercy to anyone. He had a

[3] Gold Panic Investigation: 13.

list, for example, of two hundred New York merchants who owed him gold; he proposed to print their names in the newspapers, demanding settlement at once, and would have done so, had not his lawyers advised him that the move might be adjudged criminal conspiracy.[4]

The tension, general excitement and pressure in business circles were such that President Grant decided to release some of the Government's gold, even though the reserve be diminished. In some mysterious way a hint of this reached Gould. The day before " Black Friday " he resolved to betray his partners, and secretly sell gold before the price abruptly dropped. To do this with success it was necessary to keep on buying, so that the price would be run up still higher.

Such methods were prohibited by the code of the Stock Exchange which prescribed certain rules of the game, for while the members of the Exchange allowed themselves the fullest latitude and the most unchecked deception in the fleecing of outside elements, yet among themselves they decreed a set of rules forbidding any sort of double-dealing in trading with one another. To draw an analogy, it was like a group of professional card sharps deterring themselves by no scruples in the cheating of the unwary, but who insisted that among their own kind fairness should be scrupulously observed. Yet, rules or no rules, no one could gainsay the fact that many of the foremost financiers had often and successfully used the very enfilading methods that Gould now used.

While Gould was secretly disposing of his gold holdings, he was goading on his confederates and his crowd of fifty or more brokers to buy still more.[5] By this

[4] Gold Panic Investigation, etc., 13.
[5] " Gould, the guilty plotter of all these criminal proceedings,"

time, it seems, Fisk and his partner in the brokerage business, Belden, had some stray inklings of Gould's real plan; yet all that they knew were the fragments Gould chose to tell them, with perhaps some surmises of their own. Gould threw out just enough of an outline to spur on their appetite for an orgy of spoils. Undoubtedly, Gould made a secret agreement with them by which he could repudiate the purchases of gold made in their names. Away from the Stock Exchange Fisk made a ludicrous and dissolute enough figure, with his love of tinsel, his show and braggadacio, his mock military prowess, his pompous, windy airs and his covey of harlots. But in Wall Street he was a man of affairs and power; the very assurance that in social life made him ridiculous to a degree, was transmuted into a pillar of strength among the throng of speculators who themselves were mainly arrant bluffs. A dare-devil audacity there was about Fisk that impressed, misled and intimidated; a fine screen he served for Gould plotting and sapping in the background.

## THE MEMORABLE "BLACK FRIDAY"

The next day, "Black Friday," September 24, 1869, was one of tremendous excitement and gloomy apprehension among the money changers. Even the exchanges of foreign countries reflected the perturbation. Gould gave orders to buy all gold in Fisk's name; Fisk's brokers ran the premium up to 151 and then to 161. The market prices of railroad stocks shrank rapidly; failure after failure of Wall Street firms was announced, and

reported the Congressional Investigating Committee of 1870, "determined to betray his own associates, and silent, and imperturbable, by nods and whispers directed all."—Gold Panic Investigation: 14.

fortunes were swept away.  Fearing that the price of
gold might mount to 200, manufacturers and other business concerns throughout the country frantically directed their agents to buy gold at any price.  All this
time Gould, through certain brokers, was secretly selling; and while he was doing so, Fisk and Belden by his
orders continued to buy.

The Stock Exchange, according to the descriptions of many eye-witnesses, was an extraordinary sight
that day.  On the most perfunctory occasions the scenes
enacted there might have well filled the exotic observer
with unmeasured amazement.  But never had it presented so thoroughly a riotous, even bedlamic aspect as
on this day, Black Friday; never had greed and the
fear born of greed, displayed themselves in such frightful forms.

Here could be seen many of the money masters shriek-
ing and roaring, anon rushing about with whitened faces.
indescribably contorted, and again bellowing forth this
order or that curse with savage energy and wildest ges-
ture.  The puny speculators had long since uttered their
doleful squeak and plunged down into the limbo of ruin,
completely engulfed; only the big speculators, or their
commission men, remained in the arena, and many of
these-like trapped rats scurried about from pillar to post.
The little fountain in the " Gold Room " serenely
spouted and bubbled as usual, its cadence lost in the
awful uproar; over to it rushed man after man splashing
its cooling water on his throbbing head.  Over all rose
a sickening exhalation, the dripping, malodorous sweat
of an assemblage worked up to the very limit of mental
endurance.

What, may we ask, were these men snarling, cursing
and fighting over?  Why, quite palpably over the di-

vision of wealth that masses of working men, women and children were laboriously producing, too often amid sorrow and death. While elsewhere pinioned labor was humbly doing the world's real work, here in this " Gold Room," greed contested furiously with greed, cunning with cunning over their share of the spoils. Without their structure of law, and Government to enforce it, these men would have been nothing; as it was, they were among the very crests of society; the makers of law, the wielders of power, the pretenders to refinement and culture.

Baffled greed and cunning outmatched and duplicity doubled against itself could be seen in the men who rushed from the " Gold Room " hatless and frenzied — some literally crazed — when the price of gold advanced to 162. In the surrounding streets were howling and impassable crowds, some drawn thither by curiosity and excitement, others by a fancied interest; surely, fancied, for it was but a war of eminent knaves and knavish gamblers. Now this was not a " disorderly mob " of workers such as capitalists and politicians created out of orderly workers' gatherings so as to have a pretext for clubbing and imprisoning; nay it all took place in the " conservative " precincts of sacrosant Wall Street, the abiding place of " law and order." The participants were composed of the " best classes ; " therefore, by all logic it was a scene supereminently sane, respectable and legitimate; the police, worthy defenders of the peace, treated it all with an awed respect.

Suddenly, early in the afternoon, came reports that the United States Treasury was selling gold; they proved to be true. Within fifteen minutes the whole fabric of the gold manipulation had gone to pieces. It is narrated that a mob, bent on lynching, searched for

Gould, but that he and Fisk had sneaked away through a back door and had gone uptown.

The general belief was that Gould was irretrievably ruined. That he was secretly selling gold at an exorbitant price was not known; even his own intimates, except perhaps Fisk and Belden, were ignorant of it. All that was known was that he had made contracts for the purchase of enormous quantities of fictitious gold at excessive premiums. As a matter of fact, his underhand sales had brought him eleven or twelve million dollars profit. But if his contracts for purchase were enforced, not only would these profits be wiped out, but also his entire fortune.

## ELEVEN MILLIONS POCKETED BY JUDICIAL COLLUSION.

Ever agile and resourceful, Gould quickly extricated himself from this difficulty. He fell back upon the corrupt judiciary. Upon various flimsy pretexts, he and Fisk, in a single day, procured twelve sweeping injunctions and court orders.[6] These prohibited the Stock Exchange and the Gold Board from enforcing any rules of settlement against them, and enjoined Gould and Fisk's brokers from settling any contracts. The result, in brief, was that judicial collusion allowed Gould to pocket his entire " profits," amounting, as the Congressional Committee of 1870 reported, to about eleven million dollars, while relieving him from any necessity of paying up his far greater losses. Fisk's share of the eleven millions was almost nothing; Gould retained practically the entire sum. Gould's confederates and agents were ruined, financially and morally; scores of failures,

[6] Gold Panic Investigation, etc., 18.

**JAY GOULD,**
Who, in a Brief Period, Possessed Himself of a Vast Fortune.

dozens of suicides, the despoilment of a whole people, were the results of Gould's handiwork.

From his Erie railroad thefts, the gold conspiracy and other maraudings, Gould now had about twenty-five or thirty million dollars. Perhaps the sum was much more. Having sacked the Erie previous to his being ousted in 1873, he looked out for further instruments of plunder.

Money was power; the greater the thief the greater the power; and Gould, in spite of abortive lawsuits and denunciations, had the cardinal faculty of holding on to the full proceeds of his piracies. In 1873 there was no man more rancorously denounced by the mercantile classes than Gould. If one were to be swayed by their utterances, he would be led to believe that these classes, comprising the wholesale and retail merchants, the importers and the small factory men, had an extraordinarily high and sensitive standard of honesty. But this assumption was sheer pretense, at complete variance with the facts. It was a grim sham constantly shattered by investigation. Ever, while vaunting its own probity and scoring those who defrauded it, the whole mercantile element was itself defrauding at every opportunity.

### SOME COMPARISONS WITH GOULD.

One of the numberless noteworthy and conclusive examples of the absolute truth of this generalization was that of the great frauds perpetrated by the firm of Phelps, Dodge and Company, millionaire importers of tin, copper, lead and other metals.

So far as public reputation went, the members of the house were the extreme opposites of Gould. In the wide realm of commercialism a more stable and illustrious firm could not be found. Its wealth was conventionally "solid and substantial;" its members were lauded as "high-toned" business men "of the old-fashioned school," and as consistent church communicants and expansive philanthropists. Indeed, one of them was regarded as so glorious and uplifting a model for adolescent youth, that he was chosen president of the Young Men's Christian Association; and his statue, erected by his family, to-day irradiates the tawdry surroundings of Herald Square, New York City. In the Blue Book of the elect, socially and commercially, no names could be found more indicative of select, strong-ribbed, tripledyed respectability and elegant social poise and position.

In the dying months of 1872, a prying iconoclast, unawed by the glamor of their public repute and the contemplation of their wealth, began an exhaustive investigation of their custom house invoices. This inquiring individual was B. G. Jayne, a special United States Treasury agent. He seems to have been either a dutyloving servant of the people, stubbornly bent upon ferreting out fraud wherever he found it, irrespective of whether the criminals were powerful or not, or he was prompted by the prospect of a large reward. The more he searched into this case, the more of a mountainous mass of perjury and fraud revealed itself. On January, 3, 1873, Jayne set the full facts before his superior, George S. Boutwell, Secretary of the Treasury.

". . . According to ordinary modes of reckoning," he wrote, "a house of the wealth and standing of

Phelps, Dodge and Company would be above the influences that induce the ordinary brood of importers to commit fraud.   That same wealth and standing became an almost impenetrable armor against suspicion of wrong-doing and diverted the attention of the officers of the Government, preventing that scrutiny which they give to acts of other and less favored importers."   Jayne went on to tell how he had proceeded with great caution in "establishing beyond question gross under-valuations," and how United States District Attorney Noah Davis (later a Supreme Court Justice) concurred with him that fraud had been committed.

### THE GREAT FRAUDS OF PHELPS, DODGE AND COMPANY.

The Government red tape showed signs at first of declining to unwind, but further investigation proved the frauds so great, that even the red tape was thrilled into action, and the Government began a suit in the United States District Court at New York for $1,000,-000 for penalties for fraudulent custom-house under-valuations. It sued William E. Dodge, William E. Dodge, Jr., D. Willis James, Anson Phelps Stokes, James Stokes and Thomas Stokes as the participating members of the firm.

The suit was a purely civil one; influential defrauders were not inconvenienced by Government with criminal actions and the prospect of prison lodging and fare; this punishment was reserved exclusively for petty offenders outside of the charmed circle.   The sum of $1,000,000 sued for by the Government referred to penalties due since 1871 only; the firm's duplicates of invoices covering the period before that could not be found; "they had probably been destroyed; " hence, it was impossible to ascertain how much Phelps, Dodge and Company had defrauded in the previous years.

The firm's total importations were about $6,000,000 a year; it was evident, according to the Government officials, that the frauds were not only enormous, but that they had been going on for a long time. These frauds were not so construed " by any technical construction, or far-fetched interpretation," but were committed " by the firm's deliberately and systematically stating the cost of their goods below the purchase price for no conceivable reason but to lessen the duties to be paid to the United States."

These long-continuing frauds could not have been possible without the custom-house officials having been bribed to connive. The practice of bribing customs officers was an old and common one. In his report to the House of Representatives on February 23, 1863, Representative Van Wyck, chairman of an investigating committee, fully described this system of bribery. In summarizing the evidence brought out in the examination of fifty witnesses he dealt at length with the custom house officials who for large bribes were in collusion with brokers and merchants. " No wonder," he exclaimed, " the concern [the custom house] is full of fraud, reeking with corruption." [7]

[7] The Congressional Globe, Appendix, Thirty-seventh Congress, Third Session, 1862-3, Part ii: 118.
" During the last session the Secretary had the honor of transmitting the draft of a bill for the detection and prevention of fraudulent entries at the custom-houses, and he adheres to the opinion that the provisions therein embodied are necessary for the protection of the revenue. . . . For the past year the collector, naval officer, and surveyor of New York have entertained suspicions that fraudulent collusions with some of the customs officers existed. Measures were taken by them to ascertain whether these suspicions were well founded. By per-

Great was the indignation shown at the charges by the flustered members of the firm; most stoutly these "eminently proper" men asserted their innocence.[8]  In point of fact (as has been shown in the chapters on the Astor fortune) several of them had long been slyly defrauding in other fields, particularly by the corrupt procuring of valuable city land before and during the Tweed regime.  They had also been enriching themselves by the corrupt obtaining of railroad grants.  There was a scurrying about by Phelps, Dodge and Company to explain that some mistake had been made; but the Government steadfastly pressed its action; and Secretary Boutwell curtly informed them that if they were innocent of guilt, they had the opportunity of proving so in court.  After this ultimatum their tone changed; they exerted every influence to prevent the case from coming to trial, and they announced their willingness to compromise.  The Government was induced to accept their offer; and on February 24, 1873, Phelps, Dodge and Company paid to the United States Treasury the

sistent vigilance facts were developed which have led to the arrest of several parties and the discovery that a system of fraud has been successfully carried on for a series of years. These investigations are now being prosecuted under the immediate direction of the Solicitor of the Treasury, for the purpose of ascertaining the extent of those frauds and bringing the guilty parties to punishment.  It is believed that the enactment at the last session of the bill referred to would have arrested, and that its enactment now will prevent hereafter, the frauds hitherto successfully practiced."— Annual Report for 1862 of Salmon P. Chase, Secretary of the Treasury. No matter what laws were passed, however, the frauds continued, and the importers kept on bribing.

[8] If the degree of the scandal that the unearthing of these frauds created is to be judged by the extent of space given to it by the newspapers, it must have been large and sensational. See issues of the New York "Times" and other newspapers of January 11, 1873, January 29, 1873, March 20, 1873, and April 20, 1873.  A full history of the case, with the official correspondence from the files of the Treasury Department, is to be found in the New York "Times," issue of April 28, 1873.

sum of $271,017.23 for the discontinuance of the million-dollar suit for custom-house frauds.[9]

## THEIR PRESENT WEALTH TRACED TO FRAUD.

From these persistent frauds came, to a large extent, the great collective and individual wealth of the members of this firm, and of their successors. It was also by reason of these frauds that Phelps, Dodge and Company were easily able to outdo competitors. Only recently, let it be added, they formed themselves into a corporation with a capital of $50,000,000. With the palpably great revenues from their continuous frauds, they were in an advantageous position to buy up many forms of property. Beginning in 1880 the mining of copper, they obtained hold of many very rich mining properties; their copper mines yield at present (1909) about 100,000,000 pounds a year. Phelps, Dodge and Company also own extensive coal mines and lines of railroads in the southwest Territories of the United States. Ten thousand employees are directly engaged in their copper and coal mines and smaller works, and on the 1,000 miles of railroad directly owned and operated by them.

[9] See House Executive Documents, Forty-third Congress, First Session, 1874, Doc. No. 124: 78. Of the entire sum of $271,-017.23 paid by Phelps, Dodge and Company to compromise the suit, Chester A. Arthur, then Collector of the Port, later President of the United States, received $21,906.01 as official fees; the Naval Officer and the Surveyor of the Port each were paid the same sum by the Government, and Jayne received $65,718.03 as his percentage as informer.

One of the methods of defrauding the Government was peculiar. Under the tariff act there was a heavy duty on imported zinc and lead, while works of art were admitted free of duty. Phelps, Dodge and Company had zinc and lead made into Europe into crude Dianas, Venuses and Mercurys and imported them in that form, claiming exemption from the customs duty on the ground of their being "works of art."

So greatly were the members of the firm enriched by their frauds that when D. Willis James, one of the partners sued by the Government for fraudulent undervaluations, died on September 13, 1907, he left an estate of not less than $26,967,448. John F. Farrel, the appraiser, so reported in his report filed on March 28, 1908, in the transfer tax department of the Surrogate's department, New York City. But as the transfer tax has been, and is, continuously evaded by ingenious anticipatory devices, the estate, it is probable, reached much more.

James owned (accepting the appraiser's specific report at a time when panic prices prevailed) tens of millions of dollars worth of stock in railroad, mining, manufacturing and other industries. He owned, for instance, $2,750,000 worth of shares in the Phelps-Dodge Copper Queen Mining Company; $1,419,510 in the Old Dominion Company, and millions more in other mining companies. His holdings in the Great Northern Railway, the history of which is one endless chain of fraud, amounted to millions of dollars — $3,840,000 of preferred stock; $3,924,000 of common stock; $1,715,000 of stock in the Great Northern Railway iron ore properties; $1,405,000 of Great Northern Railway shares in the form of subscription receipts, and so on. He was a large holder of stock in the Northern Pacific Railway, the development of which, as we shall see, has been one of incessant frauds. His interest in the "good will" of Phelps, Dodge and Company was appraised at $180,000; his interest in the same firm at $945,786; his cash on deposit with that firm at $475,000.[10]

[10] At his death he was eulogistically described as "the merchant philanthropist." On the day after the appraiser's report was filed, the New York "Times," issue of March 29, 1908, said: "Mr. James was senior member of the firm of Phelps,

In the defrauding of the United States Government, however, Phelps, Dodge and Company were doing no uncommon thing. The whole importing trade was incessantly and cohesively thriving upon this form of fraud. In his annual report for 1874, Henry C. Johnson, United States Commissioner of Customs, estimated that tourists returning from Europe yearly smuggled in as personal effects 257,810 trunks filled with dutiable goods valued at the enormous sum of $128,905,000. " It is well known," he added, "that much of this baggage is in reality intended to be put upon the market as merchandise, and that still other portions are brought over for third parties who have remained at home. Most of those engaged in this form of importation are people of wealth" . . .[11] Similar and additional facts were brought out in great abundance by a United States Senate committee appointed, in 1886, to investigate customs frauds in New York. After holding many sessions this committee declared that it had found " conclusive evidence that the undervaluation of certain kinds of imported merchandise is persistently practiced to an alarming extent at the port of New York."[12] At all other ports the customs frauds were notorious.

The frauds of the whiskey distillers in cheating the Government out of the internal revenue tax were so

Dodge & Co., of 99 John Street. His interest in educational and philanthropic work was very deep, and by his will he left bequests amounting to $1,195,000 to various charitable and religious institutions. The residue of the estate, amounting to $24,482,653, is left in equal shares to his widow and their son." On the same day that the appraiser's report was filed a large gathering of unemployed attempted to hold a meeting in Union Square to plead for the starting of public work, but were brutally clubbed, ridden down and dispersed by the police.

[11] Executive Documents, Forty-third Congress, Second Session, 1874, No. 2: 225.
[12] U. S. Senate Report, No. 1990, Forty-ninth Congress, Second Session, Senate Reports, iii, 1886-87.

enormous as to call forth several Congressional investigations;[18] the millions of dollars thus defrauded were used as private capital in extending the distilleries; virtually all of the fortunes in the present Whiskey Trust are derived in great part from these frauds. The banks likewise cheated the Government out of large sums in their evasion of the stamp tax. " This stamp tax," reported the Comptroller of Currency in 1874, " is to a considerable extent evaded by banks and more frequently by depositors, by drawing post notes, or bills of exchange at one day's sight, instead of on demand, and by substituting receipts for checks." [14]

It was from these various divisions of the capitalist class that the most caustic and virtuous tirades against Gould came. The boards of trade and chambers of commerce were largely made up of men who, while assuming the most vaniloquent pretensions, were themselves malodorous with fraud. To read the resolutions passed by them, and to observe retrospectively the supreme airs of respectability and integrity they individually took on, one would conclude that they were all men of whitest, most irreproachable character. But the official reports contradict their pretensions at every turn; and they are all seen in their nakedness as perjurers, cheats and frauds, far more sinister in their mask than Gould in his carelessly open career of theft and corruption. Many of the descendants of that sordid aggregation live to-day in the luxury of inherited cumulative wealth, and boast of a certain " pride of ancestry " and " refinement of social position; " it is they from whom the sneers at the " lower classes " come; and they it is

[18] Reports of Committees, Fortieth Congress, Third Session, 1869-70. Report No. 3, etc.
[14] Executive Document, No. 2, 1874: 140.

who take unto themselves the ordaining of laws and of customs and definitions of morality.[15]

From the very foundation of the United States Government, not to mention what happened before that time, the custom-house frauds have been continuous up to the very present, without any intermission. The recent suits brought by the Government against the Sugar Trust for gigantic frauds in cheating in the importation of sugar, were only an indication of the increasing frauds. The Sugar Trust was compelled to disgorge about $2,000,000, but this sum, it was admitted, was only a part of the enormous total out of which it had defrauded the Government. The further great custom-house scandals and court proceedings in 1908 and 1909 showed that the bribery of custom-house weighers and inspectors had long been in operation, and that the whole importing class, as a class, was profiting heavily by this bribery and fraud. While the trials of importers were going on in the United States Circuit Court at New York, despatches from Washington announced, on October 22, 1909, that the Treasury Department estimated that the same kind of frauds as had been uncovered at New York, had flourished for decades, although in a somewhat lesser degree, at Boston, Philadelphia, Norfolk, New Orleans, San Francisco and at other ports.

" It is probable," stated these subdued despatches,

[15] It is worthy of note that several of the descendants of the Phelps-Dodge-Stokes families are men and women of the highest character and most radical principles. J. G. Phelps Stokes, for instance, joined the Socialist party to work for the overthrow of the very system on which the wealth of his family is founded. A man more devoted to his principles, more keenly alive to the injustices and oppressions of the prevailing system, more conscientious in adhering to his views, and more upright in both public and private dealings, it would be harder to find than J. G. Phelps Stokes. He is one of the very few distinguished exceptions among his class.

"that these systematic filchings from the Government's receipts cover a period of more than fifty years, and that in this, the minor officials of the New York Custom House have been the greatest offenders, although their nefarious profits have been small in comparison with the illegitimate gains of their employers, the great importers. These are the views of responsible officials of the Treasury Department." These despatches stated the truth very mildly. The frauds have been going on for more than a century, and the Government has been cheated out of a total of hundreds upon hundreds of millions of dollars, perhaps billions.

And the thieving importers of these times comprise the respectable and highly virtuous chambers of commerce and boards of trade, as was the case in Gould's day. They are ever foremost in pompously denouncing the very political corruption which they themselves cause and want and profit from; they are the fine fellows who come together in their solemn conclaves and resolve this and resolve that against "law-defying labor unions," or in favor of "a reform in our body politic," etc., etc. A glorious crew they are of excellent, most devout church members and charity dispensers; sleek, self-sufficient men who sit on Grand Juries and Trial Juries, and condemn the petty thieves to conviction carrying long terms of imprisonment. Viewing commercial society, one is tempted to conclude that the worthiest members of society, as a whole, are to be found within the prisons; yes, indeed, the time may not be far away, when the stigma of the convict may be considered a real badge of ancestral honor.

But the comparison of Gould and the trading classes is by no means complete without adding anew a contrast between how the propertied plunderers as a class were immune from criminal prosecution, and the persecution to which the working class was subjected.

Although all sections of the commercial and financial class were cheating, swindling and defrauding with almost negligible molestation from Government, the workers could not even plead for the right to work without drawing down upon themselves the full punitive animosity of governing powers whose every move was one of deference to the interests of property. Apart from the salient fact that the prisons throughout the United States were crowded with poor criminals, while the machinery of the criminal courts was never seriously invoked against the commercial and financial classes, the police and other public functionaries would not even allow the workers to meet peacefully for the petitioning of redress. Organized expressions of discontent are ever objectionable to the ruling class, not so much for what is said, as for the movements and reconstructions they may lead to — a fact which the police authorities, inspired from above, have always well understood.

### THE CLUBBING OF THE UNEMPLOYED.

" The winter of 1873–74," says McNeill,

was one, of extreme suffering. Midwinter found tens of thousands of people on the verge of starvation, suffering for food, for the need of proper clothing, and for medical attendance. Meetings of the unemployed were held in many places, and public attention called to the needs of the poor. The men asked for work and found it not, and children cried for bread. . . . The unemployed and suffering poor of New York City determined to hold a meeting and appeal to the public by bringing to their attention the spectacle of their poverty. They gained permission from the Board of Police to parade the streets and hold a meeting in Tompkins Square on January 13, 1874, but on January 12 the Board of Police and Board of Parks revoked the order and prohibited the meeting. It was impossible to notify the scattered army of this order, and at the time of the meeting the people marched through the gates of Tompkins Square. . . . When the square was completely filled with men, women and children, without a moment's warning, the police closed in upon them on all sides.

One of the daily papers of the city confessed that the scene could not be described. People rushed from the gates and through the streets, followed by the mounted officers at full speed, charging upon them without provocation. Screams of women and children rent the air, and the blood of many stained the streets, and to the further shame of this outrage it is to be added that when the General Assembly of New York State was called to this matter they took testimony, but made no sign.[16]

Thus was the supremacy of "law and order" maintained. The day was saved for well-fed respectability, and starving humanity was forced back into its despairing haunts, there to reflect upon the club-taught lesson that empty stomachs should remain inarticulate. For the flash of a second, a nameless fright seized hold of the gilded quarters, but when they saw how well the police did their dispersing work, and choked up with their clubs the protests of aggregated suffering, self-confidence came back, revelry was resumed, and the saturnalia of theft went on unbrokenly.

And a lucky day was that for the police. The methods of the ruling class were reflected in the police force; while perfumed society was bribing, defrauding and ex-

[16] "The Labor Movement": 147-148. In describing to the committee on grievances the horrors of this outrage, John Swinton, a writer of great ability, and a man whose whole heart was with the helpless, suffering and exploited, closed his address by quoting this verse:

"There is a poor blind Samson in our land,
   Shorn of his strength and bound with bonds of steel,
Who may in some grim revel raise his hand,
   And shake the pillars of the Commonweal."

propriating, the police were enriching themselves by a perfected system of blackmail and extortion of their own. Police Commissioners, chiefs, inspectors, captains and sergeants became millionaires, or at least, very rich from the proceeds of this traffic.    Not only did they extort regular payments from saloons, brothels and other establishments on whom the penalties of law could be visited, but they had a standing arrangement with thieves of all kinds, rich thieves as well as what were classed as ordinary criminals, by which immunity was sold at specified rates.[17]    The police force did not want this system interfered with; hence at all times toadied to the rich and influential classes as the makers of law and the creators of public opinion.    To be on the good side of the rich, and to be praised as the defenders of law and order, furnished a screen of incalculable utility behind which they could carry on undisturbedly their own peculiar system of plunder.

[17] The very police captain, one Williams, who commanded the police at the Tompkins Square gathering was quizzed by the " Lexow Committee " in 1893 as to where he got his great wealth.  He it was who invented the term " Tenderloin," signifying a district from which large collections in blackmail and extortion could be made.  By 1892, the annual income derived by the police from blackmailing and other sources of extortion was estimated at $7,000,000.  (See " Investigation of the Police Department of New York City," 1894, v: 5734.)  With the establishment of Greater New York the amount about doubled, or, perhaps, trebled.

# CHAPTER XII

## THE GOULD FORTUNE AND SOME ANTECEDENT
## FACTORS

With his score or more of millions of booty, Jay Gould
now had much more than sufficient capital to compete
with many of the richest magnates; and what he might
lack in extent of capital when combated by a combination of magnates, he fully made up for by his pulverizing
methods. His acute eye had previously lit upon the
Union Pacific Railroad as offering a surpassingly prolific
field for a new series of thefts. Nor was he mistaken.
The looting of this railroad and allied railroads which
he, Russell Sage and other members of the clique proceeded to accomplish, added to their wealth, it was
estimated perhaps $60,000,000 or more, the major share
of which Gould appropriated.

It was commonly supposed in 1873 that the Union
Pacific Railroad had been so completely despoiled that
scarcely a vestige was left to prey upon. But Gould had
an extraordinary faculty for devising new and fresh
schemes of spoliation. He would discern great opportunities for pillage in places that others dismissed as
barren; projects that other adventurers had bled until
convinced nothing more was to be extracted, would be
taken up by Gould and become plethora of plunder under
his dexterous touch. Again and again Gould was charged
with being a wrecker of property; a financial beach-
comber who destroyed that he might profit. These
accusations, in the particular exclusive sense in which

they were meant, were distortions. In almost every instance the railroads gathered in by Gould were wrecked before he secured control; all that he did was to revive, continue and elaborate the process of wrecking. It had been proved so in the case of the Erie Railroad; he now demonstrated it with the Union Pacific Railroad.

## THE MISLEADING ACCOUNTS HANDED DOWN.

This railroad had been chartered by Congress in 1862 to run from a line on the one hundredth meridian in Nebraska to the western boundary of Nevada. The actual story of its inception and construction is very different from the stereotyped accounts shed by most writers. These romancers, distinguished for their syco-phancy and lack of knowledge, would have us believe that these enterprises originated as splendid and memo-rable exhibitions of patriotism, daring and ability. According to their version Congress was so solicitous that these railroads should be built that it almost implored the projectors to accept the great gifts of franchises, land and money that it proffered as assistance. A radiantly glowing description is forged of the men who succeeded in laying these railroads; how there stretched immense reaches of wilderness which would long have remained desolate had it not been for these indomitable pioneers; and how by their audacious skill and persistence they at last prevailed, despite sneers and ridicule, and gave to the United States a chain of railroads such as a few years before it had been considered folly to attempt.

Very limpidly these narratives flow; two generations have drunk so deeply of them that they have become inebriated with the contemplation of these wonderful men. When romance, however, is hauled to the arch-

**RESIDENCE OF JAY GOULD,**
759 Fifth Avenue, New York.

ives, and confronted with the frigid facts, the old dame collapses into shapeless stuffing.

In the opening chapter of the present part of this work it was pointed out by a generalization (to be frequently itemized by specifications later on) that the accounts customarily written of the origin of these railroads have been ridiculously incorrect. To prove them so it is only necessary to study the debates and the reports of Congress before, and after, the granting of the charters.

### SECTIONAL INTERESTS IN CONFLICT.

Far greater forces than individual capitalists, or isolated groups of capitalists, were at work to promote or prevent the construction of this or that Pacific road. In the struggle before the Civil War between the capitalist system of the North and the slave oligarchy of the South, the chattel slavery forces exerted every effort to use the powers of Government to build railroads in sections where their power would be extended and further intrenched. Their representatives in Congress feverishly strained themselves to the utmost to bring about the construction of a trans-continental railroad passing through the Southwest. The Northern constituents stubbornly fought the project. In reprisal, the Southern legislators in Congress frustrated every move for trans-continental railroads which, traversing hostile or too doubtful territory, would add to the wealth, power, population and interests of the North. The Government was allowed to survey routes, but no comprehensive trans-continental Pacific railroad bills were passed.

The debates in Congress during the session of 1859 over Pacific railroads were intensely aciduous. Speaking of the Southern slave holders, Senator Wilson, of

Massachusetts, denounced them as "restless, ambitious gentlemen who are organizing Southern leagues to open the African slave trade, and to conquer Mexico and Central America." He added with great acerbity: "They want a railroad to the Pacific Ocean; they want to carry slavery to the Pacific and have a base line from which they can operate for the conquest of the continent south."[1] In fiery verbiage the Southern Senators slashed back, taunting the Northerners with seeking to wipe out the system of chattel slavery, only to extend and enforce all the more effectually their own system of white slavery. The honorable Senators unleashed themselves; Senatorial dignity fell askew, and there was snarling and growling, retort and backtalk and bad blood enough.

The disclosures that day were extremely delectable. In the exchange of recriminations, many truths inadvertently came out. The capitalists of neither section, it appeared, were faithful to the interests of their constituencies. This was, indeed, no discovery; long had Northern representatives been bribed to vote for land and money grants to railroads in the South, and vice versa. But the charges further brought out by Senator Wilson angered and exasperated his Southern colleagues. "We all remember," said he, "that Texas made a grant of six thousand dollars and ten thousand acres of land a mile to a Pacific railway company." Yes, in truth, they all remembered; the South had supported that railroad project as one that would aid in the extension of her power and institutions. "I remember," Wilson went on, "that when that company was organized the men who got it up could not, by any possibility, have raised one hundred thousand dollars if they paid their honest debts.

[1] The Congressional Globe, Thirty-fifth Congress, Second Session, 1858-59, Part II, Appendix: 291.

Many of them were political bankrupts as well as pecuniary bankrupts — men who had not a dollar; and some of them were men who not only never paid a debt, but never recognized an obligation."

At this thrust a commotion was visible in the exalted chamber; the blow had struck, and not far from where Wilson stood.

"Years have passed away," continued the Senator, "and what has Texas got? Twenty-two or twenty-three miles of railway, with two cars upon it, with no depot, the company owning everything within hailing distance of the road; and they have imported an old worn-out engine from Vermont. And this is part of your grand Southern Pacific Railroad. These gentlemen are out in pamphlets, proving each other great rascals, or attempting to do so; and I think they have generally succeeded. . . . The whole thing from the beginning has been a gigantic swindle." [2]

What Senator Wilson neglected to say was that the capitalists of his own State and other Northern States had effected even greater railroad swindles; the owners of the great mills in Massachusetts were, as we shall see, likewise bribing Congress to pass tariff acts.

### A MYTH OF MODERN FABRICATION.

The myth had not then been built up of putative great constructive pioneers, risking their every cent, and racking their health and brains, in the construction of railways. It was in the very heyday of the bribing and swindling, as numerous investigating committees showed; there could be no glamour or illusion then.

The money lavishly poured out for the building of

[2] The Congressional Globe, etc., 1858–59, Part II, Appendix, 291.

railroads was almost wholly public money drawn from compulsory taxation of the whole people. At this identical time practically every railroad corporation in the country stood indebted for immense sums of public money, little of which was ever paid back. In New York State more than $40,000,000 of public funds had gone into the railroads; in Vermont $8,000,000 and large sums in every other State and Territory. The whole Legislature and State Government of Wisconsin had been bribed with a total of $800,000, in 1856, to give a large land grant to one company alone, details of which transaction will be found elsewhere.[8] The State of Missouri had already disbursed $25,000,000 of public funds; not content with these loans and donations two of its railroads demanded, in 1859, that the State pay interest on their bonds.

In both North and South the plundering was equally conspicuous. Some of the Northern Senators were fond of pointing out the incompetency and rascality of the Southern oligarchy, while ignoring the acts of the capitalists in their own section. Senator Wilson, for instance, enlarged upon the condition of the railroads in North and South Carolina, describing how, after having been fed with enormous subsidies, they were almost worthless. And if anything was calculated to infuriate the Southerners it was the boast that the capitalists of Massachusetts had $100,000,000 invested in railroads, for they knew, and often charged, that most of this sum had been cheated by legislation out of the National, State or other public treasury, and that what had not been so obtained had been extracted largely from the underpaid and overworked laborers of the mills. Often they had compared the two systems of labor, that of the North

[8] See the chapters on the Russell Sage fortune.

and that of the South, and had pointedly asked which was really the worse.

Not until after the Civil War was under way, and the North was in complete control of Congress, was it that most of the Pacific railroad legislation was secured. The time was exceedingly propitious. The promoters and advocates of these railroads could now advance the all-important argument that military necessity as well as popular need called for their immediate construction.

No longer was there any conflict at Washington over legislation proposed by warring sectional representatives. But another kind of fight in Congress was fiercely set in motion. Competitive groups of Northern capitalists energetically sought to outdo one another in getting the charters and appropriations for Pacific railroads. After a bitter warfare, in which bribery was a common weapon, a compromise was reached by which the Union Pacific Railroad Company was to have the territory west of a point in Nebraska, while to other groups of capitalists, headed by John I. Blair and others, charters and grants were given for a number of railroads to start at different places on the Missouri River, and converge at the point from which the Union Pacific ran westward.

In the course of the debate on the Pacific Railroads bill, Senator Pomeroy introduced an amendment providing for the importation of large numbers of cheap European laborers, and compelling them to stick to their work in the building of the railroads under the severest penalties for non-compliance. It was, in fact, a proposal to have the United States Government legalize the peonage system of white slavery. Pomeroy's amendment specifically provided that the troops should be called upon to enforce these civil contracts. " It strikes one as the most monstrous proposition I ever heard of," interjected

Senator Rice. " It is a measure to enslave white men, and to enforce that slavery at the point of the bayonet. I begin to believe what I have heard heretofore in the South, that the object of some of these gentlemen was merely to transfer slavery from the South to the North; and I think this is the first step toward it." [4]

The amendment was defeated. The act which Congress passed authorized the chartering of the Union Pacific Railroad with a capital of $100,000,000. In addition to granting the company the right of way, two hundred feet wide, through thousands of miles of the public domain, of arbitrary rights of condemnation, and the right to take from the public lands whatever building material was needed, Congress gave as a gift to the company alternate sections of land twenty miles wide along the entire line. Still further, the company was empowered to call upon the Government for large loans of money.

CONGRESS BRIBED FOR THE UNION PACIFIC CHARTER.

It was highly probable that this act was obtained by bribery. There is not the slightest doubt that the supplementary act of 1864 was. The directors and stockholders of the company were not satisfied with the comprehensive privileges that they had already obtained. It was very easy, they saw, to get still more. Among these stockholders were many of the most effulgent merchants and bankers in the country; we find William E. Dodge, for instance, on the list of stockholders in 1863. The pretext that they offered as a public bait was that " capital needed more inducements to encourage it to invest its money." But this assuredly was not the argument prevailing in Congress. According to the report of a Senate committee of 1873 — the " Wilson Committee "

[4] The Congressional Globe, Thirty-seventh Congress, Third Session, 1862-63. Part ii: 1241-1243.

—nearly $436,000 was spent in getting the act of July, 1864, passed.[5]

For this $436,000 distributed in fees and bribes, the Union Pacific Railroad Company secured the passage of a law giving it even more favorable government subsidies, amounting to from $16,000 to $48,000 a mile, according to the topography of the country. The land grant was enlarged from twenty to forty miles wide until it included about 12,000,000 acres, and the provisions of the original act were so altered and twisted that the Government stood little or no chance of getting back its outlays.

The capitalists behind the project now had franchises, gifts and loans actually or potentially worth many hundreds of millions of dollars. But to get the money appropriated from the National Treasury, it was necessary by the act that they should first have constructed certain miles of their railroads. The Eastern capitalists had at home so many rich avenues of plunder in which to invest their funds — money wrung out of army contracts, usury and other sources — that many of them were indisposed to put any of it in the unpopulated stretches of the far West. The banks, as we have seen, were glutting on twenty, and often fifty, and sometimes a hundred per cent.; they saw no opportunity to make nearly as much from the Pacific railroads.

### THE CREDIT MOBILIER JOBBERY.

All the funds that the Union Pacific Railroad Company could privately raise by 1865 was the insufficient

[5] Reports of Committees, Credit Mobilier Reports, Forty-second Congress, Third session, 1872-73; Doc. No. 78: xviii. The committee reported that the evidence proved that this sum had been disbursed in connection with the passage of the amendatory act of July 2, 1864.

sum of $500,000. Some greater incentive was plainly needed to induce capitalists to rush in. Oakes Ames, head of the company, and a member of Congress, finally hit upon the auspicious scheme. It was the same scheme that the Vanderbilts, Gould, Sage, Blair, Huntington, Stanford, Crocker and other railroad magnates employed to defraud stupendous sums of money.

Ames produced the alluring plan of a construction company. This corporation was to be a compact affair composed of himself and his charter associates; and, so far as legal technicalities went, was to be a corporation apparently distinct and separate from the Union Pacific Railroad Company. Its designed function was to build the railroad, and the plan was to charge the Union Pacific exorbitant and fraudulent sums for the work of construction. What was needed was a company chartered with comprehensive powers to do the constructing work. This desideratum was found in the Credit Mobilier Company of America, a Pennsylvania corporation, conveniently endowed with the most extensive powers. The stock of this company was bought in for a few thousand dollars, and the way was clear for the colossal frauds planned.

The prospects for profit and loot were so unprecedentedly great that capitalists now blithely and eagerly darted forward. One has only to examine the list of stockholders of the Credit Mobilier Company in 1867 to verify this fact. Conspicuous bankers such as Morton, Bliss and Company and William H. Macy; owners of large industrial plants and founders of multimillionaire fortunes such as Cyrus H. McCormick and George M. Pullman; merchants and factory owners and landlords and politicians — a very edifying and inspiring array of respectable capitalists was it that now hastened to buy or get gifts of Credit Mobilier stock.[6]

The contract for construction was turned over to the Credit Mobilier Company. This, in turn, engaged sub-contractors. The work was really done by these sub-contractors with their force of low-paid labor. Oakes Ames and his associates did nothing except to look on executively from a comfortable distance, and pocket the plunder. As fast as certain portions of the railroad were built the Union Pacific Railroad Company received bonds from the United States Treasury. In all, these bonds amounted to $27,213,000, out of much of which sum the Government was later practically swindled.

### GREAT CORRUPTION AND VAST THEFTS.

Charges of enormous thefts committed by the Credit Mobilier Company, and of corruption of Congress, were specifically made by various individuals and in the public press. A sensational hullabaloo resulted; Congress was stormed with denunciations; it discreetly concluded that some action had to be taken. The time-honored, mil-dewed dodge of appointing an investigating committee was decided upon.

Virtuously indignant was Congress; zealously inquis-itive the committee appointed by the United States Sen-ate professed to be. Very soon its honorable members were in a state of utter dismay. For the testimony began to show that some of the most powerful men in Congress

[6] The full lists of these stockholders can be found in Docs. No. 77 and No. 78, Reports of U. S. Senate Committees, 1872-73. Morton, Bliss & Co. held 18,500 shares; Pullman, 8,400 shares, etc. The Morton referred to — Levi P. Morton — was later (1888-1892) made Vice President of the United States by the money interests.

were implicated in Credit Mobilier corruption; men such as James G. Blaine, one of the foremost Republican politicians of the period, and James A. Garfield, who later was elevated into the White House. Every effort was bent upon whitewashing these men; the committee found that as far as their participation was concerned " nothing was proved," but, protest their innocence as they vehemently did, the tar stuck, nevertheless.

As to the thefts of the Credit Mobilier Company, the committee freely stated its conclusions. Ames and his band, the evidence showed, had stolen nearly $44,000,000 outright, more than half of which was in cash. The committee, to be sure, was not so brutal as to style it theft; with a true parliamentarian regard for sweetness and sacredness of expression, the committee's report described it as " profit."

After holding many sessions, and collating volumes of testimony, the committee found, as it stated in its report, that the total cost of building the Union Pacific Railroad was about $50,000,000. And what had the Credit Mobilier Company charged? Nearly $94,000,000 or, to be exact, $93,546,287.28.[7] The committee admitted that " the road had been built chiefly with the resources of the Government."[8] A decided mistake; it had been entirely built so. The committee itself showed how the entire cost of building the road had been " wholly reimbursed from the proceeds of the Government bonds and first mortgage bonds," and that " from the stock, income bonds, and land grant bonds, the builders received in cash value $23,366,000 as profit — about forty-eight per cent. on the entire cost."[9]

The total " profits " represented the difference between

[7] Doc. No. 78, Credit Mobilier Investigation: xiv.
[8] Ibid., xx.
[9] Ibid., xvii.

the cost of building the railroad and the amount charged
— about $44,000,000 in all, of which $23,000,000 or more
was in immediate cash. It was more than proved that
the amount was even greater; the accounts had been falsified to show that the cost of construction was $50,000,000.
Large sums of money, borrowed ostensibly to build the
road, had at once been seized as plunder, and divided in
the form of dividends upon stock for which the clique
had not paid a cent in money, contrary to law.

### THRIFTY, SAGACIOUS PATRIOTISM.

Who could deny that the phalanx of capitalists scram-
bling forward to share in this carnival of plunder were
not gifted with unerring judgment? From afar they
sighted their quarry. Nearly all of them were the fifty
per cent. "patriot" capitalists of the Civil War; and,
just as in all extant biographies, they are represented as
heroic, self-sacrificing figures during that crisis, when
in historical fact, they were defrauding and plundering
indomitably, so are they also glorified as courageous,
enterprising men of prescience, who hazarded their money
in building the Pacific railroads at a time when most of
the far West was an untenanted desert. And this string
of arrant falsities has passed as " history! "

If they had that foresight for which they are so inveterately lauded, it was a foresight based upon the certainty that it would yield them forty-eight per cent. profit
and more from a project on which not one of them did
the turn of a hand's work, for even the bribing of Congress was done by paid agents. Nor did they have to
risk the millions that they had obtained largely by fraud
in trade and other channels; all that they had to do
was to advance that money for a short time until they

got it back from the Government resources, with forty-eight per cent. profit besides.

The Senate Committee's report came out at a time of panic when many millions of men, women and children were out of work, and other millions in destitution. It was in that very year when the workers in New York City were clubbed by the police for venturing to hold a meeting to plead for the right to work. But the bribing of Congress in 1864, and the thefts in the construction of the railroad, were only parts of the gigantic frauds brought out — frauds which a people who believed themselves under a democracy had to bear and put up with, or else be silenced by force.

THE BRIBERY PERSISTENTLY CONTINUES.

When the act of 1864 was passed, Congress plausibly pointed out the wise, precautionary measures it was taking to insure the honest disbursements of the Government's appropriations. " Behold," said in effect this Congress, " the safeguards with which we are surrounding the bill. We are providing for the appointment of Government directors to supervise the work, and see to it that the Government's interests do not suffer." Very appropriate legislation, indeed, from a Congress in which $436,000 of bribe money had been apportioned to insure its betrayal of the popular interests.

But Ames and his brother capitalists bribed at least one of the Government directors with $25,000 to connive at the frauds:[10] he was a cheaply bought tool, that director. And immediately after the railroad was built and in operation, its owners scented more millions of plunder if they could get a law enacted by Congress

[10] Document No. 78, Credit Mobilier Investigation: xvii.

allowing them exorbitant rates for the transportation of troops and Government supplies and mails. They corruptly paid out, it seems, $126,000 to get this measure of March 3, 1871, passed.[11]

What was the result of all this investigation? Mere noise. The oratorical tom-toms in Congress resounded vociferously for the gulling of home constituencies, and of palaver and denunciations there was a plenitude. The committee confined itself to recommending the expulsion of Oakes Ames and James Brooks from Congress. The Government bravely brought a civil action, upon many specified charges, against the Union Pacific Railroad Company for misappropriation of funds. This action the company successfully fought; the United States Supreme Court, in 1878, dismissed the suit on the ground that the Government could not sue until the company's debt had matured in 1895.[12]

Thus these great thieves escaped both criminal and civil process, as they were confident that they would, and as could have been accurately foretold. The immense plunder and the stolen railroad property the perpetrators of these huge frauds were allowed to keep. Congress could have forfeited upon good legal grounds the charter of the Union Pacific Railroad Company then and there. So long as this was not done, and so long as they were unmolested in the possession of their loot, the participating capitalists could well afford to be curiously tolerant of verbal chastisement which soon passed away, and which had no other result than to add several more ponderous volumes to the already appallingly encumbered archives of Government investigations.

By this time — the end of 1873 — the market value

[11] Doc. No. 78, etc., xvii.
[12] 98 U. S. 569.

of the stock of the Union Pacific Railroad was at a very low point. The excessive amount of plunder appropriated by Ames and his confederates had loaded it down with debt. With fixed charges on enormous quantities of bonds to pay, few capitalists saw how the stock could be made to yield any returns — for some time, at any rate. Now was seen the full hollowness of the pretensions of the capitalists that they were inspired by a public-spirited interest in the development of the Far West. This pretext had been jockeyed out for every possible kind of service. As soon as they were convinced that the Credit Mobilier clique had sacked the railroad of all immediate plunder, the participating capitalists showed a sturdy alacrity in shunning the project and disclaiming any further connection with it. Their stock, for the most part, was offered for sale.

## JAY GOULD COMES FORWARD.

It was now that Jay Gould eagerly stepped in. Where others saw cessation of plunder, he spied the richest possibilities for a new onslaught. For years he had been a covetous spectator of the operations of the Credit Mobilier; and, of course, had not been able to contain himself from attempting to get a hand in its stealings. He and Fisk had repeatedly tried to storm their way in, and had carried trumped-up cases into the courts, only to be eventually thwarted. Now his chance came.

What if $50,000,000 had been stolen? Gould knew that it had other resources of very great value; for, in addition to the $27,000,000 Government bonds that the Union Pacific Railroad had received, it also had as asset about 12,000,000 acres of land presented by Congress. Some of this land had been sold by the railroad company at an average of about $4.50 an acre, but the greater part still remained in its ownership. And millions of acres more could be fraudulently seized, as the sequel proved.

Gould also was aware — for he kept himself well informed — that, twenty years previously, Government geologists had reported that extensive coal deposits lay in Wyoming and other parts of the West. These deposits would become of incalculable value; and while they were not included in the railroad grants, some had already been stolen, and it would be easy to get hold of many more by fraud. And that he was not in error in this calculation was shown by the fact that the Union Pacific Railroad and other allied railroads under his control, and under that of his successors, later seized hold of many of these coal deposits by violence and fraud.[18] Gould also knew that every year immigration was pouring into the West; that in time its population, agriculture and industries would form a rich field for exploitation. By the well-understood canons of capitalism, this futurity could be capitalized in advance. Moreover, he had in mind other plans by which tens of millions could be stolen under form of law.

Fisk had been murdered, but Gould now leagued himself with much abler confederates, the principal of whom was Russell Sage. It is well worth while pausing here to give some glimpses of Sage's career, for he left an immense fortune, estimated at considerably more than $100,000,000, and his widow, who inherited it, has attained the reputation of being a "philanthropist" by

[18] The Interstate Commerce Commission reported to the United States Senate in 1908 that the acquisition of these coal lands had "been attended with fraud, perjury, violence and disregard of the rights of individuals," and showed specifically how. Various other Government investigations fully supported the charges.

disbursing a few of those millions in what she considers charitable enterprises. One of her endowed "philanthropies" is a bureau to investigate the causes of poverty and to improve living conditions; another for the propagation of justice. Deeply interested as the benign Mrs. Sage professes to be in the causes producing poverty and injustice, a work such as this may peradventure tend to enlighten her. This highly desirable knowledge she can thus herein procure direct and gratuitously. Furthermore, it is necessary, before describing the joint activities of Gould and Sage, to give a prefatory account of Sage's career; what manner of man he was, and how he obtained the millions enabling him to help carry forward those operations.

END OF VOL. II.

Part III, comprising "The Great Fortunes from Railroads," is continued in Vol. III.

(The index for Volumes I, II and III will be found in Volume III.)

CPSIA information can be obtained
at www.ICGtesting.com
Printed in the USA
LVHW051640190523
747502LV00003B/234